The Black American History Edition

BLACK EXCELLENCE

Written and Organized

by

Maham the Mentor

Publisher's Cataloging-in-Publication data
Names: Maham the Mentor, author.
Title: Black excellence / written and organized by Maham the
Mentor.
Series: The Black American History Edition
Description: Dallas, TX: Maham the Mentor Books, LLC., 2022.
Identifiers: LCCN: 2022918209 | ISBN: 979-8-9860422-3-7
Subjects: LCSH African Americans--Biography. | African
Americans--History. | BISAC BIOGRAPHY &
AUTOBIOGRAPHY / Cultural, Ethnic & Regional /
African American & Black
Classification: LCC E185.96 .M 2022 | DDC 973.0496/092--dc23

DEDICATION

This Book is Dedicated to my father, John Arnold DuBriel. I'm honored to
have had you as a father and thank you for always believing in me. I was
unaware of most of your medical conditions you had because you never
complained about it. You were always positive and in good spirits.
Knowing that you were in pain and discomfort most of the time, going
back and forth between doctors your entire life. I know that you always had
death around the corner. The way you maintained your composure and
serve God, I'm proud of you. I'm grateful to have had such a great man
guide me in this life! To the DuBriel and Metoyer family of Cane River
Louisiana, we love you and you'll always be in our hearts!

CONTENTS

INTRODUCTION

Black Excellence defined by Maham the Mentor is the Excellence of Black People in America. That Excellence comes from extraordinary Black People, who accomplished great tasks or Goals, under the most extreme conditions to mankind. Black History is very important to me because I am a direct descendant of it. Most of my life, I thought my life was difficult and it may have been for me, in my mind. I could easily allow myself to believe I was this fragile, I thought I couldn't bare the treatment I received. Then I learned about Frederick Douglass and George Washington Carver, I shut up, immediately!! How dare I complain about my treatment when these great men were treated so inhumanely. My father was murdered before I was born, my mother passed away five months after I was born. I went through foster care, I was adopted, I was in Special Education by the Eighth grade. I made many mistakes which led me to prison while I was still attending High School. I was 18 years old. I couldn't read until I was 22, which brings me to meetings these ancestors through literature.

Through literature I was able to see how fortunate I was to be born in this day in time, instead of the 1700 or 1800s. I was able to see through reading, how difficult life was for them, what our ancestors really went through. How some of them contributed and never received any recognition for it? Only through over reading about a subject do I feel comfortable talking about it, if I don't really know too much about it, I'm not even going to speak on it. These people that I wrote about in this book I have research them on numerous occasions or read about them when I was passing time. They helped me go from special education to graduating college with honors twice.

Black Excellence highlights the amazing contributions of Black Americans, I selected the ones I believe should be known or mentioned. I would encourage anyone who doesn't like my selection to write or organize your own book. I would love to read it. There are no finish lines to learning. We can all participate in the uplifting and strengthening of all people. With this book, I hope and pray that we remember who we are! What gave us strength. It was unity! Unity in love and principles. Going through history, breaking down these amazing Black Americans, our ancestors. I truly hope that this inspires them to do better, as it did me. Seeing the adversity some of these people in this book faced, can enlighten a young man that his life is way better than his ancestors and he should be grateful because without their contributions we could be in the same predicament.

We should know our past to appreciate our future. As an Educated Black man in America, I'm aware of the impact and the importance of having the knowledge of our history. Having this type of knowledge in America is great for All Races when it is explained right. Which is why I have taken it upon myself to write a series of Books on Black American History. As a strong Black Man. I can honestly say, I love this country and I appreciate this country. My country is my extended family. Our America School systems have failed us on Black History. Less than 10% of class time is devoted to Black History. Only 8% of Seniors can identify slavery as a main cause of the Civil War. Each State must decide on what the students will learn. Seven of our States don't even mention Slavery in their History lessons (Alaska, Montana, Wyoming, Iowa, Maine, Vermont, and Rhode Island.) Eight of our States don't mention the Civil Rights movement. (Alaska, Oregon, Montana, Wyoming, South Dakota, Missouri, Rhode Island, and Maine) Only two States Mention White Supremacy. (Massachusetts and Maryland). There are no National Standards for Black History. No plans for one. But in 2022, in America. We are passing Laws to limit Critical Race Theories for fear of people condemning white people. Because how we tell Black People, Black History is extremely important, especially when so many lies and stereotypes running rampant. We must remember our past to truly appreciate our future. As Black people, our History in America has kind of been whitewashed, which led many to believe that Black people had no value and played no real role in building America. So much Black American History is missing from America History, it devalues the many Black people who sacrifice their lives for our freedom.

I feel it's my responsibility to educate all Human beings about Black American History, especially my young Black Men and women. This is the second book as planned. Black American History is so Rich. There's so much to learn and so much to teach. Where to begin and where to end. Since there's no right or wrong answers. I started off with Black Massacres in America, after the Civil War began. Book two is Black Excellence. I hope to enlighten us all about the real adversity Black people went through for us all to have the opportunity to have a Life, Liberty, and the pursuit of Property or the pursuit of happiness. Without Black people, there would be no America. I know and understand this to the fullest. So, I sincerely thank all the Black people who have died before me, playing their part in establishing this great Nation. Since the beginning of this country, Black people have always been the cornerstone of this society, Black people built it, period. It is that simple. "The Land in America in 1619 was unmanageable to work for white people". America's beginning time places us in Jamestown, Virginia. It was too hard for white people to work that land. Black labor was the only thing that gave the land any Value. Without that, nothing happens (Condé Nast. "James Baldwin: Letter from a Region in My Mind." The New Yorker, 10 Nov. 1962). 1619 is way before the industrial revolution that happened in the 1900s, meaning. There were no manufacturing plants or factories of this period. Everyone, everywhere had to work in the fields, agriculture was the way of life back then. Many educators claim or teach that Black people in America started in the Transatlantic Slave trade. Which is during the years of 1526-1808 AD. I believe that it started in the year 711 AD. When Black People from North Africa enslaved White people in Spain and Portugal and kept them enslaved for 700 years. I'll explain more about that later in my book called: Black Masters. When The Black People (Moors) enslaved the White People in Spain and Portugal. Let's dive into Black Excellence.

CHAPTER ONE
DRED SCOTT (1795-1858)

Credit: Missouri Historical Society

Dred Scott was an enslaved man of "100 percent pure" African descent. Dred's case was predicated on the fact that he was taken by his master, an officer in the U.S. Army, from the slave state of Missouri to the free state of Illinois and then to the free territory of Wisconsin. He lived on free soil for a long period of time.

Born in Southampton, Virginia, in his youth, Dred Scott was known as "Sam." He later changed his name to Dred Scott. He moved with his master to Huntsville, Alabama and later to St. Louis, Missouri. In 1831 his owner, Peter Blow, died and John Emerson, a surgeon in the U.S. Army, bought him. He accompanied his new master to Illinois (a free state) and Wisconsin (a territory). While in what is now Minnesota, around 1836 he met and married Harriett Robinson. In 1843 Emerson died and left his estate to his widow Irene Emerson, who refused Scott's demand for his freedom. He then obtained the assistance of two attorneys who helped him to sue for his freedom in court.

One of the most important cases ever tried in the United States was heard in St. Louis' Old Courthouse. The Supreme Court decided the case in 1857 and hastened the start of the Civil War.

When the first case was first filed in 1846, Dred Scott was in his late 40s. He was born in Virginia around 1799, and was the property, as his parents had been, of the Peter Blow family. He had spent his entire life as a slave, and never got the opportunity to learn to read. Dred Scott moved to St. Louis with the Blows in 1830 but was soon sold due to Blow's financial problems. He was purchased by Dr. John Emerson, a military surgeon stationed at Jefferson Barracks, in south St. Louis and accompanied him to posts in Illinois and the Wisconsin Territory, where slavery had been prohibited by the Missouri Compromise of 1820. During this period, Dred Scott married Harriet Robinson, also a slave, at Fort Snelling; they later had four children, two boys that died in infancy and two girls, Eliza and Lizzie. John Emerson married Irene Sanford during a brief stay in Louisiana. In 1842, the Scott's returned with Dr. and Mrs. Emerson to St. Louis. John Emerson died the following year, and it is believed that Mrs. Emerson hired out Dred Scott, Harriet, and their children to work for other families.

On April 6th, 1846, Dred Scott and his wife Harriet filed suit against Irene Emerson for their freedom. For several years, Scott had lived in free territories, yet made no attempt to end his servitude. It is not known for sure why he chose this particular time for the suit, although historians have considered three possibilities: He may have been dissatisfied with being hired out; Mrs. Emerson might have been planning to sell him; as well as he offered to buy his own freedom and been refused. It is known that the suit was not brought for political reasons. Most likely, friends in St. Louis who opposed slavery had encouraged Scott to sue for his freedom on the grounds that he had once lived in a free territory.

In the past, Missouri courts supported the doctrine of "once free, always free." Dred Scott could not read or write and had no money. He needed help with his suit. John Anderson, the Scott's minister, may have been influential in their decision to sue, and the Blow family, Dred's original owners, backed him financially. The support of such friends helped the Scotts through nearly years of complex and often disappointing litigation.

It is difficult to understand today, but under the law in 1846 whether or not the Scotts were entitled to their freedom was not as important as the consideration of property rights. If slaves were indeed valuable property, like a car or an expensive home today, could they be taken away from their owners because of where the owner had taken them? In other words, if you drove your car from Missouri to Illinois, and the State of Illinois said that it was illegal to own a car in Illinois, could the authorities take the car away from you when you returned to Missouri? These were the questions being discussed in the Dred Scott case, with one major difference: your car is not human and cannot sue you. Although few whites considered the human factor in Dred Scott's slave suit, today we acknowledge that it is wrong to hold people against their will and force them to work as people did in the days of slavery.

The Dred Scott case was first brought to trial in 1846 on the first floor, west wing courtroom of St. Louis' Old Courthouse. The Scotts lost the first trial because hearsay evidence was presented, but they were granted the right by the judge to a second trial. In the second trial, held in the same courtroom in 1850, a jury of 12 white men heard the evidence and decided that Dred Scott and his family should be free. Slaves were valuable property, and Mrs. Emerson did not want to lose the Scotts, so she appealed her case to the Missouri State Supreme Court, which in 1852 reversed the ruling made at the Old Courthouse, stating that "times now are not as they were when the previous decisions on this subject were made." The slavery issue was becoming more divisive nationwide and provided the court with political reasons to return Dred Scott to slavery. The court was saying that Missouri law allowed slavery, and it would uphold the rights of slave-owners in the state at all costs.

Dred Scott was not ready to give up in his fight for freedom for himself and his family, however. With the help of a new team of lawyers who hated slavery, Dred Scott filed suit in St. Louis Federal Court in 1854 against John F. A. Sanford, Mrs. Emerson's brother, and executor of the Emerson estate. Since Sanford resided in New York, the case was taken to the Federal courts due to diversity of residence. The suit was heard not in the Old Courthouse but in the Papin Building, near the area where the north leg of the Gateway Arch stands today. The case was decided in favor of Sanford, but Dred Scott appealed to the U.S. Supreme Court.

On March 6, 1857, Chief Justice Roger B. Taney delivered the majority opinion of the U.S. Supreme Court in the Dred Scott case. Seven of the nine justices agreed that Dred Scott should remain a slave, but Taney did not stop there. He also ruled that as a slave, Dred Scott was not a citizen of the United States, and therefore had no right to bring suit in the federal courts on any matter. In addition, he declared that Scott had never been free, due to the fact that slaves were personal property; thus, the Missouri Compromise of 1820 was unconstitutional, and the Federal Government had no right to prohibit slavery in the new territories. The court appeared to be sanctioning slavery under the terms of the Constitution itself and saying that slavery could not be outlawed or restricted within the United States.

The American public reacted very strongly to the Dred Scott Decision. Antislavery groups feared that slavery would spread unchecked. The new Republican Party, founded in 1854 to prohibit the spread of slavery, renewed their fight to gain control of Congress and the courts. Their well-planned political campaign of 1860, coupled with divisive issues that split the Democratic Party, led to the election of Abraham Lincoln as President of the United States and South Carolina's secession from the Union. The Dred Scott Decision moved the country to the brink of Civil War.

Ironically, Irene Emerson was remarried in 1850 to Calvin C. Chaffee, a northern congressman opposed to slavery. After the Supreme Court decision, Mrs. Chaffee turned Dred and Harriet Scott and their two daughters over to Dred's old friends, the Blows, who gave the Scotts their freedom on May 26, 1857. On September 17, 1858, Dred Scott died of tuberculosis and was buried in St. Louis at the old Weslyan Cemetery near the streets that are now Laclede and Grand. His grave was moved in the 1860s to Calvary Cemetery in northern St. Louis. His grave site at Calvary was marked due to the efforts of the Rev. Edward Dowling in 1957 of the Baden Historical Society.

Dred Scott did not live to see the fratricidal war touched off at Fort Sumter in 1861 but did live to gain his freedom. The ultimate result of the war, the end of slavery throughout the United States, was not something

Dred Scott could have foreseen in 1846, when he decided to sue for his freedom in St. Louis' Old Courthouse.

However, his life, his purpose and indeed his destiny was to be forever a most integral part of the destruction of an institution that when abolished, in large part because of the perseverance of Dred and Harriet Scott, freed not only a people but a nation from the grip of an unspeakable evil.

https://www.thedredscottfoundation.org/dshf/index.php?option=com_content&view=article&id=50&Itemid=93

CHAPTER TWO
SOJOURNER TRUTH (1797-1883)

Credit: Hulton Archive/Getty Images

Sojourner Truth was born in 1797 as Isabella, a Dutch-speaking slave in rural New York. Separated from her family at age nine, she was sold several times before ending up on the farm of John and Sally Dumont. As was the case for most slaves in the rural North, Isabella lived isolated from other Black Americans, and she suffered from physical and sexual abuse at the hands of her masters. Inspired by her conversations with God, which she held alone in the woods, Isabella walked to freedom in 1826. Although tempted to return to Dumont's farm, she was struck by a vision of Jesus, during which she felt "baptized in the Holy Spirit," and she gained the strength and confidence to resist her former master. In this experience, Isabella was like countless black Americans who called on the supernatural for the power to survive injustice and oppression.

In 1828, Isabella moved to New York City and soon thereafter became a preacher in the "perfectionist," or Pentecostal tradition. Her faith and preaching brought her into contact with abolitionists and women's rights crusaders, and Truth became a powerful speaker on both subjects. She traveled extensively as a lecturer, particularly after the publication of The Narrative of Sojourner Truth, which detailed her suffering as a slave. Her speeches were not political but were based on her unique interpretation-as a woman and a former slave-of the Bible.

With the start of the Civil War, Truth became increasingly political in her work. She agitated for the inclusion of blacks in the Union Army, and, once they were permitted to join, volunteered by bringing them food and clothes. She became increasingly involved in the issue of women's suffrage but broke with leaders Susan B. Anthony and Elizabeth Cady Stanton when Stanton stated that she would not support the black vote if women were not also granted the right. Truth also fought for land to resettle freed slaves, and she saw the 1879 Exodus to Kansas as part of God's divine plan. Truth's famous "Ar'n't I a Woman?" speech, delivered in 1851 at the Ohio Women's Rights Convention, is a perfect example of how, as Nell Painter puts it, "at a time when most Americans thought of slaves as male and women as white, Truth embodied a fact that still bears repeating: Among blacks are women; among the women, there are blacks."

Sojourner Truth was born Isabella, the youngest of 12 children, in Ulster County, NY, in 1797. When she was nine, Isabella was sold from her family to an English speaking-family called Neely. Like many black New Yorkers, Isabella spoke only Dutch. Her new owners beat her for not understanding their commands. She was sold twice more before arriving at the Dumont farm, at 14. which she worked for 17 years. John Dumont beat her, and there is evidence that his wife, Sally, sexually abused her. Of this time in her life,

Isabella wrote: "Now the war begun." It was a war both with her masters, and herself.

Alone on John Dumont's farm with little contact with other black New Yorkers, Isabella found her own ways to worship God. She built a temple of brush in the woods, an African tradition she may have learned from her mother and bargained with God as if he were a familiar presence. Even though she had worked hard to please her master for 16 years, Isabella listened to God when He told her to walk away from slavery. With her baby, Sophia, Isabella left Dumont's farm in 1826 and walked to freedom.

Like thousands of slaves, free blacks, and poor whites in the early nineteenth century, Isabella was swept up by the tide the Second Great Awakening, a Protestant evangelical movement that emphasized living simply and following the Holy Spirit. In 1827, newly-free Isabella considered returning to the Dumont farm to attend Pinkster, a celebration of New York slaves. She was saved from joining her ex-master by a frightening vision of God, followed by the calming presence of an intercessor, whom Isabella recognized as Jesus. With Jesus as her "soul-protecting fortress," Isabella gained the power to rise "above the battlements of fear."

In 1826, Isabella was living with the Van Wagenens, white Methodists, when she learned that her son, Peter, had been illegally sold into slavery in Alabama. An outraged Isabella had no money to regain her son, but with God on her side she said she felt "so tall within, as if the power of a nation was within [her]." She acquired money for legal fees and filed a complaint with the Ulster County grand jury. Peter was returned to her in the spring of 1828, marking the first step in a life of activism inspired by religious faith.

In the late 1820s, Isabella moved to New York City and lived among a community of Methodist Perfectionists, men and women who met outside of the church for ecstatic worship and emphasized living simply through the power of the Holy Spirit. Through the perfectionists, Isabella fell under the spell of the "Prophet Matthias," and lived with his cult from 1833 to 1834. This experience suggests that Isabella, although on her way to self-confidence and independence, still yearned for structure and family, but chose an abusive situation - Matthias often beat her - that felt familiar to her experience as John Dumont's slave.

While living in New York, Isabella attended the many camp meetings held around the city, and she quickly established herself as a powerful speaker, capable of converting many. In 1843, she was "called in spirit" on the day of Pentecost. The spirit instructed her to leave New York, a "second Sodom," and travel east to lecture under the name Sojourner Truth. This new name signified her role as an itinerant preacher, her preoccupation with truth and justice, and her mission to teach people "to embrace Jesus, and refrain from sin." Sojourner Truth set off on her journey during a period of millennial fervor, with many poised to hear her call to Jesus before the Day of Judgement.

Sojourner Truth first met the abolitionist Frederick Douglass while she was living at the Northampton Association. Although he admired her speaking ability, Douglass was patronizing of Truth, whom he saw as "uncultured." Years later, however, Truth would use her plain talk to challenge Douglass. At an 1852 meeting in Ohio, Douglass spoke of the need for blacks to seize freedom by force. As he sat down, Truth asked "Is God gone?" Although much exaggerated by Harriet Beecher Stowe and other writers, this exchange made Truth a symbol for faith in nonviolence and God's power to right the wrongs of slavery.

The 1879 spontaneous exodus of tens of thousands of freed people from southern states to Kansas was the culmination of one of Sojourner Truth's most fervent prayers. After the Civil War, Truth had traveled to Washington to work among destitute freed people. Inspired by divine command, Truth began agitating for their resettlement to western lands. She drew up a petition (which probably never reached Congress, as intended) and traveled extensively, promoting her plan and collecting signatures. Truth saw the Exodusters, fleeing violence and abuse in the Reconstruction South, as evidence that God had a plan for Black People.

During the Civil War, Sojourner Truth took up the issue of women's suffrage. She was befriended by Susan B. Anthony and Elizabeth Cady Stanton, but disagreed with them on many issues, most notably Stanton's threat that she would not support the black vote if women were denied it. Although she remained supportive of women's suffrage throughout her life, Truth distanced herself from the increasingly racist language of the women's groups. Truth died on November 26, 1883. In her old age, she had let go of Pentecostal judgement and embraced spiritualism. Her last words were "be a follower of the Lord Jesus."

https://www.pbs.org/thisfarbyfaith/people/sojourner_truth.html

CHAPTER THREE
NAT TURNER (1800–1831)

Nat Turner was an enslaved person who became a preacher and made history as the leader of one of the bloodiest enslaved revolts in America on August 21, 1831. Following the insurrection, Turner hid for six weeks, but he was eventually caught and later hanged. The incident ended the emancipation movement in that region and led to even harsher laws against the enslaved. While Turner became an icon of the 1960s Black power movement, others have criticized him for using violence as a means of demanding change.

Turner was born on October 2, 1800, in Southampton County, Virginia, on the plantation of Benjamin Turner. His mother was named Nancy, but nothing is known about his father. Turner's owner, Benjamin, allowed him to be instructed in reading, writing and religion.

As a small child, Turner was thought to have some special talent because he could describe things that happened before he was even born. Some even remarked that he "surely would be a prophet," according to his later confession. His mother and grandmother told Turner that he "was intended for some great purpose." Turner was deeply religious and spent much of his time reading the Bible, praying and fasting.

Over the years, Turner worked on a number of different plantations. He ran away from Samuel Turner, his former owner's brother, in 1821. After 30 days of hiding in the woods, Turner came back to Samuel's plantation after he received what he believed to be a sign from God. After Samuel's death, Turner became the enslaved person of Thomas Moore and then the property of his widow. When she married John Travis, Turner went to work on Travis' lands

On August 21, 1831, Turner and his supporters began a revolt against white owners with the killing of his owners, the Travis family.

Turner believed in signs and heard divine voices, and he had a vision in 1825 of a bloody conflict between Black and white spirits. Three years later, he had what he believed to be another message from God. In his later confession, Turner explained: "the Spirit instantly appeared to me and said the Serpent was loosened, and Christ had laid down the yoke he had borne for the sins of men, and that I should take it on and fight against the Serpent." Turner would receive another sign to tell him when to fight, but this latest message meant "I should arise and prepare myself and slay my enemies with their own weapons."

Turner took a solar eclipse that occurred in February 1831 as a signal that the time to rise up had come. He recruited several other enslaved people to join him in his cause. Turner gathered more supporters — growing to a group of up to 40 or 50 enslaved people — as he and his men continued their violent spree through the county. They were able to secure arms and horses from those they killed. Most sources say that about 55 white men, women and children died during Turner's rebellion.

Initially, Turner had planned to reach the county seat of Jerusalem and take over the armory there, but he and his men were foiled in this plan. They faced off against a group of armed white men at a plantation near Jerusalem, and the conflict soon dissolved into chaos. Turner himself fled into the woods.

While Turner hid, white mobs took their revenge on the Black people of Southampton County. Estimates range from approximately 100 to 200 Black Americans who were slaughtered after the rebellion.

Turner was eventually captured on October 30, 1831. He was represented by lawyer Thomas R. Gray, who wrote down Turner's confession. Turner pled not guilty during his trial, believing that his rebellion was the work of God. He was sentenced to death by hanging, and this sentence was carried out on November 11, 1831. Many of his co-conspirators met the same fate.

The incident put fear in the heart of Southerners, ending the organized emancipation movement in that region. Southern states enacted even harsher laws against the enslaved instead. Turner's actions also added fuel to the abolitionist movement in the North. Noted abolitionist William Lloyd Garrison even published an editorial in his newspaper The Liberator in support of Turner to some degree

Over the years, Turner has emerged as a hero, a religious fanatic and a villain. Turner became an important icon to the 1960s Black power movement as an example of a Black American standing up against white oppression.

Others have objected to Turner's indiscriminate slaughtering of men, women, and children to try to achieve this end. As historian Scot French told The New York Times, "To accept Nat Turner and place him within the pantheon of American revolutionary heroes is to sanction violence as a means of social change. He has a kind of radical consciousness that to this day troubles advocates of a racially reconciled society. The story lives because it's relevant today to questions of how to organize for change."

Turner was the subject of William Styron's 1967 Pulitzer Prize-winning novel Confessions of Nat Turner.

Turner's life and uprising was also the subject of the 2016 film, The Birth of a Nation, which was directed, written by and starring Nate Parker. The film won the Audience Award and Grand Jury Prize at the 2016 Sundance Film Festival.

https://www.biography.com/activist/nat-turner

CHAPTER FOUR
FREDERICK DOUGLASS (1818-1895)

Douglass was born enslaved as Frederick Augustus Washington Bailey on Holme Hill Farm in Talbot County, Maryland. Although the date of his birth was not recorded, Douglass estimated that he had been born in February 1818, and he later celebrated his birthday on February 14. (The best source for the events in Douglass's life is Douglass himself in his oratory and writings, especially his three autobiographies, the details of which have been checked when possible and have largely been confirmed, though his biographers have contributed corrections and clarifications.) Douglass was owned by Capt. Aaron Anthony, who was the clerk and superintendent of overseers for Edward Lloyd V (also known as Colonel Lloyd), a wealthy landowner and slaveholder in eastern Maryland. Like many other enslaved children, Douglass was separated from his mother, Harriet Bailey, when he was very young. He spent his formative years with his maternal grandmother, Betsey Bailey, who had the responsibility of raising young, enslaved children.

Harriet Bailey worked as a field hand on a neighboring plantation and had to walk more than 12 miles to visit her son, whom she met with only a few times in his life. He described her as "tall and finely proportioned, of dark, glossy complexion, with regular features, and amongst the slaves was remarkably sedate and dignified." She died when he was about seven years old. As an adult, Douglass learned that his mother had been the only Black person in what was then Talbot County who could read, an extraordinarily rare achievement for a field hand.

When Douglass was age five or six, he was taken to live on Colonel Lloyd's home plantation, Wye House. Lloyd's plantation functioned like a small town. Young Douglass found himself among several other enslaved children competing for food and other comforts. In 1826 at approximately age eight, he was sent to live with Hugh and Sophia Auld at Fells Point, Baltimore. Hugh's brother Capt. Thomas Auld was the son-in-law of Douglass's owner, Aaron Anthony. Douglass's responsibility in Baltimore was to care for Hugh and Sophia's young son, Thomas. Sophia began teaching Douglass how to read, along with her son. The lessons ended abruptly, however, when Hugh discovered what had been going on and informed Sophia that literacy would "spoil" a slave. According to Douglass, Hugh stated that if a slave were given an inch, he would "take an ell [a unit of measure equal to about 45 inches]." In Maryland, as in many other slaveholding states, it was forbidden to teach enslaved people how to read and write. Douglass continued his learning in secret, by exchanging bread for lessons from the poor white boys he played with in the neighborhood and by tracing the letters in Thomas's old schoolbooks.

In March 1832 Douglass was sent from Baltimore to St. Michaels, on

Maryland's Eastern Shore. After both Aaron Anthony and his daughter Lucretia died, her husband, Capt. Thomas Auld, became Douglass's owner. Teenage Douglass experienced harsher living conditions with Auld, who was known for his abusive practices.

In January 1833 Douglass was leased to local farmer Edward Covey. Leasing or hiring out enslaved persons was a common revenue-generating practice. Farmers would pay slaveholders a monthly fee for enslaved people and take responsibility for their care, food, and lodging. Covey was known as a "slave breaker," someone who abused slaves physically and psychologically in order to make them more compliant. According to Douglass, Covey's abuse led to a climactic confrontation six months into Douglass's time with the farmer. One day Covey attacked Douglass, and Douglass fought back. The two men engaged in an epic two-hour-long physical struggle. Douglass ultimately won the fight, and Covey never attacked him again. Douglass emerged from the incident determined to protect himself from any physical assault from anyone in the future.

In January 1834 Douglass was sent to William Freeland's farm. Living and working conditions were better under Freeland; however, Douglass still desired his freedom. While living with Freeland, he started a Sabbath school at which he taught area Blacks how to read and write. Along with four other enslaved men, Douglass plotted to escape north by taking a large canoe up the coast of Maryland and to proceed to Pennsylvania, but their plot was discovered. Douglass and the other participants were arrested. Captain Auld then sent Douglass back to Baltimore to live again with Hugh and Sophia Auld and to learn a trade.

Hugh Auld hired out Douglass to local shipyards as a ship caulker. Now working as a skilled tradesman, Douglass was paid by the shipyards for his efforts. He would then submit his earnings to Auld, who gave Douglass a small percentage of the wages. Douglass would eventually hire out his own time, which meant that he paid Auld a set amount every week but was responsible for maintaining his own food and clothing. During this time, Douglass became more involved in Baltimore's Black community, which led him to meet Anna Murray, a freeborn Black woman, whom he would eventually marry.

Douglass moved about Baltimore with few restrictions, but that privilege came to an end when he decided to attend a religious meeting outside of Baltimore on a Saturday evening and postpone paying Auld his weekly fee. The following Monday, when Douglass returned, Auld threatened him. After that encounter, Douglass was determined to escape his bondage. He escaped in September 1838 by dressing as a sailor and traveling from Baltimore to Wilmington, Delaware, by train, then on to Philadelphia by steamboat, and from there to New York City by train. Black sailors in the 19th century traveled with documents granting them protection under the American flag. Douglass used such documents to secure his passage north with the help of Anna, who, according to family lore, had sold her feather bed to help finance his passage.

New York City was a dangerous place for enslaved people seeking freedom. Numerous slave catchers traveled to the city to track down those who had escaped. Many locals, Black and white, were willing, for money, to tell the authorities about people trying to escape enslavement. For his own protection, Douglass (still months from assuming that name) changed his name from Frederick Bailey to Frederick Johnson. A chance meeting with Black abolitionist David Ruggles led Douglass to safety. Anna arrived in New York several days later, and the two were married by the Reverend J.W.C. Pennington.

At Ruggles's recommendation, the couple quickly left New York City for New Bedford, Massachusetts. Ruggles had determined that New Bedford's shipping industry would offer Douglass the best chance to find work as a ship caulker. In New Bedford the couple stayed with a local Black married couple, Nathan and Polly Johnson. Because many families in New Bedford had the surname Johnson, Douglass chose to change his name again. Nathan Johnson suggested the name Douglass, which was inspired by the name of an exiled nobleman in Sir Walter Scott's poem The Lady of the Lake. The newly minted Frederick Douglass earned money for the first time as a free man. However, despite Douglass's previous work experience, racial prejudice in New Bedford prevented him from working as a ship caulker (white caulkers refused to work with Black caulkers). Consequently, Douglass spent his first years in Massachusetts working as a common laborer.

Douglass remained an avid reader throughout his adult life. When he escaped to New York, he carried with him a copy of The Columbian Orator. In New Bedford he discovered William Lloyd Garrison's abolitionist newspaper, The Liberator. Inspired by it, Douglass attended a Massachusetts Anti-Slavery Society convention in Nantucket in the summer of 1841. At the meeting, abolitionist William C. Coffin, having heard Douglass speak in New Bedford, invited him to address the general body. Douglass's extemporaneous speech was lauded by the audience, and he was recruited as an agent for the group.

As an agent of both the Massachusetts Anti-Slavery Society and the

American Anti-Slavery Society, Douglass traveled the country promoting abolition and the organizations' agenda. He and other people who had escaped conditions of enslavement frequently described their own experiences under those conditions. The American Anti-Slavery Society supported "moral suasion" abolition, the belief that slavery was a moral wrong that should be resisted through nonviolent means. Douglass strongly promoted this philosophy during the early years of his abolitionist career. In his speech at the 1843 National Convention of Colored Citizens in Buffalo, New York, Black abolitionist, and minister Henry Highland Garnet proposed a resolution that called for enslaved people to rise up against their masters. The controversial resolution ignited a tense debate at the convention, with Douglass rising in firm opposition. His belief in moral suasion would repeatedly place him at odds with other Black abolitionists during this phase of his career. Work as an agent provided Douglass with the means to support his family. He and Anna had five children: Rosetta (born 1839), Lewis (born 1840), Frederick, Jr. (born 1842), Charles (born 1844), and Annie (born 1849).

In 1845 Douglass published his first autobiography, Narrative of the Life of Frederick Douglass, an American Slave, Written by Himself. Prior to its publication, audiences at Douglass's lectures had questioned his authenticity as an ex-slave because of his eloquence, refusal to use "plantation speech," and unwillingness to provide details about his origins. The Narrative settled these disputes by naming people and locations in Douglass's life. The book also challenged the conventional employment of ghostwriters for slave narratives by boldly acknowledging that Douglass wrote it himself. Douglass would publish two additional autobiographies: My Bondage and My Freedom (1855) and Life and Times of Frederick Douglass (1881). The Narrative quickly became popular, especially in Europe, but the book's success contributed to Hugh Auld's determination to return Douglass to the conditions of enslavement.

The threat of capture, as well as the book's excellent performance in Europe, prompted Douglass to travel abroad from August 1845 to 1847, and he lectured throughout the United Kingdom. His English supporters, led by Ellen and Anna Richardson, purchased Douglass from Hugh Auld, giving him his freedom. In the spring of 1847, Douglass returned to the United States a free man with the funding to start his own newspaper.

Douglass moved to Rochester, New York, to publish his newspaper, The North Star, despite objections from Garrison and others. Basing the newspaper in Rochester ensured that The North Star did not compete with the distribution of The Liberator and the National Anti-Slavery Standard in New England. The North Star's first issue appeared on December 3, 1847. In 1851 the paper merged with the Liberty Party Paper to form Frederick Douglass' Paper, which ran until 1860. Douglass would publish two additional newspapers during his life, Douglass' Monthly (1859–63) and New National Era (1870–74).

The move to Rochester surrounded Douglass with political abolitionists such as Gerrit Smith. During his first few years in Rochester, Douglass remained loyal to Garrison's philosophy, which promoted moral suasion, stated that the U.S. Constitution was an invalid document, and discouraged participation in American politics because it was a system corrupted by slavery. In 1851, however, Douglass announced his split from Garrison when he declared that the Constitution was a valid legal document that could be used on behalf of emancipation. Consequently, Douglass became more engaged in American politics and constitutional interpretation

The country's tension around slavery rapidly increased in the 1850s. Douglass's Rochester home was part of the Underground Railroad and hosted numerous fellow abolitionists. In 1859 Douglass met with abolitionist John Brown in a quarry in Chambersburg, Pennsylvania. Brown invited Douglass to participate in the planned raid on the federal arsenal in Harpers Ferry, Virginia (now in West Virginia), which Brown hoped would inspire a massive uprising by enslaved people. Douglass declined the invitation. Shortly after the raid (October 16–19), Douglass received word that the authorities were looking to arrest him as an accomplice. He quickly fled to Canada before heading to Europe for a scheduled lecture tour. Douglass returned home in April 1860 after learning that his youngest daughter, Annie, had died.

With the outbreak of the Civil War, Douglass strongly advocated for inclusion of Black soldiers in the Union army. He became a recruiter for the Massachusetts 54th, an all-Black infantry regiment in which his sons Lewis and Charles served. In 1863 Douglass visited the White House to meet with Pres. Abraham Lincoln to advocate for better pay and conditions for the soldiers. Lincoln then invited Douglass to the White House in 1864 to discuss what could be done for Blacks in the case of a Union loss. Douglass would meet with Lincoln a third time, after the president's second inauguration and about a month before his assassination.

The Emancipation Proclamation and the Union's victory presented a new reality: millions of Black people were free. Douglass dedicated himself to securing the community's rights to this new freedom. He strongly supported the Fourteenth Amendment, which granted Blacks citizenship, but he realized that this new citizenship status needed to be protected by suffrage. Initially Douglass supported a constitutional amendment supporting suffrage for all men and women. Having attended the 1848 women's rights convention in Seneca Falls, New York, he was a longtime supporter of women's rights, joining Elizabeth Cady Stanton and Susan B. Anthony in this stance. Reconstruction politics, however, indicated that a universal suffrage amendment would fail. Douglass then supported Black male suffrage with the idea that Black men could help women secure the right to vote later. This placed him at odds with Stanton and Anthony. Douglass hoped that the passage of the Fifteenth Amendment would encourage Black Americans to stay in the South to consolidate their power as a voting bloc, but the region's high levels of violence against Black people led him to support Black migration to safer areas of the country.

After a fire destroyed his Rochester home, Douglass moved in 1872 to Washington, D.C., where he published his latest newspaper venture, New National Era. The newspaper folded in 1874 because of its poor fiscal health. That same year Douglass was appointed president of the Freedman's Savings & Trust, also known as the Freedman's Bank. The bank failed four months after he became president because of the years of corruption that predated his association with the bank. The bank's failure harmed his reputation, but Douglass worked with the U.S. Congress to remedy the damage caused by the bank.

After the Freedman's Bank debacle, Douglass held numerous government appointments. He became the first Black U.S. marshal in 1877 when he was appointed to that post for the District of Columbia by Pres. Rutherford B. Hayes. He served in that capacity until 1881, when Pres. James A. Garfield appointed him to the high-paying position of recorder of deeds for the District of Columbia. In 1889 Pres. Benjamin Harrison selected Douglass as the U.S. minister resident and consul general to the Republic of Haiti. The major controversy during Douglass's tenure was the quest by the United States to acquire the port town of Môle Saint-Nicolas as a refueling station for the U.S. Navy. Douglass disagreed with the Harrison administration's approach, preferring to promote the autonomy of the Haitian government. He resigned the position in 1891 and returned to his home in Washington, D.C.

Douglass spent the last 17 years of his life at Cedar Hill, his home in the Anacostia neighborhood of Washington, D.C., to which he had moved in 1878. On August 4, 1882, Anna Murray Douglass died in the home after suffering a stroke. In 1884 Douglass married Helen Pitts, his white secretary, who was about 20 years younger than her husband. The marriage was controversial for its time, and it resulted in Douglass's temporary estrangement from some friends and family.

During the latter years of his life, Douglass remained committed to social justice and the Black community. His prominence and work resulted in his being the most photographed American man in the 19th century. His distinguished photographs were deliberate contradictions to the visual stereotypes of Black American men, at the time, which often exaggerated their facial features, skin color, and physical bodies and demeaned their intelligence. He served on Howard University's board of trustees from 1871 to 1895. Douglass cultivated relationships with younger activists, most notably Ida B. Wells, who featured his letter to her in her book Southern Horrors: Lynch Law in All Its Phases. He also contributed to her pamphlet protesting the exclusion of exhibits dedicated to Black culture from the 1893 World's Columbian Exposition, The Reason Why the Colored American Is Not in the World's Columbian Exposition.

Douglass died in his Cedar Hill home on February 20, 1895. After his death, Helen Pitts Douglass established the Frederick Douglass Memorial and Historical Association to preserve his legacy. She bequeathed the home and its belongings to the organization in her will. Cedar Hill became part of the National Park system in 1962, and it was designated the Frederick Douglass National Historic Site in 1988. The U.S. Library of Congress digitized its holdings of Douglass's papers, which include letters, speeches, and personal documents.

At the end of his life, Douglass, an American icon who fought for social justice and equity, became known as the "Lion of Anacostia." Through his writings, speeches, and photographs, he boldly challenged the racial stereotypes of Black Americans. Douglass's contributions to the Black American community and American history were recognized in the early 20th century during Negro History Week, the predecessor of Black History Month, which many communities anchored to the day on which his birthday was celebrated, February 14. Today Douglass is renowned not just for his rise from slavery to the highest levels of American society but also for his dedication to challenging the country to recognize the rights of all people and be consistent with its ideals.

https://www.britannica.com/biography/Frederick-Douglass

CHAPTER FIVE
HARRIET TUBMAN (1820-1913)

Harriet Tubman circa 1885

Harriet Tubman was an escaped enslaved woman who became a "conductor" on the Underground Railroad, leading enslaved people to freedom before the Civil War, all while carrying a bounty on her head. But she was also a nurse, a Union spy and a women's suffrage supporter. Tubman is one of the most recognized icons in American history and her legacy has inspired countless people from every race and background.

Harriet Tubman was born around 1820 on a plantation in Dorchester County, Maryland. Her parents, Harriet ("Rit") Green and Benjamin Ross, named her Araminta Ross and called her "Minty."

Rit worked as a cook in the plantation's "big house," and Benjamin was a timber worker. Araminta later changed her first name to Harriet in honor of her mother.

Harriet had eight siblings, but the realities of slavery eventually forced many of them apart, despite Rit's attempts to keep the family together. When Harriet was five years old, she was rented out as a nursemaid where she was whipped when the baby cried, leaving her with permanent emotional and physical scars.

Around age seven Harriet was rented out to a planter to set muskrat traps and was later rented out as a field hand. She later said she preferred physical plantation work to indoor domestic chores.

Harriet's desire for justice became apparent at age 12 when she spotted an overseer about to throw a heavy weight at a fugitive. Harriet stepped between the enslaved person and the overseer—the weight struck her head.

She later said about the incident, "The weight broke my skull ... They carried me to the house all bleeding and fainting. I had no bed, no place to lie down on at all, and they laid me on the seat of the loom, and I stayed there all day and the next."

Harriet's good deed left her with headaches and narcolepsy the rest of her life, causing her to fall into a deep sleep at random. She also started having vivid dreams and hallucinations which she often claimed were religious visions (she was a staunch Christian). Her infirmity made her unattractive to potential slave buyers and renters.

In 1840, Harriet's father was set free, and Harriet learned that Rit's owner's last will had set Rit and her children, including Harriet, free. But Rit's new owner refused to recognize the will and kept Rit, Harriett, and the rest of her children in bondage.

Around 1844, Harriet married John Tubman, a free Black man, and changed her last name from Ross to Tubman. The marriage was not good, and the knowledge that two of her brothers—Ben and Henry—were about to be sold provoked Harriet to plan an escape.

On September 17, 1849, Harriet, Ben, and Henry escaped their Maryland plantation. The brothers, however, changed their minds and went back. With the help of the Underground Railroad, Harriet persevered and traveled 90 miles north to Pennsylvania and freedom.

Tubman found work as a housekeeper in Philadelphia, but she wasn't satisfied living free on her own—she wanted freedom for her loved ones and friends, too.

She soon returned to the south to lead her niece and her niece's children to Philadelphia via the Underground Railroad. At one point, she tried to bring her husband John north, but he'd remarried and chose to stay in Maryland with his new wife.

The 1850 Fugitive Slave Act allowed fugitive and freed workers in the north to be captured and enslaved. This made Harriet's role as an Underground Railroad conductor much harder and forced her to lead enslaved people further north to Canada, traveling at night, usually in the spring or fall when the days were shorter.

She carried a gun for both her own protection and to "encourage" her charges who might be having second thoughts. She often drugged babies and young children to prevent slave catchers from hearing their cries.

Over the next 10 years, Harriet befriended other abolitionists such as Frederick Douglass, Thomas Garrett, and Martha Coffin Wright, and established her own Underground Railroad network. It's widely reported she emancipated 300 enslaved people; however, those numbers may have been estimated and exaggerated by her biographer Sarah Bradford, since Harriet herself claimed the numbers were much lower.

Nevertheless, it's believed Harriet personally led at least 70 enslaved people to freedom, including her elderly parents, and instructed dozens of others on how to escape on their own. She claimed, "I never ran my train off the track, and I never lost a passenger."

When the Civil War broke out in 1861, Harriet found new ways to fight slavery. She was recruited to assist fugitive enslaved people at Fort Monroe and worked as a nurse, cook and laundress. Harriet used her knowledge of herbal medicines to help treat sick soldiers and fugitive enslaved people.

In 1863, Harriet became head of an espionage and scout network for the Union Army. She provided crucial intelligence to Union commanders about Confederate Army supply routes and troops and helped liberate enslaved people to form Black Union regiments.

Though just over five feet tall, she was a force to be reckoned with, although it took over three decades for the government to recognize her military contributions and award her financially.

After the Civil War, Harriet settled with family and friends on land she owned in Auburn, New York. She married former enslaved man and Civil War veteran Nelson Davis in 1869 (her husband John had died 1867) and they adopted a little girl named Gertie a few years later.

Harriet had an open-door policy for anyone in need. She supported her philanthropy efforts by selling her home-grown produce, raising pigs and accepting donations and loans from friends. She remained illiterate yet toured parts of the northeast speaking on behalf of the women's suffrage movement and worked with noted suffrage leader Susan B. Anthony.

In 1896, Harriet purchased land adjacent to her home and opened the Harriet Tubman Home for Aged and Indigent Colored People. The head injury she suffered in her youth continued to plague her and she endured brain surgery to help relieve her symptoms. But her health continued to deteriorate and eventually forced her to move into her namesake rest home in 1911.

Pneumonia took Harriet Tubman's life on March 10, 1913, but her legacy lives on. Schools and museums bear her name, and her story has been revisited in books, movies, and documentaries.

Tubman even had a World War II Liberty ship named after her, the SS Harriet Tubman.

In 2016, the United States Treasury announced that Harriet's image will replace that of former President and slaveowner Andrew Jackson on the $20 bill. Treasury Secretary Steven Mnuchin (who served under President Trump) later announced the new bill would be delayed until at least 2026. In January 2021, President Biden's administration announced it would speed up the design process to mint the bills honoring Tubman's legacy.

BLACK EXCELLANCE

https://www.history.com/topics/black-history/harriet-tubman

CHAPTER SIX
BOOKER T. WASHINGTON (1856-1915)

Credit: Library of Congress

Born April 5, 1856, in Franklin County, Virginia, Booker Taliaferro was the son of an unknown White man and Jane, an enslaved cook of James Burroughs, a small planter.

Jane named her son Booker Taliaferro but later dropped the second name. Booker gave himself the surname "Washington" when he first enrolled in school. Sometime after Booker's birth, his mother was married to Washington Ferguson, a slave. A daughter, Amanda, was born to this marriage. James, Booker's younger half-brother, was adopted. Booker's elder brother, John, was also the son of a White man.

Booker spent his first nine years as a slave on the Burroughs farm. In 1865, his mother took her children to Malden, West Virginia, to join her husband, who had gone there earlier and found work in the salt mines. At age nine, Booker was put to work packing salt. Between the ages of ten and twelve, he worked in a coal mine. He attended school while continuing to work in the mines. In 1871, he went to work as a houseboy for the wife of Gen. Lewis Ruffner, owner of the mines.

In 1872, at age sixteen, Booker T. Washington entered Hampton Normal and Agricultural Institute in Virginia. The dominant personality at the school, which had opened in 1868 under the auspices of the American Missionary Association, was the principal, Samuel Chapman Armstrong, the son of American missionaries in Hawaii.

Armstrong, who had commanded Black troops in the Civil War, believed that the progress of freedmen and their descendants depended on education of a special sort, which would be practical and utilitarian and would at the same time inculcate character and morality.

Washington traveled most of the distance from Malden to Hampton on foot, arriving penniless. His entrance examination to Hampton was to clean a room. The teacher inspected his work with a spotless, white handkerchief. Booker was admitted. He was given work as a janitor to pay the cost of his room and board, and Armstrong arranged for a White benefactor to pay his tuition.

At Hampton, Washington studied academic subjects and agriculture, which included work in the fields and pigsties. He also learned lessons in personal cleanliness and good manners. His special interest was public speaking and debate. He was jubilant when he was chosen to speak at his commencement.

The most important part of his experience at Hampton was his association with Armstrong, who he described in his autobiography as "a great man - the noblest, rarest human being it has ever been my privilege to meet." From Armstrong, Washington derived much of his educational philosophy.

After graduating from Hampton with honors in 1875, Washington returned to Malden to teach. For eight months he was a student at Wayland Seminary, an institution with a curriculum that was entirely academic. This experience reinforced his belief in an educational system that emphasized practical skills and self-help. In 1879, Washington returned to Hampton to teach in a program for American Indians.

In 1880, a bill that included a yearly appropriation of $2,000 was passed by the Alabama State Legislature to establish a school for Blacks in Macon County. This action was generated by two men - Lewis Adams, a former slave, and George W. Campbell, a former slave owner. On February 12, 1881, Governor Rufus Willis Cobb signed the bill into law, establishing the Tuskegee Normal School for the training of Black teachers.

Armstrong was invited to recommend a White teacher as principal of the school. Instead, he suggested Washington, who was accepted. When Washington arrived at Tuskegee, he found that no land or buildings had been acquired for the projected school, nor was there any money for these purposes since the appropriation was for salaries only. Undaunted, Washington began selling the idea of the school, recruiting students and seeking support of local Whites.

The school opened July 4, 1881, in a shanty loaned by a Black church, Butler A.M.E. Zion. With money borrowed from Hampton Institute's treasurer, Washington purchased an abandoned 100-acre plantation on the outskirts of Tuskegee. Students built a kiln, made bricks for buildings and sold bricks to raise money. Within a few years, they built a classroom building, a dining hall, a girl's dormitory and a chapel.

By 1888, the 540-acre Tuskegee Normal and Industrial Institute had an enrollment of more than 400 and offered training in such skilled trades as carpentry, cabinet-omaking, printing, shoemaking and tinsmithing. Boys also studied farming and dairying, while girls learned such domestic skills as cooking and sewing.

Through their own labor, students supplied a large part of the needs of the school. In the academic departments, Washington insisted that efforts be made to relate the subject matter to the actual experiences of the students. Strong emphasis was placed on personal hygiene, manners and character building.

Students followed a rigid schedule of study and work, arising at five in the morning and retiring at nine-thirty at night. Although Tuskegee was non-denominational, all students were required to attend chapel daily and a series of religious services on Sunday. Washington himself usually spoke to the students on Sunday evening.

Olivia Davidson, a graduate of Hampton and Framingham State Normal School in Massachusetts, became teacher and assistant principal at Tuskegee in 1881. In 1885, Washington's older brother John, also a Hampton graduate, came to Tuskegee to direct the vocational training program.

Other notable additions to the staff were acclaimed scientist Dr. George Washington Carver, who became director of the agriculture program in 1896; Emmett J. Scott, who became Washington 's private secretary in 1897; and Monroe Nathan Work, who became head of the Records and Research Department in 1908.

On Tuskegee's 25th anniversary, Washington had transformed an idea into a 2,000-acre, eighty-three building campus that, combined with such personal property as equipment, livestock and stock in trade, was valued at $831,895. Tuskegee's endowment fund was $1,275,644 and training in thirty-seven industries was available for the more than 1,500 students enrolled that year.

Through progress at Tuskegee, Washington showed that an oppressed people could advance. His concept of practical education was a contribution to the general field of education. His writings, which included 40 books, were widely read and highly regarded. Among his works was an autobiography titled "Up From Slavery" (1901), "Character Building" (1902), "My Larger Education" (1911), and "The Man Farthest Down" (1912).

Washington settled into the national scene on opening day of the Atlanta Exposition in 1895 when he spoke about "The New Negro," one with "the knowledge of how to live ... how to cultivate the soil, to husband their resources, and make the most of their opportunities."

Eyebrows raised again on Oct. 16, 1901, when Washington became the first Black person to dine at the White House. Counsel to many U.S. presidents, he was there at the invitation of President Theodore Roosevelt.

Washington was married three times. In 1882, he married his Malden sweetheart, Fannie Norton Smith. She died two years later, leaving an infant daughter, Portia (who married William Sidney Pittman, an architect, in 1907).

In 1885, Washington married Hampton graduate Olivia Davidson, the assistant principal of Tuskegee, who died in 1889. Two sons were born to this marriage: Booker Taliaferro, Jr. and Ernest Davidson.

In 1893, Washington married Fisk University graduate Margaret James Murray, who had come to Tuskegee as lady principal in 1889 and directed the programs for female students and initiated the Women's Meetings. Margaret Murray Washington died in 1925.

Margaret and her husband's three children and four grandchildren survived Washington, who died November 14, 1915, at age fifty-nine of arteriosclerosis and exhaustion. He died after an illness in St. Luke's hospital, New York City, where he had been admitted on November 5. Aware that the end was near, he left with his wife and his physician, Dr. John A. Kennedy, Sr., on November 12, so that he could die in Tuskegee.

Booker T. Washington's funeral on November 17, 1915, was held in the Tuskegee Institute Chapel, and was attended by nearly 8,000 people. He was buried on campus in a brick tomb, made by students, on a hill commanding a view of the entire campus.

https://www.tuskegee.edu/discover-tu/tu-presidents/booker-t-washington

CHAPTER SEVEN
GEORGE WASHINGTON CARVER (1864-1943)

George Washington Carver was born on a farm near Diamond, Missouri, in Newton County about 1865. His mother, Mary, was owned by Moses and Susan Carver. His father, a slave on a neighboring farm, died before George was born. When George was just a few months old, he and his mother were kidnapped from the Carver farm by a band of men who roamed Missouri during the Civil War era. These outlaws hoped to sell George and his mother elsewhere. Young George was recovered by a neighbor and returned to the Carvers, but his mother was not. George and his older brother, Jim, were raised by Moses and Susan Carver.

While Jim helped Moses Carver with farm work, George, who was frail and sickly, spent much of his time helping Susan Carver with chores around the cabin. He learned how to perform many domestic tasks such as cooking, mending, and doing laundry. He also tended the garden and became fascinated with plants.

Susan Carver taught George to read and write at home. When he was about eleven, George went to Neosho to attend a school for Black Americans. There he boarded with Andrew and Mariah Watkins, a childless black couple. He stayed in Neosho for at least two years until the late 1870s, when he decided to move to Kansas with other Black Americans who were traveling west.

Over the next ten years, George traveled from one midwestern town to another, working and attending school. He often used his domestic skills to make money. By the late 1880s, George moved to Winterset, Iowa. George was befriended by a white couple, John and Helen Milholland. They encouraged George to enroll in nearby Simpson College where he studied piano and art. After a year, however, George transferred to the State Agricultural College at Ames, Iowa, to study agriculture. He earned his bachelor's degree in 1894 and a graduate degree in 1896.

In 1896, George Washington Carver left Iowa to take a job with Booker T. Washington at Tuskegee Institute in Alabama. There he conducted agricultural research and taught students until his death. George's research and instruction helped poor southern farmers, both white and black, change their farming practices and improve their diets. He stressed the importance of planting peanuts to upgrade the quality of the soil, which had been depleted from years of planting cotton. George found many practical uses for peanuts, sweet potatoes, and other agricultural products. He also created and tested many recipes in his laboratory. George's ideas and discoveries helped farmers improve their lives. His work also helped revitalize the depressed southern economy.

As George worked tirelessly in his laboratory from 1900 to 1920, his fame grew. He became widely known for his agricultural experiments. He also became known as a promoter of racial equality. People who wanted to improve race relations in America asked for George's help. George was a deeply religious man and agreed to share his belief in racial equality. During the 1920s and 1930s, he traveled throughout the South delivering his message of racial harmony.

George drew more public attention during the mid-1930s when the polio virus struck in America. George offered a treatment of peanut-oil massages that he believed helped many people, especially children, gain relief from the painful and paralyzing effects of polio. As word of George's treatment spread, people flocked to the Tuskegee campus for George's "cure."

George Washington Carver's reputation also grew larger during the 1930s because of the Great Depression. This was a period of great economic decline caused partly from generations of poor farming practices and years of drought. People from all over the world asked George for agricultural advice because he was able to show farmers how to maximize plant production and improve the soil at very little cost.

George lived a simple and industrious life. A skilled artist and musician who never married, George lived out his life in a dormitory at Tuskegee Institute. He became friends with many people, some of whom were quite rich and famous. One of his closest friends was the automobile manufacturer Henry Ford. Ford made sure that an elevator was installed in George's dormitory so that George could get to his laboratory more easily in his later years.

George Washington Carver changed the agricultural and economic life of many poor farmers. From ordinary peanuts he made hundreds of useful products, including milk, cheese, soap, and grease. He also made over a hundred products from sweet potatoes. Though he was offered positions at many other laboratories, George always declined, preferring to continue his work among his own race at Tuskegee.

George died on January 5, 1943, at Tuskegee Institute. He is buried on that campus near the grave of Booker T. Washington. The George Washington Carver National Monument in Diamond was created soon after his death. Established by legislation sponsored by Senator Harry S. Truman, it was the first national memorial to an Black American. It stands on the farm where George was born.

BLACK EXCELLANCE

CHAPTER EIGHT
W.E.B. DU BOIS (1868-1963)

Credit: National Park Service

W.E.B. Du Bois wasn't just an influential black man and leader, he held numerous titles, he was a scholar, writer, editor, and civil rights pioneer, was born William Edward Burghardt Du Bois in Great Barrington, Massachusetts, the son of Mary Silvina Burghardt, a domestic worker, and Alfred Du Bois, a barber and itinerant laborer. In later life Du Bois made a close study of his family origins, weaving them rhetorically and conceptually—if not always accurately—into almost everything he wrote. Born in Haiti and descended from mixed race Bahamian slaves, Alfred Du Bois enlisted during the Civil War as a private in a New York regiment of the Union army but appears to have deserted shortly afterward. He also deserted the family less than two years after his son's birth, leaving him to be reared by his mother and the extended Burghardt kin. Long resident in New England, the Burghardts descended from a freedman of Dutch slave origin who had fought briefly in the American Revolution. Under the care of his mother and her relatives, young Will Du Bois spent his entire childhood in that small western Massachusetts town, where probably fewer than two-score of the four thousand inhabitants were Black American. He received a classical, college preparatory education in Great Barrington's racially integrated high school, from whence, in June 1884, he became the first Black American graduate. A precocious youth, Du Bois not only excelled in his high school studies but also contributed numerous articles to two regional newspapers, the Springfield Republican and the black-owned New York Globe, then edited by T. Thomas Fortune.

In 1888 Du Bois enrolled at Harvard as a junior. He received a BA cum laude, in 1890, an MA in 1891, and a PhD in 1895. Du Bois was strongly influenced by the new historical work of the German-trained Albert Bushnell Hart and the philosophical lectures of William James, both of whom became friends and professional mentors. Other intellectual influences came with his studies and travels between 1892 and 1894 in Germany, where he was enrolled at the Friedrich-Wilhelm III Universität (then commonly referred to as the University of Berlin but renamed the Humboldt University after World War II). Because of the expiration of the Slater Fund fellowship that supported his stay in Germany, Du Bois could not meet the residency requirements that would have enabled him formally to stand for the degree in economics, despite his completion of the required doctoral thesis (on the history of southern U.S. agriculture) during his tenure. Returning to the United States in the summer of 1894, Du Bois taught classics and modern languages for two years at Wilberforce University in Ohio. While there, he met Nina Gomer, a student at the college, whom he married in 1896 at her home in Cedar Rapids, Iowa. The couple had two children. By the end of his first year at Wilberforce, Du Bois had completed his Harvard doctoral thesis, "The Suppression of the African Slave Trade to the United States of America,

1638–1870," which was published in 1896 as the inaugural volume of the Harvard Historical Studies series.

In high school Du Bois came under the influence of and received mentorship from the principal, Frank Hosmer, who encouraged his extensive reading and solicited scholarship aid from local worthies that enabled Du Bois to enroll at Fisk University in September 1885, six months after his mother's death. One of the best of the southern colleges for newly freed slaves founded after the Civil War, Fisk offered a continuation of his classical education and the strong influence of teachers who were heirs to New England and Western Reserve (Ohio) abolitionism. It also offered the northern-reared Du Bois an introduction to southern American racism and Black American culture. His later writings and thought were strongly marked, for example, by his experiences teaching school in the hills of eastern Tennessee during the summers of 1886 and 1887.

Although he had written his Berlin thesis in economic history, received his Harvard doctorate in history, and taught languages and literature at Wilberforce, Du Bois made some of his most important early intellectual contributions to the emerging field of sociology. In 1896 he was invited by the University of Pennsylvania to conduct a study of the Seventh Ward in Philadelphia. There, after an estimated 835 hours of door-to-door interviews in 2,500 households, Du Bois completed the monumental study, The Philadelphia Negro (1899). The Philadelphia study was both highly empirical and hortatory, a combination that prefigured much of the politically engaged scholarship that Du Bois pursued in the years that followed and that reflected the two main strands of his intellectual engagement during this formative period: the scientific study of the so-called Negro Problem and the appropriate political responses to it. While completing his fieldwork in Philadelphia, Du Bois delivered to the Academy of Political and Social Science in November 1896 an address, "The Study of the Negro Problem," a methodological manifesto on the purposes and appropriate methods for scholarly examination of the condition of black people. In March 1897, addressing the newly founded American Negro Academy in Washington, D.C., he outlined for his black intellectual colleagues, in "The Conservation of the Races," both a historical sociology and theory of race as a concept and a call to action in defense of Black American culture and identity. During the following July and August, he undertook for the U.S. Bureau of Labor the first of several studies of southern Black American households, which was published as a bureau bulletin the following year under the title The Negroes of Farmville, Virginia: A Social Study. During that same summer, Atlantic Monthly published the essay "The Strivings of the Negro People," a slightly revised version of which later opened The Souls of Black Folk (1903).

Together these works frame Du Bois's evolving conceptualization of, methodological approach to, and political values and commitments regarding the problem of race in America. His conceptions were historical and global, his methodology empirical and intuitive, his values and commitments involving both mobilization of an elite vanguard to address the issues of racism and the conscious cultivation of the values to be drawn from Black American folk culture.

After the completion of the Philadelphia study in December 1897, Du Bois began the first of two long tenures at Atlanta University, where he taught sociology and directed empirical studies—modeled loosely on his Philadelphia and Farmville work—of the social and economic conditions and cultural and institutional lives of southern Black Americans. During this first tenure at Atlanta, he also wrote two more books, The Souls of Black Folk, a collection of poignant essays on race, labor, and culture, and John Brown (1909), an impassioned interpretation of the life and martyrdom of the militant abolitionist. He also edited two short-lived magazines, Moon (1905–1906) and Horizon (1907–1910), which represented his earliest efforts to establish journals of intellectual and political opinion for a black readership.

With the publication of Souls of Black Folk, Du Bois emerged as the most prominent spokesperson for the opposition to Booker T. Washington's policy of political conservatism and racial accommodation. Ironically, Du Bois had kept a prudent distance from Washington's opponents and had made few overt statements in opposition to the so-called Wizard of Tuskegee. In fact, his career had involved a number of near-misses whereby he himself might have ended up teaching at Tuskegee. Having applied to Washington for a job shortly after returning from Berlin, he had to decline Tuskegee's superior monetary offer because he had already accepted a position at Wilberforce. On a number of other occasions Washington— sometimes prodded by Albert Bushnell Hart—sought to recruit Du Bois to join him at Tuskegee, a courtship he continued at least until the summer of 1903, when Du Bois taught summer school at Tuskegee. Early in his career, moreover, Du Bois's views bore a superficial similarity to Washington's. In fact, he had praised Washington's 1895 "Atlanta Compromise" speech, which proposed to southern white elites a compromise wherein blacks would forswear political and civil rights in exchange for economic opportunities. Like many elite blacks at the time, Du Bois was not averse to some form of franchise restriction, so long as it was based on educational qualifications and applied equally to white and black. Du Bois had been charged with overseeing the Black American Council's efforts to encourage black economic enterprise and worked with Washington's partisans in that effort. By his own account his overt rupture with Washington was sparked by the growing evidence of a conspiracy, emanating from Tuskegee, to dictate speech and opinion in all of black America and to crush any opposition to Washington's leadership. After the collapse of efforts to compromise their differences through a series of meetings in 1904, Du Bois joined William Monroe Trotter and other Washington opponents to form the Niagara Movement, an organization militantly advocating full civil and political rights for Black Americans.

Although it enjoyed some success in articulating an alternative vision of how black Americans should respond to the growing segregation and racial violence of the early twentieth century, the Niagara Movement was fatally hampered by lack of funds and the overt and covert opposition of Washington and his allies. Indeed, the vision and program of the movement were fully realized only with the founding of a new biracial organization, the National Association for the Advancement of Colored People (NAACP). The NAACP grew out of the agitation and a 1909 conference called to protest the deteriorating status of and escalating violence against black Americans. Racial rioting in August 1908 in Springfield, Illinois, the home of Abraham Lincoln, sparked widespread protest among blacks and liberal whites appalled at the apparent spread of southern violence and lynch law into northern cities. Although its officers made some initial efforts to maintain a détente with Booker T. Washington, the NAACP represented a clear opposition to his policy of accommodation and political quietism. It launched legal suits, legislative lobbying, and propaganda campaigns that embodied uncompromising, militant attacks on lynching, Jim Crow, and disfranchisement. In 1910 Du Bois left Atlanta to join the NAACP as an officer, its only black board member, and to edit its monthly magazine, The Crisis.

As editor of The Crisis Du Bois finally established the journal of opinion that had so long eluded him, one that could serve as a platform from which to reach a larger audience among Black Americans and one that united the multiple strands of his life's work. In its monthly issues he rallied black support for NAACP policies and programs and excoriated white opposition to equal rights. But he also opened the journal to discussions of diverse subjects related to race relations and black cultural and social life, from black religion to new poetic works. The journal's cover displayed a rich visual imagery embodying the sheer diversity and breadth of the black presence in America. Thus, the journal constituted, simultaneously, a forum for multiple expressions of and the coherent representation and enactment of black intellectual and cultural life. A mirror for and to black America, it inspired a black intelligentsia and its public.

From his vantage as an officer of the NAACP, Du Bois also furthered another compelling intellectual and political interest, Pan-Africanism. He had attended the first conference on the global condition of peoples of African descent in London in 1900. Six other gatherings followed between 1911 and 1945, including the First Universal Races Congress in London in 1911, and Pan-African congresses held in Paris in 1919; London, Brussels, and Paris in 1921; London and Lisbon in 1923; New York City in 1927; and in Manchester, England, in 1945. Each conference focused in some fashion on the fate of African colonies in the postwar world, but the political agendas of the earliest meetings were often compromised by the ideological and political entanglements of the elite delegates chosen to represent the African colonies. The Jamaican black nationalist Marcus Garvey enjoyed greater success in mobilizing a mass base for his version of Pan-Africanism and posed a substantial ideological and political challenge to Du Bois. Deeply suspicious of Garvey's extravagance and flamboyance, Du Bois condemned his scheme to collect funds from Black Americans to establish a shipping line that would aid their "return" to Africa, his militant advocacy of racial separatism, and his seeming alliance with the Ku Klux Klan. Although he played no role in the efforts to have Garvey jailed and eventually deported for mail fraud, Du Bois was not sorry to see him go. (In 1945, however, Du Bois joined Garvey's widow, Amy Jacques Garvey, and George Padmore to sponsor the Manchester Pan-African conference that demanded African independence. Du Bois cochaired the opening session of the conference with Garvey's first wife, Amy Ashwood Garvey.)

The rupture in world history that was World War I and the vast social and political transformations of the decade that followed were reflected in Du Bois's thought and program in other ways as well. During the war he had written "Close Ranks," a controversial editorial in The Crisis (July 1918), which urged Black Americans to set aside their grievances for the moment and concentrate their energies on the war effort. In fact, Du Bois and the NAACP fought for officer training and equal treatment for black troops throughout the war, led a silent protest march down Fifth Avenue in 1917 against racism, and in 1919 launched an investigation into charges of discrimination against black troops in Europe. Meanwhile, the unprecedented scope and brutality of the war itself stimulated changes in Du Bois's evolving analyses of racial issues and phenomena. Darkwater: Voices within the Veil (1920) reflects many of these themes, including the role of African colonization and the fundamental role of the international recruitment and subjugation of labor in causing the war and in shaping its aftermath. His visit to Liberia in 1923 and the Soviet Union in 1926, his subsequent study of Marxism, his growing awareness of Freud, and the challenges posed by the Great Depression all brought him to question the NAACP's largely legalistic and propagandistic approach to fighting racism.

In the early 1930s Du Bois opened the pages of The Crisis to wide-ranging discussions of the utility of Marxian thought and of racially based economic cooperatives and other institutions in the fight against race prejudice. This led to increasing antagonism between him and his colleagues at the NAACP, especially the executive director Walter White, and to his resignation in June 1934.

Du Bois accepted an appointment as chair of the sociology department at Atlanta University, where he had already been teaching as a visiting professor during the winter of 1934. There he founded and edited a new scholarly journal, Phylon, from 1940 to 1944. There, too, he published his most important historical work, Black Reconstruction in America: An Essay toward a History of the Part Which Black Folk Played in the Attempt to Reconstruct Democracy in America, 1860–1880 (1935), and Dusk of Dawn: An Essay toward an Autobiography of a Race Concept (1940), his most engaging and poignant autobiographical essay since Souls of Black Folk. During this period Du Bois continued to be an active lecturer and an interlocutor with young scholars and activists; he also deepened his studies of Marxism and traveled abroad. He sought unsuccessfully to enlist the aid of the Phelps-Stokes Fund in launching his long-dreamed-of project to prepare an encyclopedia of black peoples in Africa and the diaspora. By 1944, however, Du Bois had lost an invaluable supporter and friend with the death of John Hope, the president of Atlanta University, leaving him vulnerable to dismissal following sharp disagreements with Hope's successor.

Far from acceding to a peaceful retirement, however, in 1944 Du Bois (now seventy-six years old) accepted an invitation to return to the NAACP to serve in the newly created post of director of special research. Although the organization was still under the staff direction of Du Bois's former antagonist, Walter White, the 1930s Depression and World War II had induced some modifications in the programs and tactics of the NAACP, perhaps in response to challenges raised by Du Bois and other younger critics. It had begun to address the problems of labor as well as legal discrimination, and even the court strategy was becoming much more aggressive and economically targeted. In hiring Du Bois, the board appears to have anticipated that other shifts in its approach would be necessary in the coming postwar era. Clearly it was Du Bois's understanding that his return portended continued study of and agitation around the implications of the coming postwar settlement as it might affect black peoples in Africa and the diaspora, and that claims for the representation of African and Black American interests in that settlement were to be pressed. He represented the NAACP in 1945 as a consultant to the U.S. delegation at the founding conference of the United Nations in San Francisco. In 1947 he prepared and presented to that organization An Appeal to the World, a ninety-four-page, militant protest against American racism as an international violation of human rights. During this period and in support of these activities he wrote two more books, Color and Democracy: Colonies and Peace (1945) and The World and Africa: An Inquiry into the Part Which Africa Has Played in World History (1947), each of which addressed some aspect of European and American responsibilities for justice in the colonial world.

As ever, Du Bois learned from and was responsive to the events and developments of his time. Conflicts with the U.S. delegation to the United Nations (which included Eleanor Roosevelt, who was also a member of the NAACP board) and disillusionment with the evolving role of America as a postwar world power reinforced his growing radicalism and refusal to be confined to a safe domestic agenda. He became a supporter of the leftist Southern Negro Youth Congress at a time of rising hysteria about Communism and the onset of the cold war. In 1948 he was an active supporter of the Progressive Party and Henry Wallace's presidential bid. All of this put him at odds with Walter White and the NAACP board, who were drawn increasingly into collusion with the Harry S. Truman administration and into fierce opposition to any leftist associations. In 1948, after an inconclusive argument over assigning responsibility for a leak to the New York Times of a Du Bois memorandum critical of the organization and its policies, he was forced out of the NAACP for a second time.

After leaving the NAACP, Du Bois joined the Council on African Affairs, where he chaired the Africa Aid Committee and was active in supporting the early struggle of the African National Congress of South Africa against apartheid. The council had been organized in London in the late 1930s by Max Yergan and Paul Robeson to push decolonization and to educate the general public about that issue. In the postwar period it, too, became tainted by charges of Communist domination and lost many former supporters (including Yergan and Ralph Bunche); it dissolved altogether in 1955. Having linked the causes of decolonialization and antiracism to the fate of peace in a nuclear-armed world, Du Bois helped organize the Cultural and Scientific Conference for World Peace in March 1949, was active in organizing its meetings in Paris and Mexico City later that year and attended its Moscow conference that August. Subsequently this group founded the Peace Information Center in 1950, and Du Bois was chosen to chair its Advisory Council. The center endorsed and promoted the Stockholm Peace Appeal, which called for banning atomic weapons, declaring their use a crime against humanity and demanding international controls. During this year Du Bois, who actively opposed the Korean War and Truman's foreign policy more generally, accepted the nomination of New York's Progressive Party to run for the U.S. Senate on the platform "Peace and Civil Rights." Although he lost, his vote total ran considerably ahead of the other candidates on the Progressive ticket.

During the campaign, on 25 August 1950, the officers of the Peace Information Center were directed to register as "agents of a foreign principal" under terms of the Foreign Agents Registration Act of 1938. Their distribution of the Stockholm Appeal, alleged to be a Soviet-inspired manifesto, was the grounds for these charges, although the so-called foreign principal was never specifically identified in the subsequent indictment. Although the center disbanded on 12 October 1950, indictments against its officers, including Du Bois, were handed down on 9 February 1951. Du Bois's lawyers won a crucial postponement of the trial until the following 18 November 1951, by which time national and international opposition to the trial had been mobilized. Given the good fortune of a weak case and a fair judge, Du Bois and his colleagues were acquitted. Meanwhile, following the death of his wife, Nina, in July 1950, Du Bois married Shirley Graham, the daughter of an old friend, in 1951. Although the union bore no children, David, Shirley Du Bois's son from an earlier marriage, took Du Bois's surname.

After the trial, Du Bois continued to be active in the American Peace Crusade and received the International Peace Prize from the World Council of Peace in 1953. With Shirley, a militant leftist activist in her own right, he was drawn more deeply into leftist and Communist Party intellectual and social circles during the 1950s. He was an unrepentant supporter of and apologist for Joseph Stalin, arguing that though Stalin's methods might have been, they were necessitated by unprincipled and implacable opposition from the West and by U.S. efforts to undermine the regime. He was also convinced that American news reports about Stalin and the Soviet bloc were unreliable at best and sheer propaganda or falsehoods at worst. His views do not appear to have been altered by the Soviets' own exposure and condemnation of Stalin after 1956.

From February 1952 to 1958 both W. E. B. and Shirley were denied passports to travel abroad. Thus, he could not accept the many invitations to speak abroad or participate in international affairs, including most notably the 1957 independence celebrations of Ghana, the first of the newly independent African nations. When these restrictions were lifted in 1958, the couple traveled to the Soviet Union, Eastern Europe, and China. While in Moscow, Du Bois was warmly received by Nikita Khrushchev, whom he strongly urged to promote the study of African civilization in Russia, a proposal that eventually led to the establishment in 1962 of the Institute for the Study of Africa. While there, he also received the Lenin Peace Prize.

But continued cold war tensions and their potential impact on his ability to travel and remain active in the future led Du Bois to look favorably on an invitation in May 1961 from Kwame Nkrumah and the Ghana Academy of Sciences to move to Ghana and undertake direction of the preparation of an "Encyclopedia Africana," a project much like one he had long contemplated. Indeed, his passport had been rescinded again after his return from China (travel to that country was barred at the time), and it was only restored after intense lobbying by the Ghanaian government. Before leaving the United States for Ghana on 7 October 1961, Du Bois officially joined the American Communist Party, declaring in his 1 October 1961 letter of application that it and socialism were the only viable hope for black liberation and world peace. His desire to travel and work freely also prompted his decision two years later to become a citizen of Ghana.

In some sense these actions brought full circle some of the key issues that had animated Du Bois's life. Having organized his life's work around the comprehensive, empirically grounded study of what had once been called the Negro Problem, he ended his years laboring on an interdisciplinary and global publication that might have been the culmination and symbol of that ambition: to document the experience and historical contributions of African peoples in the world. Having witnessed the formal détente among European powers by which the African continent was colonized in the late nineteenth century, he lived to taste the fruits of the struggle to decolonize it in the late twentieth century and to become a citizen of the first new African nation. Having posed at the end of the nineteenth century the problem of black identity in the diaspora, he appeared to resolve the question in his own life by returning to Africa. Undoubtedly the most important modern Black American intellectual, Du Bois virtually invented modern Black American letters and gave form to the consciousness animating the work of practically all other modern Black American intellectuals to follow. He authored seventeen books, including five novels; founded and edited four different journals; and pursued two full-time careers: scholar and political organizer. But more than that, he reshaped how the experience of America and Black America could be understood; he made us know both the complexity of who black Americans have been and are, and why it matters; and he left Americans—black and white—a legacy of intellectual tools, a language with which they might analyze their present and imagine a future.

From late 1961 to 1963 Du Bois lived a full life in Accra, the Ghanaian capital, working on the encyclopedia, taking long drives in the afternoon, and entertaining its political elite and the small colony of Black Americans during the evenings at the comfortable home the government had provided him. Du Bois died the day before his American compatriots assembled for the March on Washington for Jobs and Freedom. It was a conjunction more than rich with historical symbolism. It was the beginning of the end of the era of segregation that had shaped so much of Du Bois's life, but it was also the beginning of a new era when "the Negro Problem" could not be confined to separable terrains of the political, economic, domestic, or international, or to simple solutions such as integration or separatism, rights or consciousness. The life and work of Du Bois had anticipated this necessary synthesis of diverse terrains and solutions. On 29 August 1963 Du Bois was interred in a state funeral outside Castle Osu, formerly a holding pen for the slave cargoes bound for America.

https://hutchinscenter.fas.harvard.edu/web-dubois

CHAPTER NINE
JACK JOHNSON (1878-1946)

Credit: Copyright © The British Library Board

Jack Johnson was one of the toughest boxers who ever lived. In nearly a half century of boxing he was only knocked out three times.

John Arthur Johnson, better known as Jack Johnson and nicknamed the "Galveston Giant," was an American boxer and arguably the best heavyweight of his generation. He was the first black Heavyweight Champion of the World, 1908-1915 and became infamous for his interracial relationships with white women. For more than a decade, Johnson was probably the most famous, and certainly the most notorious Black American in the world.

From 1902-1907 Johnson won over 50 matches, some of them against other Black American boxers such as Joe Jeannette, Sam Langford, and Sam McVey. Johnson's career was legendary—in 47 years of fighting, he was only knocked out three times—but his life was full of problems. Johnson was not fully accepted as champion and white supremacists searched methodically for what they termed a "great white hope" to take the title away from him. They arranged for ex-heavyweight champion James Jeffries to fight Johnson in Reno, Nevada, in 1910, in what was billed at "The Fight of the Century." However, their "hope" was dashed in the fifteenth round. The aftermath of the fight left at least 23 blacks and two whites dead in racial incidents around the country.

Johnson had the quality to endure, both inside the ring out outside of it. As a boxer, some of his greatest victories came after he himself had been knocked down and appeared to be nearing defeat. Outside the ring, he took the worst that America's racists could give him and gave it right back to them by his haughty attitude and public breaking of racial taboos.

After his career in boxing, Johnson, an amateur cellist and fiddler who was a connoisseur of Harlem night life, eventually opened his own supper club, Club Deluxe, at 142nd Street and Lenox Avenue. He died as the result of an automobile accident near Raleigh, North Carolina, in June 1946. The play, The Great White Hope, by Howard Sackler, which was also made into a movie starring James Earl Jones, is based on his life. Johnson was admitted to the Boxing Hall of Fame in 1954.

Jack Johnson was born in Galveston, Texas on March 31, 1878, as the second child and first son of Henry and Tina "Tiny" Johnson, former slaves, and faithful Methodists, who both worked blue-collar jobs to earn enough to raise six children (the Johnsons had nine children, five of whom lived to adulthood, and an adopted son) and taught them how to read and write. Jack Johnson had five years of formal education. He rebelled against religion, however, and was kicked out of church when he stated that God did not exist and that the church dominated people's lives.

Johnson fought his first bout, a 16-round victory, at age 15. He turned professional around 1897, fighting in private clubs and making more money than he had ever seen. In 1901, Joe Choynski, small but powerful Jewish heavyweight, came to Galveston and fought a match with Johnson, knocking him out in round three. They were both arrested for "engaging in an illegal contest" and jailed for 23 days. (Although boxing was one of the three most popular sports in America at the time, along with baseball and horse-racing, the practice was officially illegal in most states, including Texas.) Choynski began training Johnson in jail and helped him develop his style, especially when fighting larger men.

Johnson's fighting style was very distinctive. He developed a more patient approach than was customary in that day: playing defensively, waiting for a mistake, and then capitalizing on it. Johnson always began a bout cautiously, slowly building up over the rounds into a more aggressive fighter. He often fought to punish his opponents rather than knock them out, endlessly avoiding their blows and striking with swift counters. He often gave the impression of having much more to offer and, if pushed, he could punch quite powerfully.

Johnson's style was very effective, but it was criticized in the white press as being cowardly and devious. However, World Heavyweight Champion "Gentleman" Jim Corbett, who was white, had used many of the same techniques a decade earlier, and was praised by the white press as "the cleverest man in boxing."

By 1902, Johnson had won at least 50 fights against both white and black opponents. He won his first title on February 3, 1903, beating "Denver" Ed Martin over 20 rounds for the "Colored Heavyweight Championship." His efforts to win the full title were thwarted as World Heavyweight Champion James J. Jeffries refused to face him. Blacks could box whites for other titles, but the heavyweight championship was such a respected and coveted position that blacks were not deemed worthy to compete for it. Johnson was, however, able to fight former champion Bob Fitzsimmons in July 1907, and knocked him out in two rounds.

He eventually won the World Heavyweight Title on December 26, 1908, when he fought the Canadian world champion Tommy Burns in Sydney, Australia, after following him all over the world, taunting him in the press for a match. The fight lasted 14 rounds before being stopped by the police. The title was awarded to Johnson on a referee's decision as a T.K.O, and he had severely beaten the champion. During the fight, Johnson had mocked both Burns and his ringside crew. Every time Burns was about to go down, Johnson would hold him up, punishing him more.

After Johnson's victory over Burns, racial animosity among whites ran so deep that even a socialist like novelist Jack London called for a "Great White Hope" to take the title away from Johnson—who was crudely caricatured as a subhuman "ape"—and return it to where it supposedly belonged, with the "superior" white race. As title holder, Johnson thus had to face a series of fighters billed by boxing promoters as "great white hopes," often in exhibition matches. In 1909, he beat Victor McLaglen, Frank Moran, Tony Ross, Al Kaufman, and the middleweight champion, Stanley Ketchel.

The match with Ketchel was keenly fought by both men until the twelfth and last round, when Ketchel threw a right to Johnson's head, knocking him down. Slowly regaining his feet, Johnson countered by throwing a straight to Ketchel's jaw, knocking him out, along with several of his teeth. His later fight with middleweight star "Philadelphia" Jack O'Brien was a disappointing one for Johnson: though scaling 205 pounds to O'Brien's 161, he could only achieve a six-round draw.

In 1910, former heavyweight champion James J. Jeffries came out of retirement and said, "I am going into this fight for the sole purpose of proving that a white man is better than a Negro." Jeffries had not fought in six years and had to lose around 100 pounds to get back to his championship fighting weight.

At the fight, which took place on July 4, 1910, in front of 22,000 people, at a ring built just for the occasion in downtown Reno, Nevada, the ringside band played, "All coons look alike to me." The fight had become a hotbed of racial tension, and the promoters incited the all-white crowd to chant "kill the nigger." Johnson, however, proved stronger and more nimble than Jeffries. In the fifteenth round, after he had been knocked down twice for the first time in his career, Jeffries' people called it quits to prevent Johnson from knocking him out.

The "Fight of the Century" earned Johnson $225,000 and silenced the critics, who had belittled Johnson's previous victory over Tommy Burns as "empty," claiming that Burns was a false champion since Jeffries had retired undefeated.

The outcome of the fight triggered race riots that evening—the Fourth of

July—all across the United States, from Texas and Colorado to New York and Washington, D.C. Johnson's victory over Jeffries had dashed white dreams of a finding a "great white hope" to defeat him. Many whites felt humiliated by the defeat of Jeffries and were incensed by Johnson's own haughty attitude during and after the fight.

Blacks, on the other hand, were jubilant, celebrating Johnson's great victory as a triumph for their entire long-suffering race. Black poet William Waring Cuney later highlighted the Black American reaction to the fight in his poem, "My Lord, What a Morning."

Around the country, blacks organized spontaneous parades, gathered in prayer meetings, and purchased goods with their newly won, gambling earnings. These celebrations often drew a violent response from white people. Some "riots" were simply Black Americans celebrating in the streets. In certain cities, like Chicago, the police allowed the celebrants to continue their festivities. But in other cities, the police and angry white citizens tried to subdue the celebrations. Innocent black people were often attacked on the streets, and in some cases, gangs of whites entered black neighborhoods and tried to burn down apartment buildings. Police interrupted several attempted lynchings. In all, riots occurred in more than 25 states and 50 cities. At least 23 blacks and two whites died in the riots, and hundreds more were injured. A few white people were also injured when they tried to intervene in a crowd's beating of a black man.

Some states reacted by banning the filming of Johnson's victories over white fighters. Black American newspapers stated that white people were afraid to circulate images of obvious black superiority and argued that the white press was hypocritical by condemning fight films while allowing lynchings to occur without criticism. The Washington Bee wrote, "The white man cannot expect always to be in the front rank without competition, and we all should look at things this way."

On April 5, 1915, Johnson lost his title to Jess Willard, a huge working cowboy who did not start boxing until he was almost 30 years old. With a crowd of 25,000 at the Vedado Racetrack in Havana, Cuba, Johnson was K.O.'d in the twenty-sixth round of the scheduled 45-round fight, which was co-promoted by Roderick James "Jess" McMahon and a partner. Johnson found that he could not knock out the giant Willard, who fought as a counterpuncher, making Johnson do all the leading. Johnson began to tire after the twentieth round and was visibly hurt by heavy body punches from Willard in rounds preceding the twenty-sixth-round knockout. Johnson is said to have spread rumors that he took a dive, but Willard is widely regarded as winning fairly. Willard said, "If he was going to throw the fight, I wish he'd done it sooner. It was 105 degrees out."

Johnson was an early example of the celebrity athlete, appearing regularly in the press and later on radio and in motion pictures. He earned considerable sums endorsing various products, including patent medicines, and indulged several expensive hobbies such as automobile racing and tailored clothing, as well as purchasing jewelry and furs for his wives. Once, when he was pulled over for a $50.00 speeding ticket (a large sum at the time), he gave the officer a $100.00 bill, telling him to keep the change as he was going to make his return trip at the same speed. Johnson was also interested in the opera, (his favorite being Il Trovatore) and in history—he was an admirer of Napoleon Bonaparte, believing that he arose from similar origins as the French dictator.

Johnson flouted conventions regarding the social and economic "place" of Black Americans in American society. As a black man, he broke a powerful taboo in consorting with white women and would verbally taunt men (both white and black) inside and outside the ring. Johnson was not shy about his affection for white women, nor modest about his physical prowess, both in and out of the ring.

Johnson married Etta Duryea in late 1910 or early 1911. She committed suicide in September of 1911, and Johnson quickly remarried, to Lucille Cameron. Both women were white, a fact that caused considerable controversy at the time. After Johnson married Cameron, two ministers in the South recommended that Johnson be lynched. The couple fled via Canada to France soon after their marriage to escape criminal charges in the U.S.

In 1920, Johnson opened a night club in Harlem; he sold it three years later to a white gangster, Owney Madden, who renamed it the Cotton Club.

After fighting a number of bouts in Mexico, Johnson returned to the United States on July 20, 1920, and surrendered to federal agents for allegedly violating the Mann Act against "transporting women across state lines for immoral purposes" by sending his white girlfriend, Belle Schreiber, a railroad ticket to travel from Pittsburgh to Chicago. This prosecution is generally considered an intentional misuse of the Act, which was intended to stop interstate traffic in prostitutes. He was sent to the United States Penitentiary, Leavenworth to serve his sentence of one year, and was released on July 9, 1921. There have been recurring proposals to grant Johnson a posthumous Presidential pardon.

In 1924, Lucille Cameron divorced Johnson on the grounds of infidelity. Johnson then married an old friend, Irene Pineau, in 1925, a marriage which lasted until his death.

Johnson continued fighting, but age was catching up with him. After two losses in 1928, he participated only in exhibition bouts.

In 1946, Johnson died in a car crash near Raleigh, North Carolina at age 68, just one year before Jackie Robinson broke the "color line" in Major League Baseball. He was buried next to Etta Duryea at Graceland Cemetery in Chicago. His grave is unmarked, but a stone that bears only the name "Johnson" stands above the plots of him and two of his wives. Johnson had no known children

Johnson's skill as a fighter and the money that it brought made it impossible for him to be ignored by the white establishment. In a time when Black Americans enjoyed few civil rights, and in which lynching was an accepted, extra-legal means of social coercion in many parts of the United States, his success and defiant behavior were a serious threat to the racist status quo.

In the short term, the boxing world reacted against Johnson's legacy. Joe Louis, later, was not able to box for the heavyweight title until he proved he could "act white," and was warned against gloating over fallen opponents or having his picture taken with a white woman. Johnson foreshadowed, in many ways, perhaps the most famous boxer of all time, Muhammad Ali. In fact, Ali often spoke of how he was influenced by Jack Johnson. He identified with him because he felt white America ostracized him in the same manner because of his membership in the Nation of Islam and his opposition to the war in Vietnam. In his autobiography, Ali relates how he and Joe Frazier agreed that Johnson and Joe Louis were the greatest boxers of old.

https://www.newworldencyclopedia.org/entry/Jack_Johnson_(boxer)

CHAPTER TEN
DUKE ELLINGTON (1899-1974)

Credit: Discography | Discogs

Considered one of the greatest jazz composers of all time, Duke Ellington had an enormous impact on the popular music of the late 20th century. Among his more than two thousand songs are such hits as "In A Sentimental Mood," "Sophisticated Lady," "I Got It Bad And That Ain't Good," and "I'm Beginning To See The Light." For almost fifty years he toured the world as a band leader and piano player. Today his recordings remain among the most popular jazz of the big-band era.

Born in Washington D.C. in 1899, Edward Kennedy Ellington, better known as "Duke," began playing piano as a child. His mother, who also played the piano, oversaw his education, and by the time he was seventeen he began playing professionally. Making his name as a piano player in Washington, Ellington started to compose his own music. In 1923 he moved to New York, and the following year formed his own band, the Washingtonians. By 1927, Ellington's band had found a small base of fans and secured an engagement at Harlem's famous Cotton Club. This proved to be a major turning point in Ellington's career, providing him with access to larger audiences through radio and recordings.

In 1931 Ellington left the Cotton Club and began a series of extended tours that would continue for the rest of his life. For Ellington, the big band was not simply made up of five reeds, four trumpets, three trombones, drums, a bass, and a piano; it was made up of individuals. Where other composers had concerned themselves with creating a sound that unified the many instruments into one voice, Ellington believed in letting the dissonant voices of each musician play against each other. He wrote music that capitalized on the particular style and skills of his soloists. For this and many other reasons, his soloists often stayed with him for extended periods. Among the best members of his band were Jimmy Blanton, Johnny Hodges, Cootie Williams, and Harry Carney (who was in the band for nearly every one of its forty-seven years).

In 1939, Billy Strayhorn joined the band as an arranger, composer, and sometimes pianist. The two worked well together, continuing in the tradition that Ellington had built. Strayhorn's contribution to Ellington's achievements at the time were significant, and even some of their most popular tunes (such as "Take The A Train") were written by Strayhorn. Though not as well-known as much of Ellington's other work, pieces such as "Jack the Bear," "Ko-ko," and "Cotton Tail" (done between 1939 and 1942), had a profound influence on much of the jazz composition and performance that followed. Though Ellington continued to compose and perform regularly throughout the 1940s and 1950s, the public demand for big-band music had faded. It was not until 1956, with a triumphant performance at the Newport Jazz Festival, that Ellington re-emerged as an important voice in contemporary music.

For most of his time as a composer and bandleader, Ellington underplayed his role as a pianist. Throughout the 1950s and early 1960s he began performing with a number of the other great musicians and composers of the time, making albums that included DUKE ELLINGTON AND JOHN COLTRANE (1962), MONEY JUNGLE (1962, with Max Roach and Charles Mingus), and DUKE ELLINGTON MEETS COLEMAN HAWKINS. Among the younger generations, Ellington was both a symbol of the traditional modes of jazz music and the finest example of how to transcend those modes. The beauty and energy of earlier pieces such as "Mood Indigo" remained alive in even the final years of his life. In May of 1974, Ellington died of lung cancer in New York City. In his more than fifty years as a professional musician, Ellington had been nominated for a Pulitzer Prize, elected to the National Institute of Arts and Letters, awarded a doctor of music degree from Yale University, given the Medal of Freedom, and, most importantly, built the foundations from which much of the best American music consequently grew.

https://www.pbs.org/wnet/americanmasters/duke-ellington-about-duke-ellington/586/

CHAPTER 11
LOUIS ARMSTRONG (1901-1971)

Credit: Library of Congress's Prints and Photographs division

Louis Armstrong nicknamed "Satchmo," "Pops" and, later, "Ambassador Satch," was a native of New Orleans, Louisiana. An all-star virtuoso, he came to prominence in the 1920s, influencing countless musicians with both his daring trumpet style and unique vocals.

Armstrong's charismatic stage presence impressed not only the jazz world but all of popular music. He recorded several songs throughout his career, including he is known for songs like "Star Dust," "La Vie En Rose" and "What a Wonderful World."

Louis Armstrong was born on August 4, 1901, in New Orleans, Louisiana, in a neighborhood so poor that it was nicknamed "The Battlefield."

Armstrong had a difficult childhood: His father was a factory worker and abandoned the family soon after Louis's birth. His mother, who often turned to prostitution, frequently left him with his maternal grandmother. Armstrong was obligated to leave school in the fifth grade to begin working.

A local Jewish family, the Karnofskys, gave young Armstrong a job collecting junk and delivering coal. They also encouraged him to sing and often invited him into their home for meals.

On New Year's Eve in 1912, Armstrong fired his stepfather's gun in the air during a New Year's Eve celebration and was arrested on the spot. He was then sent to the Colored Waif's Home for Boys.

There, he received musical instruction on the cornet and fell in love with music. In 1914, the home released him, and he immediately began dreaming of a life making music.

While he still had to work odd jobs selling newspapers and hauling coal to the city's famed red-light district, Armstrong began earning a reputation as a fine blues player.

One of the greatest cornet players in town, Joe "King" Oliver, began acting as a mentor to the young Armstrong, showing him pointers on the horn and occasionally using him as a sub.

By the end of his teens, Armstrong had grown up fast. In 1918, he married Daisy Parker, a prostitute, commencing a stormy union marked by many arguments and acts of violence.

During this time, Armstrong adopted a three-year-old boy named

Clarence. The boy's mother, Armstrong's cousin, had died in childbirth. Clarence, who had become mentally disabled from a head injury he had suffered at an early age, was taken care of by Armstrong his entire life.

Meanwhile, Armstrong's reputation as a musician continued to grow: In 1918, he replaced Oliver in Kid Ory's band, then the most popular band in New Orleans.

He was soon able to stop working manual labor jobs and began concentrating full-time on his cornet, playing parties, dances, funeral marches and at local "honky-tonks"—a name for small bars that typically host musical acts.

Beginning in 1919, Armstrong spent his summers playing on riverboats with a band led by Fate Marable. It was on the riverboat that Armstrong honed his music reading skills and eventually had his first encounters with other jazz legends, including Bix Beiderbecke and Jack Teagarden.

Though Armstrong was content to remain in New Orleans, in the summer of 1922, he received a call from Oliver to come to Chicago and join his Creole Jazz Band on second cornet.

Armstrong accepted, and he was soon taking Chicago by storm with both his remarkably fiery playing and the dazzling two-cornet breaks that he shared with Oliver. He made his first recordings with Oliver on April 5, 1923; that day, he earned his first recorded solo on "Chimes Blues."

Armstrong soon began dating the female pianist in the band, Lillian Hardin. After they married in 1924, Hardin made it clear that she felt Oliver was holding Armstrong back. She pushed her husband to cut ties with his mentor and join Fletcher Henderson's Orchestra, the top Black American dance band in New York City at the time.

Armstrong joined Henderson in the fall of 1924 and immediately made his presence felt with a series of solos that introduced the concept of swing music to the band. Armstrong had a great influence on Henderson and his arranger, Don Redman, both of whom began integrating Armstrong's swinging vocabulary into their arrangements—transforming Henderson's band into what is generally regarded as the first jazz big band.

However, Armstrong's southern background didn't mesh well with the more urban, Northern mentality of Henderson's other musicians, who sometimes gave Armstrong a hard time over his wardrobe and the way he talked. Henderson also forbade Armstrong from singing, fearing that his rough way of vocalizing would be too coarse for the sophisticated audiences at the Roseland Ballroom.

Unhappy, Armstrong left Henderson in 1925 to return to Chicago, where he began playing with his wife's band at the Dreamland Café.

While in New York, Armstrong cut dozens of records as a sideman, creating inspirational jazz with other greats such as Sidney Bechet, and backing numerous blues singers including Bessie Smith.

Back in Chicago, OKeh Records decided to let Armstrong make his first records with a band under his own name: Louis Armstrong and his Hot Five. From 1925 to 1928, Armstrong made more than 60 records with the Hot Five and, later, the Hot Seven.

Today, these are generally regarded as the most important and influential recordings in jazz history; on these records, Armstrong's virtuoso brilliance helped transform jazz from an ensemble music to a soloist's art. His stop-time solos on numbers like "Cornet Chop Suey" and "Potato Head Blues" changed jazz history, featuring daring rhythmic choices, swinging phrasing and incredible high notes.

He also began singing on these recordings, popularizing wordless "scat singing" with his hugely popular vocal on 1926's "Heebie Jeebies."

The Hot Five and Hot Seven were strictly recording groups; Armstrong performed nightly during this period with Erskine Tate's orchestra at the Vendome Theater, often playing music for silent movies. While performing with Tate in 1926, Armstrong finally switched from the cornet to the trumpet.

Armstrong's popularity continued to grow in Chicago throughout the decade, as he began playing other venues, including the Sunset Café and the Savoy Ballroom. A young pianist from Pittsburgh, Earl Hines, assimilated Armstrong's ideas into his piano playing.

Together, Armstrong and Hines formed a potent team and made some of the greatest recordings in jazz history in 1928, including their virtuoso duet, "Weather Bird," and "West End Blues."

The latter performance is one of Armstrong's best-known works, opening with a stunning cadenza that features equal helpings of opera and the blues;

with its release, "West End Blues" proved to the world that the genre of fun, danceable jazz music was also capable of producing high art.

In the summer of 1929, Armstrong headed to New York, where he had a role in a Broadway production of Connie's Hot Chocolates, featuring the music of Fats Waller and Andy Razaf. Armstrong was featured nightly on Ain't Misbehavin', breaking up the crowds of (mostly white) theatergoers nightly.

That same year, he recorded with small New Orleans-influenced groups, including the Hot Five, and began recording larger ensembles. Instead of doing strictly jazz numbers, OKeh began allowing Armstrong to record popular songs of the day, including "I Can't Give You Anything But Love," "Star Dust" and "Body and Soul."

Armstrong's daring vocal transformations of these songs completely changed the concept of popular singing in American popular music, and had lasting effects on all singers who came after him, including Bing Crosby, Billie Holiday, Frank Sinatra and Ella Fitzgerald

By 1932, Armstrong, who was now known as Satchmo, had begun appearing in movies and made his first tour of England. While he was beloved by musicians, he was too wild for most critics, who gave him some of the most racist and harsh reviews of his career.

Satchmo didn't let the criticism stop him, however, and he returned an even bigger star when he began a longer tour throughout Europe in 1933. In a strange turn of events, it was during this tour that Armstrong's career fell apart: Years of blowing high notes had taken a toll on Armstrong's lips, and, following a fight with his manager Johnny Collins — who already managed to get Armstrong into trouble with the Mafia — he was left stranded overseas by Collins.

Armstrong decided to take some time off soon after the incident and spent much of 1934 relaxing in Europe and resting his lip.

When Armstrong returned to Chicago in 1935, he had no band, no engagements, and no recording contract. His lips were still sore, and there were still remnants of his mob troubles and with Lil, who, following the couple's split, was suing Armstrong.

He turned to Joe Glaser for help; Glaser had mob ties of his own, having been close with Al Capone, but he had loved Armstrong from the time he met him at the Sunset Café (Glaser had owned and managed the club).

Armstrong put his career in Glaser's hands and asked him to make his troubles disappear. Glaser did just that; within a few months, Armstrong had a new big band and was recording for Decca Records.

During this period, Armstrong set a number of Black American "firsts." In 1936, he became the first Black American jazz musician to write an autobiography: Swing That Music.

That same year, he became the first Black American to get featured billing in a major Hollywood movie with his turn in Pennies from Heaven, starring Bing Crosby. Additionally, he became the first Black American entertainer to host a nationally sponsored radio show in 1937, when he took over Rudy Vallee's Fleischmann's Yeast Show for 12 weeks.

Armstrong continued to appear in major films with the likes of Mae West, Martha Raye and Dick Powell. He was also a frequent presence on radio, and often broke box-office records at the height of what is now known as the "Swing Era."

Armstrong's fully healed lip made its presence felt on some of the finest recordings of career, including "Swing That Music," "Jubilee" and "Struttin' with Some Barbecue."

In 1938, Armstrong finally divorced Lil Hardin and married Alpha Smith, whom he had been dating for more than a decade. Their marriage was not a happy one, however, and they divorced in 1942.

That same year, Armstrong married for the fourth — and final — time; he wed Lucille Wilson, a Cotton Club dancer.

When Wilson tired of living out of a suitcase during endless strings of one-nighters, she convinced Armstrong to purchase a house at 34-56 107th Street in Corona, Queens, New York. The Armstrongs moved into the home, where they would live for the rest of their lives, in 1943.

By the mid-'40s, the Swing Era was winding down and the era of big bands was almost over. Seeing "the writing on the wall," Armstrong scaled down to a smaller six-piece combo, the All Stars; personnel would frequently change, but this would be the group Armstrong would perform live with until the end of his career.

Members of the group, at one time or another, included Jack Teagarden, Earl Hines, Sid Catlett, Barney Bigard, Trummy Young, Edmond Hall, Billy Kyle and Tyree Glenn, among other jazz legends.

Armstrong continued recording for Decca in the late 1940s and early '50s, creating a string of popular hits, including "Blueberry Hill," "That Lucky Old Sun," "La Vie En Rose," "A Kiss to Build a Dream On" and "I Get Ideas."

Armstrong signed with Columbia Records in the mid-'50s, and soon cut some of the finest albums of his career for producer George Avakian, including Louis Armstrong Plays W.C. Handy and Satch Plays Fats. It was also for Columbia that Armstrong scored one of the biggest hits of his career: His jazz transformation of Kurt Weill's "Mack the Knife."

During the mid-'50s, Armstrong's popularity overseas skyrocketed. This led some to alter his long-time nickname, Satchmo, to "Ambassador Satch."

He performed all over the world in the 1950s and '60s, including throughout Europe, Africa and Asia. Legendary CBS newsman Edward R. Murrow followed Armstrong with a camera crew on some of his worldwide excursions, turning the resulting footage into a theatrical documentary, Satchmo the Great, released in 1957.

Though his popularity was hitting new highs in the 1950s, and despite breaking down so many barriers for his race and being a hero to the Black American community for so many years, Armstrong began losing his standing with two segments of his audience: Modern jazz fans and young Black Americans.

Bebop, a new form of jazz, had blossomed in the 1940s. Featuring young geniuses such as Dizzy Gillespie, Charlie Parker and Miles Davis, the younger generation of musicians saw themselves as artists, not as entertainers.

They saw Armstrong's stage persona and music as old-fashioned and criticized him in the press. Armstrong fought back, but for many young jazz fans, he was regarded as an out-of-date performer with his best days behind him.

The civil rights movement was growing stronger with each passing year, with more protests, marches and speeches from Black Americans wanting equal rights. To many young jazz listeners at the time, Armstrong's ever-smiling demeanor seemed like it was from a bygone era, and the trumpeter's refusal to comment on politics for many years only furthered perceptions that he was out of touch.

These views changed in 1957, when Armstrong saw the Little Rock Central High School integration crisis on television. Arkansas Governor Orval Faubus sent in the National Guard to prevent the Little Rock Nine — nine Black American students — from entering the public school.

When Armstrong saw this — as well as white protesters hurling invective at the students — he blew his top to the press, telling a reporter that President Dwight D. Eisenhower had "no guts" for letting Faubus run the country, and stating, "The way they are treating my people in the South, the government can go to hell."

Armstrong's words made front-page news around the world. Though he had finally spoken out after years of remaining publicly silent, he received criticism at the time from both Black and white public figures.

Not a single jazz musician who had previously criticized him took his side — but today, this is seen as one of the bravest, most definitive moments of Armstrong's life.

Armstrong's four marriages never produced any children, and because he and wife Lucille Wilson had actively tried for years to no avail, many believed him to be sterile, incapable of having children.

However, controversy regarding Armstrong's fatherhood struck in 1954, when a girlfriend that the musician had dated on the side, Lucille "Sweets" Preston, claimed she was pregnant with his child. Preston gave birth to a daughter, Sharon Preston, in 1955.

Shortly thereafter, Armstrong bragged about the child to his manager, Joe Glaser, in a letter that would later be published in the book Louis Armstrong In His Own Words (1999). Thereafter until his death in 1971, however, Armstrong never publicly addressed whether he was in fact Sharon's father.

In recent years, Armstrong's alleged daughter, who now goes by the name Sharon Preston Folta, has publicized various letters between her and her father. The letters, dated as far back as 1968, prove that Armstrong had indeed always believed Sharon to be his daughter, and that he even paid for her education and home, among several other things, throughout his life. Perhaps most importantly, the letters also detail Armstrong's fatherly love for Sharon.

While only a DNA test could officially prove whether a blood relationship does exist between Armstrong and Sharon — and one has never been conducted between the two — believers and skeptics can at least agree on one thing: Sharon's uncanny resemblance to the jazz legend.

Armstrong continued a grueling touring schedule into the late '50s, and it caught up with him in 1959, when he had a heart attack while traveling in Spoleto, Italy. The musician didn't let the incident stop him, however, and after taking a few weeks off to recover, he was back on the road, performing 300 nights a year into the 1960s.

Armstrong was still a popular attraction around the world in 1963 but hadn't made a record in two years. In December of that year, he was called into the studio to record the title number for a Broadway show that hadn't opened yet: Hello, Dolly!

The record was released in 1964 and quickly climbed to the top of the pop music charts, hitting the No. 1 slot in May 1964, and knocking the Beatles off the top at the height of Beatlemania.

This newfound popularity introduced Armstrong to a new, younger audience, and he continued making both successful records and concert appearances for the rest of the decade, even cracking the "Iron Curtain" with a tour of Communist countries such as East Berlin and Czechoslovakia in 1965.

In 1967, Armstrong recorded a new ballad, "What a Wonderful World." Different from most of his recordings of the era, the song features no trumpet and places Armstrong's gravelly voice in the middle of a bed of strings and angelic voices.

Armstrong sang his heart out on the number, thinking of his home in Queens as he did so, but "What a Wonderful World" received little promotion in the United States.

The tune did, however, become a No. 1 hit around the world, including in England and South Africa, and eventually became one of Armstrong's most-beloved songs after it was used in the 1986 Robin Williams film Good Morning, Vietnam.

By 1968, Armstrong's grueling lifestyle had finally caught up with him. Heart and kidney problems forced him to stop performing in 1969. That same year, his longtime manager, Joe Glaser, passed away. Armstrong spent much of that year at home but managed to continue practicing the trumpet daily.

By the summer of 1970, Armstrong was allowed to perform publicly again and play the trumpet. After a successful engagement in Las Vegas, Armstrong began taking engagements around the world, including in London and Washington, D.C. and New York (he performed for two weeks at New York's Waldorf-Astoria). However, a heart attack two days after the Waldorf gig sidelined him for two months.

Armstrong returned home in May 1971, and though he soon resumed playing again and promised to perform in public once more, he died in his sleep on July 6, 1971, at his home in Queens, New York.

Since his death, Armstrong's stature has only continued to grow. In the 1980s and '90s, younger Black American jazz musicians like Wynton Marsalis, Jon Faddis and Nicholas Payton began speaking about Armstrong's importance, both as a musician and a human being.

A series of new biographies on Armstrong made his role as a civil rights pioneer abundantly clear and, subsequently, argued for an embrace of his entire career's output, not just the revolutionary recordings from the 1920s.

Armstrong's home in Corona, Queens was declared a National Historic Landmark in 1977; today, the house is home to the Louis Armstrong House Museum, which annually receives thousands of visitors from all over the world.

One of the most important figures in 20th century music, Armstrong's innovations as a trumpeter and vocalist are widely recognized today and will continue to be for decades to come.

https://www.biography.com/musician/louis-armstrong

CHAPTER 12
LANGSTON HUGHES (1902-1967)

Credit: Underwood Archives / Getty Images

Langston Hughes, in full James Mercer Langston Hughes, American writer who was an important figure in the Harlem Renaissance and made the Black American experience the subject of his writings, which ranged from poetry and plays to novels and newspaper columns.

While it was long believed that Hughes was born in 1902, new research released in 2018 indicated that he might have been born the previous year. His parents separated soon after his birth, and he was raised by his mother and grandmother. After his grandmother's death, he and his mother moved to half a dozen cities before reaching Cleveland, where they settled. He wrote the poem "The Negro Speaks of Rivers" the summer after his graduation from high school in Cleveland; it was published in The Crisis in 1921 and brought him considerable attention. After attending Columbia University in New York City in 1921–22, he explored Harlem, forming a permanent attachment to what he called the "great dark city," and worked as a steward on a freighter bound for Africa. Back in New York City from seafaring and sojourning in Europe, he met in 1924 the writers Arna Bontemps and Carl Van Vechten, with whom he would have lifelong influential friendships. Hughes won an Opportunity magazine poetry prize in 1925. That same year, Van Vechten introduced Hughes's poetry to the publisher Alfred A. Knopf, who accepted the collection that Knopf would publish as The Weary Blues in 1926.

While working as a busboy in a hotel in Washington, D.C., in late 1925, Hughes put three of his own poems beside the plate of Vachel Lindsay in the dining room. The next day, newspapers around the country reported that Lindsay, among the most popular white poets of the day, had "discovered" a Black American busboy poet, which earned Hughes broader notice. Hughes received a scholarship to, and began attending, Lincoln University in Pennsylvania in early 1926. That same year, he received the Witter Bynner Undergraduate Poetry Award, and he published "The Negro Artist and the Racial Mountain" in The Nation, a manifesto in which he called for a confident, uniquely Black literature:

By the time Hughes received his degree in 1929, he had helped launch the influential magazine Fire!!, in 1926, and he had also published a second collection of poetry, Fine Clothes to the Jew (1927), which was criticized by some for its title and for its frankness, though Hughes himself felt that it represented another step forward in his writing.

A few months after Hughes's graduation, Not Without Laughter (1930), his first prose volume, had a cordial reception. In the 1930s he turned his poetry more forcefully toward racial justice and political radicalism. He traveled in the American South in 1931 and decried the Scottsboro case; he then traveled widely in the Soviet Union, Haiti, Japan, and elsewhere and served as a newspaper correspondent (1937) during the Spanish Civil War. He published a collection of short stories, The Ways of White Folks (1934), and became deeply involved in theatre. His play Mulatto, adapted from one of his short stories, premiered on Broadway in 1935, and productions of several other plays followed in the late 1930s. He also founded theatre companies in Harlem (1937) and Los Angeles (1939). In 1940 Hughes published The Big Sea, his autobiography up to age 28. A second volume of autobiography, I Wonder As I Wander, was published in 1956.

Hughes documented Black American literature and culture in works such as A Pictorial History of the Negro in America (1956) and the anthologies The Poetry of the Negro (1949) and The Book of Negro Folklore (1958; with Bontemps). He continued to write numerous works for the stage, including the lyrics for Street Scene, an opera with music by Kurt Weill that premiered in 1947. Black Nativity (1961; film 2013) is a gospel play that uses Hughes's poetry, along with gospel standards and scriptural passages, to retell the story of the birth of Jesus. It was an international success, and performances of the work—often diverging substantially from the original—became a Christmas tradition in many Black churches and cultural centers. He also wrote poetry until his death; The Panther and the Lash, published posthumously in 1967, reflected and engaged with the Black Power movement and, specifically, the Black Panther Party, which was founded the previous year.

Among his other writings, Hughes translated the poetry of Federico García Lorca and Gabriela Mistral. He was also widely known for his comic character Jesse B. Semple, familiarly called Simple, who appeared in Hughes's columns in the Chicago Defender and the New York Post and later in book form and on the stage. The Collected Poems of Langston Hughes, edited by Arnold Rampersad and David Roessel, appeared in 1994. Some of his political exchanges were collected as Letters from Langston: From the Harlem Renaissance to the Red Scare and Beyond (2016).

https://www.britannica.com/biography/Winold-Reiss

CHAPTER 13
THURGOOD MARSHALL (1908-1993)

Credit: Library of Congress's Prints and Photographs division

Thurgood Marshall had a fresh, passionate voice and became a champion of civil rights, both on the bench and through almost 30 Supreme Court victories before his appointment, during times of severe racial strains. Marshall was born in Baltimore, Maryland, on July 2, 1908, to Norma Arica and William Canfield Marshall. Marshall's mother was a kindergarten teacher, and his father was an amateur writer who worked as a dining-car waiter on a railroad, later becoming a chief steward at a ritzy club. When Marshall's father had a day off, he would occasionally take his sons to court so they could watch the legal procedure and arguments presented. Afterwards, the three would debate legal issues and current events together. Marshall's father would challenge his sons on the points they made, constantly encouraging them to prove their case.

Growing up in Baltimore, Marshall experienced the racial discrimination that shaped his passion for civil rights early on. The city had a death rate for Black Americans that was twice that of Caucasians, and due to school segregation, Marshall was forced to go to an all-black grade school. Once, he was unable to use the bathroom because all public restrooms were reserved for whites. Despite the times, Marshall's parents tried to shelter him from the reality of racism. They earned enough money to live in a nice area, and he was able to attend a first-rate high school. He was often mischievous and sent out of class to read the Constitution for misbehavior. When Marshall graduated high school in 1925, he knew the Constitution backwards and forwards. Marshall was accepted to Lincoln University in Oxford, Pennsylvania, from where his brother had just graduated. It was known as the black counterpart to Princeton, and one of his classmates was the famous writer Langston Hughes. Marshall chose to focus more on the social life of college. Because of his intelligence, he was able to get through with little effort, but after getting suspended for hazing with his fraternity, he began to focus on academics. Marshall joined the debate club, which helped him realize his passion for becoming a lawyer. He also became more involved with civil rights and helped desegregate a movie theater, which he later described as one of the happiest moments in his life. Marshall met his wife, Vivian Burey, while taking a weekend trip with his friends to Philadelphia. They soon married on September 4, 1929, before Marshall started his last semester. He graduated college in 1930 as a top-notch student.

After being denied by his first choice, the University of Maryland Law School, due to the color of his skin, Marshall decided to go to Howard University. He and his wife moved in with his parents, and his mother sold her wedding ring to help pay for his law school. There he learned about civil rights law and began to think of the Constitution as a living document. His mentors introduced him to the world of the NAACP, often bringing him to attend meetings and watch lawyers discuss key issues. One of the mentors who made the biggest impression upon Marshall was Charles Houston, who taught him to defeat racial discrimination through the use of existing laws. Marshall graduated as valedictorian of his class in 1933 and moved back to Baltimore.

Marshall denied a postgraduate scholarship to Harvard in order to start his own practice and opened an office in east Baltimore. A few people did come to him for help, though unable to pay. Marshall turned none of them away. He began to develop his style as he took cases dealing with police brutality, evictions and harsh landlords. Marshall was respectful but forceful in presenting his case. As his name began to gain notice, he earned big clients such as labor organizations, building associations, and corporations. Marshall started to volunteer with the NAACP and eventually became one of their attorneys, joining his mentor Houston to argue cases together. He won his first case arguing that the University of Maryland Law School should allow an Black American admission. In 1935, Houston got Marshall appointed as Assistant Special Counsel for New York in the organization. From then on, the two began planning on how to have the Supreme Court overrule the separate but equal doctrine. After Houston resigned and Marshall took over as Special Counsel in 1938, he traveled to dangerous areas in the South in order to investigate lynching, the denial of voting rights, jury service, and fair trials to Black Americans. The face of the NAACP had soon become that of Marshall's. In 1940, the NAACP set up a legal activist organization known as Fund, Inc., of which Marshall was hired to be special counsel. He was able to work toward his goal of challenging segregation in education. He won his first Supreme Court case dealing with forced confession; and after President Truman rejected the separate but equal doctrine in relation to the G.I. Bill, Marshall was ready to bring the education issue into full light. Marshall finally got the case he had been hoping for, and in 1952 argued Brown v. Board of Education. The case was reargued in 1953, and after 5 months of waiting, the Supreme Court delivered its opinion that invalidated the separate but equal doctrine. In 1961, President Kennedy appointed Marshall as federal judge to the Second Circuit Court of Appeals in New York City. Marshall spent four years on the court, and none of his opinions were reversed on appeal to the Supreme Court. In 1965, President Johnson called upon Marshall to be the country's next Solicitor General. Marshall was sworn into office, but only spent two years in the position. In 1967, the President appointed him as the first Black American to be an Associate Justice on the U.S. Supreme Court.

Marshall's voice was a liberal one which held great influence early on in his term. As a proponent of judicial activism, he believed that the United States had a moral imperative to move progressively forward. He staunchly supported upholding individual rights, expanding civil rights, and limiting the scope of criminal punishment. Justice William Brennan shared many of Marshall's opinions and they usually voted in the same bloc. In Furman v. Georgia, these justices argued the death penalty was unconstitutional in all circumstances, and dissented from the subsequent overruling opinion, Gregg v. Georgia, a few years later. He also made separate contributions to labor law (Teamsters v. Terry), securities law (TSC Industries, Inc. v. Northway, Inc.), and tax law (Cottage Savings Ass'n v. Commissioner of Internal Revenue). He had strong views on affirmative action and contributed greatly to opinions on constitutional law. Marshall maintained a down-to-earth style and would often joke with Chief Justice Burger as they passed in the hallways by asking "What's shakin', Chief baby?" As the court made a shift towards conservatism, however, Marshall became frustrated, and his influence weakened. Despite the change of currents, Marshall's voice remained strong until his retirement, when Associate Justice Clarence Thomas succeeded him. Marshall died on January 24, 1993, of heart failure in Bethesda, Maryland

https://www.oyez.org/justices/thurgood_marshall

CHAPTER 14
ROSA PARKS (1913-2005)

Credit: © Alabama Department of Archives

Most historians date the beginning of the modern civil rights movement in the United States to December 1, 1955. That was the day when an unknown seamstress in Montgomery, Alabama refused to give up her bus seat to a white passenger. This brave woman, Rosa Parks, was arrested and fined for violating a city ordinance, but her lonely act of defiance began a movement that ended legal segregation in America and made her an inspiration to freedom-loving people everywhere.

Rosa Parks was born Rosa Louise McCauley in Tuskegee, Alabama to James McCauley, a carpenter, and Leona McCauley, a teacher. At the age of two she moved to her grandparents' farm in Pine Level, Alabama with her mother and younger brother, Sylvester. At the age of 11 she enrolled in the Montgomery Industrial School for Girls; a private school founded by liberal-minded women from the northern United States.

The school's philosophy of self-worth was consistent with Leona McCauley's advice to "take advantage of the opportunities, no matter how few they were." Opportunities were few indeed. "Back then," Mrs. Parks recalled in an interview, "we didn't have any civil rights. It was just a matter of survival, of existing from one day to the next. I remember going to sleep as a girl hearing the Klan ride at night and hearing a lynching and being afraid the house would burn down." In the same interview, she cited her lifelong acquaintance with fear as the reason for her relative fearlessness in deciding to appeal her conviction during the bus boycott. "I didn't have any special fear," she said. "It was more of a relief to know that I wasn't alone." After attending Alabama State Teachers College, the young Rosa settled in Montgomery, with her husband, Raymond Parks. The couple joined the local chapter of the NAACP and worked quietly for many years to improve the lives of Black Americans in the segregated South.

"I worked on numerous cases with the NAACP," Mrs. Parks recalled, "but we did not get the publicity. There were cases of flogging, peonage, murder, and rape. We didn't seem to have too many successes. It was more a matter of trying to challenge the authorities, and to let it be known that we did not wish to continue being second-class citizens."

The bus incident led to the formation of the Montgomery Improvement Association, led by the young pastor of the Dexter Avenue Baptist Church, Dr. Martin Luther King, Jr. The association called for a boycott of the city-owned bus company. The boycott lasted 381 days and brought Mrs. Parks, Dr. King, and their cause to the attention of the world. A Supreme Court decision struck down the Montgomery ordinance under which Mrs. Parks had been fined, and outlawed racial segregation on public transportation.

In 1957, Mrs. Parks and her husband moved to Detroit, Michigan, where Mrs. Parks served on the staff of U.S. Representative John Conyers. The Southern Christian Leadership Council established an annual Rosa Parks Freedom Award in her honor.

After the death of her husband in 1977, Mrs. Parks founded the Rosa and Raymond Parks Institute for Self-Development. The Institute sponsors an annual summer program for teenagers called Pathways to Freedom. The young people tour the country in buses, under adult supervision, learning the history of their country and of the civil rights movement. President Clinton presented Rosa Parks with the Presidential Medal of Freedom in 1996. She received a Congressional Gold Medal in 1999.

When asked if she was happy living in retirement, Rosa Parks replied, "I do the very best I can to look upon life with optimism and hope and looking forward to a better day, but I don't think there is any such thing as complete happiness. It pains me that there is still a lot of Klan activity and racism. I think when you say you're happy, you have everything that you need and everything that you want, and nothing more to wish for. I haven't reached that stage yet."

Mrs. Parks spent her last years living quietly in Detroit, where she died in 2005 at the age of 92. After her death, her casket was placed in the rotunda of the United States Capitol for two days, so the nation could pay its respects to the woman whose courage had changed the lives of so many. She was the first woman and the second Black American to lie in honor at the Capitol, a distinction usually reserved for Presidents of the United States.

https://achievement.org/achiever/rosa-parks/

CHAPTER 15
BILLIE HOLIDAY (1915-1959)

Credit: @UNFspinnaker

Billie Holiday, birth name Elinore Harris, byname Lady Day. American jazz singer, one of the greatest from the 1930s to the '50s. Eleanora (her preferred spelling) Harris was the daughter of Clarence Holiday, a professional musician who for a time played guitar with the Fletcher Henderson band. She and her mother used her maternal grandfather's surname, Fagan, for a time; then in 1920 her mother married a man surnamed Gough, and both she and Eleanora adopted his name. It is probable that in neither case did her mother have Eleanora's name legally changed. The singer later adopted her natural father's last name and took the name Billie from a favorite movie actress, Billie Dove. In 1928 she moved with her mother from Baltimore, Maryland (where she had spent her childhood), to New York City, and after three years of subsisting by various means, she found a job singing in a Harlem nightclub. She had had no formal musical training, but, with an instinctive sense of musical structure and with a wealth of experience gathered at the root level of jazz and blues, she developed a singing style that was deeply moving and individual.

In 1933 Holiday made her first recordings, with Benny Goodman and others. Two years later a series of recordings with Teddy Wilson and members of Count Basie's band brought her wider recognition and launched her career as the leading jazz singer of her time. She toured with Basie and with Artie Shaw in 1937 and 1938 and in the latter year opened at the plush Café Society in New York City. About 1940 she began to perform exclusively in cabarets and in concert. Her recordings between 1936 and 1942 marked her peak years. During that period, she was often associated with saxophonist Lester Young, who gave her the nickname "Lady Day."

In 1947 Holiday was arrested for a narcotics violation and spent a year in a rehabilitation centre. No longer able to obtain a cabaret license to work in New York City, Holiday nonetheless packed New York's Carnegie Hall 10 days after her release. She continued to perform in concert and in clubs outside of New York City, and she made several tours during her later years. Her constant struggle with heroin addiction ravaged her voice, although not her technique.

Holiday's dramatic intensity rendered the most banal lyric profound. Among the songs identified with her were "Strange Fruit," "Fine and Mellow," "The Man I Love," "Billie's Blues," "God Bless the Child," and "I Wished on the Moon." The vintage years of Holiday's professional and private liaison with Young were marked by some of the best recordings of the interplay between a vocal line and an instrumental obbligato. In 1956 she wrote an autobiography, Lady Sings the Blues (with William Dufty), that was made into a motion picture starring Diana Ross in 1972. Holiday's health began to fail because of drug and alcohol abuse, and she died in 1959.

https://www.britannica.com/biography/Billie-Holiday

CHAPTER 16
JACKIE ROBINSON (1919-1972)

Credit: Regents of University of California

On April 15, 1947, Jackie Robinson became the first Black American to play Major League Baseball in the modern era. He would later become the first Black American named a vice president at a fortune 500 company; serve as an advisor to politicians; start a bank and a housing development company; and, was a key figure in advancing equal opportunity and first-class citizenship for all Americans during the Civil Rights Movement of the 1950s and 60s. Hailed a "..freedom rider before freedom rides," Robinson's name has become synonymous with breaking barriers.

Jackie Robinson was born on January 31, 1919, in Cairo, Georgia, the son of a sharecropper and the grandson of former slaves. Young Jackie grew up in Pasadena, California, raised by a single working mother of five. After graduating from Pasadena Junior College, Jackie attended the University of California Los Angeles. A star athlete, Jackie became the university's first four-sport letter winner, excelling in football, basketball, track and field, and baseball. After leaving UCLA, he served in the U.S. Army during World War II, but was court marshalled and honorably discharged for standing up for his rights and refusing to move to the back of a segregated military bus.

In 1944, upon returning home from the military, Jackie Robinson set his sights on joining baseball's Negro Leagues and began playing shortstop for the Kansas City Monarchs. In 1945, opportunity beckoned when Branch Rickey, the general manager of the Brooklyn Dodgers, invited Robinson to become the first Black American to play with the all-white Dodgers' farm team, the Montreal Royals. Anticipating the great adversity that Robinson would face as he integrated modern baseball, Rickey professed he needed a player who could bear the torment, famously telling Robinson he was "looking for a ballplayer with guts enough not to fight back."

On April 15, 1947, Jackie Robinson stepped onto Ebbets Field for his first game with the Brooklyn Dodgers. It was the beginning of an unparalleled career in baseball. At the end of his explosive nine years as a Dodger, his record included a .311 batting average, 137 home runs, 734 runs batted in, and 197 stolen bases. In 1955, he helped the Dodgers beat the New York Yankees to win their first World Series Championship. Robinson took home the Rookie of the Year Award in 1947, the Most Valuable Player Award in 1949, and in 1962 became the first Black American inducted into the Baseball Hall of Fame.

After integrating baseball, Robinson became a full-fledged leader in the Civil Rights movement. He used his celebrity status to further human rights and endeavored to change the landscape of race relations in the United States.

Upon retiring from the game in 1957, Robinson was hired to serve as the Vice President for Personnel at Chock Full O'Nuts, the first Black American to be named a Vice President of a major American company. He used his position at Chock Full O' Nuts to improve working conditions for employees.

An active member of the NAACP, Robinson was often a featured speaker at civil rights rallies including the famed March on Washington in 1963, and frequently participated in picket lines. As a nationally syndicated columnist for the New York Post and New York Amsterdam News, Robinson wrote passionately on social issues, sports, and family life, always encouraging people in his community to become active in politics and business.

In 1964, Robinson co-founded Freedom National Bank of Harlem, a Black owned and operated bank created for the express purpose of financially aiding Black urban communities. In 1970, he founded the Jackie Robinson Construction Company, which sought to provide housing for low-income people.

In 1972, just twenty-five years after the start of the "Great Experiment," Jackie Robinson died following his decade long battle with diabetes.

Following Robinson's death, Rachel Robinson became President of the Jackie Robinson Construction Corporation and renamed the company the Jackie Robinson Development Corporation. The company, responsible for building 1,600 units, specialized in building low-to-moderate income housing.

In 1973, with the assistance of Martin L. Edelman, Charles Williams and Franklin H. Williams, Mrs. Robinson honored her husband's memory by establishing The Jackie Robinson Foundation (JRF). As Robinson's living legacy, JRF provides four-year scholarships and a host of support services, including career guidance, internship placement, and leadership development opportunities to talented college students with limited financial resources. To date, 1,700 college scholars from 45 states who have attended 260 colleges and universities have benefitted from JRF's Scholars Program.

Jackie Robinson's achievements have been honored by three Presidents: On March 26, 1984, President Ronald Reagan posthumously awarded him the Presidential Medal of Freedom; during the celebration of the 50th anniversary of Jackie Robinson's historic entry into baseball, President William J. Clinton led a ceremony with Major League Baseball to honor his number "42" in perpetuity; and on October 10, 2003, the Congressional Gold Medal, the nation's highest civilian award bestowed by Congress, was awarded posthumously to Jackie Robinson. President George W. Bush and the leadership of the United States Congress presented the award to Rachel Robinson during a ceremony held in the Capitol Rotunda on March 2, 2005.

https://jackierobinson.org/jackie-robinson/

CHAPTER 17
NAT KING COLE (1919-1965)

Credit: William P. Gottlieb Collection/Library of Congress, Washington, D.C. (Neg no. LC-GLB23- 0151)

Nat King Cole became the first Black American performer to host a variety TV series in 1956. He's best known for his soft baritone voice and for singles like "The Christmas Song," "Mona Lisa" and "Nature Boy."

Nat King Cole was an American musician who first came to prominence as a jazz pianist. He owes most of his popular musical fame to his soft baritone voice, which he used to perform in big band and jazz genres. In 1956, Cole became the first Black American performer to host a variety television series, and for many white families, he was the first Black man welcomed into their living rooms each night. He has maintained worldwide popularity since his death in 1965.

Cole was born on March 17, 1919, in Montgomery, Alabama. Known for his smooth and well-articulated vocal style, Cole actually started out as a piano man. He first learned to play around the age of four with help from his mother, a church choir director. The son of a Baptist pastor, Cole may have started out playing religious music.

In his early teens, Cole had formal classical piano training. He eventually abandoned classical for his other musical passion — jazz. Earl Hines, a leader of modern jazz, was one of Cole's biggest inspirations. At 15, he dropped out of school to become a jazz pianist full time. Cole joined forces with his brother Eddie for a time, which led to his first professional recordings in 1936. He later joined a national tour for the musical revue Shuffle Along, performing as a pianist.

The following year, Cole started to put together what would become the King Cole Trio, the name being a play on the children's nursery rhyme. They toured extensively and finally landed on the charts in 1943 with "That Ain't Right," penned by Cole. "Straighten Up and Fly Right," inspired by one of his father's sermons, became another hit for the group in 1944. The trio continued its rise to the top with such pop hits as the holiday classic "The Christmas Song" and the ballad "(I Love You) For Sentimental Reasons."

By the 1950s, Cole emerged as a popular solo performer. He scored numerous hits, with such songs as "Nature Boy," "Mona Lisa," "Too Young" and "Unforgettable." In the studio, Cole got to work with some of the country's top talent, including Louis Armstrong and Ella Fitzgerald, and famous arrangers such as Nelson Riddle. He also met and befriended other stars of the era, including popular crooner Frank Sinatra.

As a Black American performer, Cole struggled to find his place in the Civil Rights movement. He had encountered racism firsthand, especially while touring in the South. In 1956, Cole had been attacked by white supremacists during a mixed-race performance in Alabama. He was rebuked by other Black Americans, however, for his less-than-supportive comments about racial integration made after the show. Cole basically took the stance that he was an entertainer, not an activist.

Cole's presence on the record charts dwindled in the late 1950s. But this decline did not last long. His career returned to top form in the early 1960s. The 1962 country-influenced hit "Rambin' Rose" reached the number two spot on the Billboard pop charts. The following spring, Cole won over music fans with the light-hearted tune "Those Lazy-Hazy-Crazy Days of Summer." He made his last appearances on the pop charts in his lifetime in 1964. Modest successes compared to his earlier hits, Cole delivered two ballads — "I Don't Want to Hurt Anymore" and "I Don't Want to See Tomorrow" — in his signature smooth style.

Cole made television history in 1956 when he became the first Black American performer to host a variety TV series. The Nat King Cole Show featured many of the leading performers of the day, including Count Basie, Peggy Lee, Sammy Davis Jr. and Tony Bennett. Unfortunately, the series didn't last long, going off the air in December 1957. Cole blamed the show's demise on the lack of a national sponsor. The sponsorship problem has been seen as a reflection of the racial issues of the times with no company seemingly wanting to back a program that featured Black entertainers.

After his show went off the air, Cole continued to be a presence on television. He appeared on such popular programs as The Ed Sullivan Show and The Garry Moore Show.

On the big screen, Cole had first started out in small roles in the 1940s, largely playing some version of himself. He landed some sizable parts in the late 1950s, appearing in the Errol Flynn drama Istanbul (1957). That same year, Cole appeared in the war drama China Gate with Gene Barry and Angie Dickinson. His only major starring role came in 1958, in the drama St. Louis Blues, also starring Eartha Kitt and Cab Calloway. Cole played the role of blues great W.C. Handy in the film. His final film appearance came in 1965: He performed alongside Jane Fonda and Lee Marvin in the light-hearted Western Cat Ballou.

In 1964, Cole discovered that he had lung cancer. He succumbed to the disease just months later, on February 15, 1965, at the age of 45, in Santa Monica, California. A "who's who" of the entertainment world, including the likes of Rosemary Clooney, Sinatra and Jack Benny, attended the legendary musician's funeral, held a few days later in Los Angeles. Released around this time, L-O-V-E proved to be Cole's final recording. The title track of the album remains hugely popular to this day and has been featured on a number of film soundtracks.

Since his death, Cole's music has endured. His rendition of "The Christmas Song" has become a holiday classic and many of his other signature songs are frequently selected for film and television soundtracks. His daughter Natalie Cole also carried on the family profession, becoming a successful singer in her own right. In 1991, she helped her father achieve a posthumous hit. Natalie recorded his hit "Unforgettable" and put their vocals together as a duet.

Cole married for the first time when he was only 17. He and his first wife, Nadine Robinson, divorced in 1948. Only a short time later, Cole married singer Maria Hawkins Ellington, with whom he raised five children. The couple had three biological children, daughters Natalie, Casey, and Timolin, and two adopted children, daughter Carol and son Nat Kelly.

https://www.biography.com/musician/nat-king-cole

CHAPTER 18
MALCOLM X (1925-1965)

Credit: reproduction rights transferred to Library of Congress

Malcolm X, one of the most influential Black American leaders of the 20th Century, was born Malcolm Little in Omaha, Nebraska on May 19, 1925, to Earl Little, a Georgia native and itinerant Baptist preacher, and Louise Norton Little who was born in the West Indian Island of Grenada. Shortly after Malcolm was born the family moved to Lansing, Michigan. Earl Little joined Marcus Garvey's Universal Negro Improvement Association (UNIA) where he publicly advocated black nationalist beliefs, prompting the local white supremacist Black Legion to set fire to their home. Little was killed by a streetcar in 1931. Authorities ruled it a suicide, but the family believed he was killed by white supremacists.

Although an academically gifted student, Malcolm dropped out of high school after a teacher ridiculed his aspirations to become a lawyer. He then moved to the Roxbury district of Boston, Massachusetts to live with an older half-sister, Ella Little Collins. Malcolm worked odd jobs in Boston and then moved to Harlem in 1943 where he drifted into a life of drug dealing, pimping, gambling, and other forms of "hustling." He avoided the draft in World War II by declaring his intent to organize black soldiers to attack whites which led to his classification as "mentally disqualified for military service."

Malcolm was arrested for burglary in Boston in 1946 and received a ten-year prison sentence. There he joined the Nation of Islam (NOI). Upon his parole in 1952, Malcolm was called to Chicago, Illinois by NOI leader, the Honorable Elijah Muhammad. Like other converts, he changed his surname to "X," symbolizing, he said, the rejection of "slave names" and his inability to claim his ancestral African name.

Recognizing his promise as a speaker and organizer for the Nation of Islam, Muhammad sent Malcolm to Boston to become the Minister of Temple Number Eleven. His proselytizing success earned a reassignment in 1954 to Temple Number Seven in Harlem. Although New York's one million blacks comprised the largest Black American urban population in the United States, Malcolm noted that "there weren't enough Muslims to fill a city bus." "Fishing" in Christian storefront churches and at competing black nationalist meetings, Malcolm built up the membership of Temple Seven. He also met his future wife, Sister Betty X, a nursing student who joined the temple in 1956. They married and eventually had six daughters.

Malcolm X quickly became a national public figure in July 1959 when CBS aired Mike Wallace's expose on the NOI, "The Hate That Hate Produced." This documentary revealed the views of the NOI, of which Malcolm was the principal spokesperson and showed those views to be in sharp contrast to those of most well-known Black American leaders of the time. Soon, however, Malcolm was increasingly frustrated by the NOI's bureaucratic structure and refusal to participate in the Civil Rights Movement. His November 1963 speech in Detroit, "Message to the Grass Roots," a bold attack on racism and a call for black unity, foreshadowed the split with his spiritual mentor, Elijah Muhammad. However, Malcolm on December 1, in response to a reporter's question about the assassination of President John F. Kennedy, used the phrase "chickens coming home to roost" which to Muslims meant that Allah was punishing white America for crimes against black people. Whatever the personal views of Muslims about Kennedy's death, Elijah Muhammad had given strict orders to his ministers not to comment on the assassination. Malcolm defied the order and was suspended from the NOI for ninety days.

Malcolm used the suspension to announce on March 8, 1964, his break with the NOI and his creation of the Muslim Mosque, Inc. Three months later he formed a strictly political group (an action expressly banned by the NOI), called the Organization of Afro American Unity (OAAU) which was roughly patterned after the Organization of African Unity (OAU).

His dramatic political transformation was revealed when he spoke to the Militant Labor Forum of the Socialist Worker's Party. Malcolm placed the Black Revolution in the context of a worldwide anti-imperialist struggle taking place in Africa, Asia, and Latin America, noting that "when I say black, I mean non-white—black, brown, red or yellow." By April 1964, while speaking at a CORE rally in Cleveland, Ohio, Malcolm gave his famous "The Ballot or the Bullet" speech in which he described black Americans as "victims of democracy."

Malcolm traveled to Africa and the Middle East in late Spring 1964 and was received like a visiting head of state in many countries including Egypt, Nigeria, Tanzania, Kenya, and Ghana. While there, Malcolm made his hajj to Mecca, Saudi Arabia and added El-Hajj to his official NOI name Malik El-Shabazz. The tour forced Malcolm to realize that one's political position as a revolutionary superseded "color."

The transformed Malcolm reiterated these views when he addressed an OAAU rally in New York, declaring for a pan-African struggle "by any means necessary." Malcolm spent six months in Africa in 1964 in an unsuccessful attempt to get international support for a United Nations investigation of human rights violations of Afro Americans in the United States. In February 1965, Malcolm flew to Paris, France to continue his efforts but was denied entry amidst rumors that he was on a Central Intelligence Agency (CIA) hit list.   Upon his return to New York, his home was firebombed.   Events continued to spiral downward and on February 21, 1965, Malcolm X was assassinated at the Audubon Ballroom in the Washington Heights section of Manhattan.

https://www.blackpast.org/african-american-history/x-malcolm-1925-1965/

CHAPTER 19
MEDGAR EVERS (1925-1963)

Credit: Hulton Archive/Getty Images

Medgar Wiley Evers was born on July 2, 1925, in the town of Decatur, in East-Central Mississippi. Growing up, Evers regularly witnessed the pervasive and violent racism directed at Black Americans. When Evers was young, a white mob lynched a family friend, and Evers frequently saw gangs of white men looking for black people to assault.

In 1943, at the age of 17, Evers dropped out of high school to get a full-time job. The following year, he volunteered for service in the US Army and was inducted at Camp Shelby. During World War II, the vast majority of Black Americans in the segregated US military were relegated to support units because white officers regarded black men as inferior combat soldiers. Consequently, the Army assigned Evers to an all-black port battalion in the Quartermaster Corps. Evers' battalion was likely charged with unloading weapons, supplies, and vehicles from Allied ships onto trucks that then transported them to the front lines via convoys such as the Red Ball Express.

While serving in England and France, Technician Fifth Grade Evers grew frustrated with the demeaning treatment that he and other black servicemembers received while serving their country. He resolved to return to his home state of Mississippi and fight for the rights of Black Americans. Shortly after Evers was discharged in 1946, he and his brother led a group of black veterans to the Newton County courthouse in Decatur to register to vote. Evers' small group was met by armed white men who threatened the veterans with violence if they did not leave. Undeterred, Evers continued to advocate for the full citizenship rights of Black Americans.

After returning to high school and obtaining his diploma, Evers attended Alcorn Agricultural and Mechanical College, where he met and married fellow student Myrlie Beasley. Upon graduating in 1952, the couple moved to Philadelphia, Mississippi, where Evers found work as an insurance salesman. Following the Supreme Court's 1954 landmark decision Brown v. Board of Education, which declared segregation in schools to be unconstitutional, Evers applied to the University of Mississippi Law School. Although Evers was still denied admission because of his race, he later helped James Meredith become the first person of color admitted to the school in 1962.

Although Evers was unsuccessful in his bid to personally desegregate the University of Mississippi Law School, he caught the attention of leaders from the National Association for the Advancement of Colored People (NAACP). In 1954, Evers became the first state field secretary for the NAACP in Mississippi. Evers and his wife moved to Jackson to take up the new post. Myrlie Evers became an important part of the Civil Rights Movement in her own right as a researcher, musician, hostess, and secretary for the NAACP.

Evers' work for the NAACP took him all over the state of Mississippi. He organized boycotts, voter-registration drives, and demonstrations, as well as investigated violence against Black Americans, such as the 1955 murder of 14-year-old Emmett Till. Evers' prominent position in the NAACP and advocacy for the rights of Black Americans prompted numerous threats from white supremacist groups. Other civil rights activists, and even Evers' own family, urged him to leave Mississippi for his own safety, but Evers refused to abandon the cause of freedom that he had fought for during World War II. Evers survived several attempts on his life, including nearly being run down by a car and having his home firebombed in May 1963. Myrlie Evers later remembered that other Black Americans would cross the street just so they would not be seen close to her husband, lest they become targets as well.

At 8 p.m. on June 11, 1963, President John F. Kennedy, himself a decorated WWII veteran, delivered a live televised speech to the nation on the issue of civil rights. Kennedy implored his fellow Americans to examine their consciences in the wake of protests requiring the deployment of the 101st Airborne Division to desegregate schools in Birmingham, Alabama. Kennedy unequivocally stated that "the rights of every man are diminished when the rights of one man are threatened." He claimed that discrimination was not a sectional issue, but a problem that existed in every city, in every state. It was a bold speech that all but one of his advisors tried to dissuade him from delivering. They knew there was little support for the civil rights legislation then being considered by Congress, and they advised the president against wasting valuable political capital.

Later that night, Evers was returning to the quiet suburban home he shared with his wife and three young children. As he stepped out of his car and made his way to the front door, he was shot in the back by a sniper concealed in a grove of trees several hundred feet away. His family heard the shot and ran outside to his aid. Evers died less than one hour later at the University of Mississippi Medical Center. Medgar Evers was just 37 years old.

The murder of one of the nation's most prominent civil rights activist shocked many. Evers was laid to rest with full military honors in Arlington National Cemetery on June 19. Three thousand people attended the ceremony. On June 28, the cover of Life magazine bore the image of Myrlie Evers comforting her bereaved son at the funeral.

. Meanwhile, the FBI promptly took over the hunt for Evers' killer. Within hours of the shooting, police had recovered the rifle used to kill Evers in the woods where his assassin had dropped it. The rifle bore a distinct fingerprint, which matched the WWII service record of a US Marine and self-proclaimed white supremacist named Byron De La Beckwith. Two weeks later, agents arrested Beckwith and charged him with the murder of Medgar Evers. Multiple eyewitnesses placed Beckwith and his car at the scene on the night of Evers' murder, but two police officers mysteriously came forward to say they had seen Beckwith 100 miles away the night of Evers' murder. Two all-white male juries failed to convict Beckwith despite the evidence against him. The governor of Mississippi at the time, Ross Barnett, even visited the courtroom during the trial to shake Beckwith's hand.

For the next 30 years, Beckwith openly bragged about killing Evers and plotted to kill other activists as well. Finally, in 1989, calls to retry Beckwith prompted his arrest and extradition from Tennessee to Mississippi. Because Beckwith's previous trials had resulted in hung juries, and therefore mistrials, the state of Mississippi was able to once again file charges against him. Hinds County assistant district attorney Bobby DeLaughter, who built the case against Beckwith for the new trial, explained its significance by saying "When you have somebody just shot from ambush in the back, while his wife and kids are right there in the house—shot not for anything violent that he did but just for what he believes—that leaves a great, gaping wound in a society."

DeLaughter reconstructed the case against Beckwith nearly from scratch. He obtained a transcript of the original trial from Myrlie Evers, and by a stroke of sheer luck, DeLaughter discovered that one of his own family members had saved the murder weapon as a souvenir after the original trial. DeLaughter's efforts paid off when a jury of black and white men and women convicted Beckwith of the murder of Medgar Evers in 1994. Beckwith received a life sentence and died in prison in 2001. DeLaughter's successful prosecution of Beckwith in the high-profile case prompted more than 20 other trials aimed at bringing the murderers of Black Americans to justice.

While Evers' memory was honored with songs, statues, and in the name of a new college, his family resolved to carry on his work. His older brother, Charles Evers, assumed Medgar Evers' former post in the NAACP and subsequently served as the mayor of Fayette, Mississippi. Myrlie Evers-Williams later became the first chairwoman of the NAACP.

Medgar Evers once said, "you can kill a man, but you can't kill an idea." Evers' death helped bolster public support for the Civil Rights Act that President John F. Kennedy had proposed, and which was ultimately signed into law in 1964. The bill formally banned discrimination and segregation in jobs, housing, and education. The following year, the Voting Rights Act of

1965 finally outlawed poll taxes and literacy tests, which many states used to disenfranchise Black Americans. The struggle for equal rights was far from over, however, as many more people lost their lives fighting for the full realization of the rights these bills promised.

https://www.nationalww2museum.org/war/articles/medgar-evers-us-army-veteran-and-civil-rights-leader

CHAPTER 20
MILES DAVIS (1926-1991)

Credit: Michael Ochs Archives/Getty Images

Miles Davis, in full Miles Dewey Davis III, American jazz musician, a great trumpeter who as a bandleader and composer was one of the major influences on the art from the late 1940s.

Davis grew up in East St. Louis, Illinois, where his father was a prosperous dental surgeon. (In later years he often spoke of his comfortable upbringing, sometimes to rebuke critics who assumed that a background of poverty and suffering was common to all great jazz artists.) He began studying trumpet in his early teens; fortuitously, in light of his later stylistic development, his first teacher advised him to play without vibrato. Davis played with jazz bands in the St. Louis area before moving to New York City in 1944 to study at the Institute of Musical Art (now the Juilliard School)— although he skipped many classes and instead was schooled through jam sessions with masters such as Dizzy Gillespie and Charlie Parker. Davis and Parker recorded together often during the years 1945–48.

Davis's early playing was sometimes tentative and not always fully in tune, but his unique, intimate tone and his fertile musical imagination outweighed his technical shortcomings. By the early 1950s Davis had turned his limitations into considerable assets. Rather than emulate the busy, wailing style of such bebop pioneers as Gillespie, Davis explored the trumpet's middle register, experimenting with harmonies and rhythms and varying the phrasing of his improvisations. With the occasional exception of multitone flurries, his melodic style was direct and unornamented, based on quarter notes and rich with inflections. The deliberation, pacing, and lyricism in his improvisations are striking.

In the summer of 1948, Davis formed a nonet that included the renowned jazz artists Gerry Mulligan, J.J. Johnson, Kenny Clarke, and Lee Konitz, as well as players on French horn and tuba, instruments rarely heard in a jazz context. Mulligan, Gil Evans, and pianist John Lewis did most of the band's arrangements, which juxtaposed the flexible, improvisatory nature of bebop with a thickly textured orchestral sound. The group was short-lived but during its brief history recorded a dozen tracks that were originally released as singles (1949–50). These recordings changed the course of modern jazz and paved the way for the West Coast styles of the 1950s. The tracks were later collected in the album Birth of the Cool (1957).

During the early 1950s Davis struggled with a drug addiction that affected his playing, yet he still managed to record albums that rank among his best, including several with such jazz notables as Sonny Rollins, Milt Jackson, and Thelonious Monk. In 1954, having overcome the addiction, Davis embarked on a two-decade period during which he was considered the most innovative musician in jazz. He formed classic small groups in the 1950s that featured saxophone legends John Coltrane and Cannonball Adderley, pianists Red Garland and Bill Evans, bassist Paul Chambers, and drummers "Philly" Joe Jones and Jimmy Cobb. Davis's albums recorded during this era, including 'Round About Midnight (1956), Workin' (1956), Steamin' (1956), Relaxin' (1956), and Milestones (1958), affected the work of numerous other artists. He capped this period of his career with Kind of Blue (1959), perhaps the most celebrated album in the history of jazz. A mellow, relaxed collection, the album includes the finest recorded examples of modal jazz, a style in which improvisations are based upon sparse chords and nonstandard scales rather than on complex, frequently changing chords. The modal style lends itself to solos that are focused on melody; this accessible quality ensured Kind of Blue's popularity with jazz fans.

Released concurrently with the small-group recordings, Davis's albums with pieces arranged and conducted by Gil Evans—Miles Ahead (1957), Porgy and Bess (1958), and Sketches of Spain (1960)—were also monuments of the genre. The Davis-Evans collaborations were marked by complex arrangements, a near-equal emphasis on orchestra and soloist, and some of Davis's most soulful and emotionally powerful playing. Davis and Evans occasionally collaborated in later years, but never again so memorably as on these three masterful albums.

The early 1960s were transitional, less-innovative years for Davis, although his music and his playing remained top-calibre. He began forming another soon-to-be-classic small group in late 1962 with bassist Ron Carter, pianist Herbie Hancock, and teenage drummer Tony Williams; tenor saxophonist Wayne Shorter joined the lineup in 1964. Davis's new quintet was characterized by a light, free sound and a repertoire that extended from the blues to avant-garde and free jazz. Compared with the innovations of other modern jazz groups of the 1960s, the Davis quintet's experimentations in polyrhythm and polytonality were more subtle but equally daring. Live at the Plugged Nickel (1965), E.S.P. (1965), Miles Smiles (1966), and Nefertiti (1967) were among the quintet's timeless, influential recordings. About the time of Miles in the Sky and Filles de Kilimanjaro (both 1968), Davis began experimenting with electronic instruments. With other musicians, including keyboardists Chick Corea and Joe Zawinul and guitarist John McLaughlin, Davis cut In a Silent Way (1969), regarded as the seminal album of the jazz fusion movement. It was considered by purists to be Davis's last true jazz album.

Davis won new fans and alienated old ones with the release of Bitches Brew (1969), an album on which he fully embraced the rhythms, electronic instrumentation, and studio effects of rock music. A cacophonous kaleidoscope of layered sounds, rhythms, and textures, the album's influence was heard in such 1970s fusion groups as Weather Report and Chick Corea's Return to Forever. Davis continued in this style for a few years, with the album Live-Evil (1970) and the film soundtrack A Tribute to Jack Johnson (1970) being particular highlights.

Davis was injured in an auto accident in 1972, curtailing his activities, then retired from 1975 through 1980. When he returned to public notice with The Man with the Horn (1981), critics felt that Davis's erratic playing showed the effects of his five-year layoff, but he steadily regained his powers during the next few years. He dabbled in a variety of musical styles throughout the 1980s, concentrating mostly on jazz-rock dance music, but there were also notable experiments in other styles, such as a return to his blues roots (Star People, 1982) and a set of Gil Evans-influenced orchestral numbers (Music from Siesta, 1987). Davis won several Grammy Awards during this period for such albums as We Want Miles (1982), Tutu (1986), and Aura (1989). One of the most-memorable events of Davis's later years occurred at the Montreux Jazz Festival in 1991, when he joined with an orchestra conducted by Quincy Jones to perform some of the classic Gil Evans arrangements of the late 1950s. Davis died less than three months later. His final album, Doo-Bop (1992), was released posthumously.

Although critics dismissed much of the music Davis released after Bitches Brew, his excursions helped keep jazz popular with mainstream audiences. In later years he ignored the critics, and he defied convention by wandering around the stage, often playing with his back to the audience. In his much praised and revealing autobiography, Miles (1989; with Quincy Troupe), he wrote frankly of his hedonistic past and of the racism he saw in the music industry. Along with Louis Armstrong, Duke Ellington, and Charlie Parker, Davis is regarded as one of the four most important and influential musicians in jazz history, as well as the music's most eclectic practitioner.

https://www.britannica.com/biography/Miles-Davis

CHAPTER 21
CHUCK BERRY (1926-2017)

Credit: Michael Ochs Archives/Getty Images

Chuck Berry is the greatest of the rock and rollers. Elvis competes with Frank Sinatra, Little Richard camps his way to self-negation, Fats Domino looks old, and Jerry Lee Lewis looks down his noble honker at all those who refuse to understand that Jerry Lee has chosen to become a great country singer. But for a fee--which went up markedly after the freak success of "My Ding-a-Ling," his first certified million-seller, in 1972, and has now diminished again--Chuck Berry will hop on a plane with his guitar and go play some rock and roll. He is the symbol of the music--the first man elected to a Rock Music Hall of Fame that exists thus far only in the projections of television profiteers; the man invited to come steal the show at the 1975 Grammys, although he has never been nominated for one himself, not even in the rock and roll or rhythm and blues categories. More important, he is also the music's substance--he taught George Harrison and Keith Richard to play guitar long before he met either, or his songs are still claimed as encores by everyone from folkies to heavy-metal kids. But Chuck Berry isn't merely the greatest of the rock and rollers, or rather, there's nothing mere about it. Say rather that unless we can somehow recycle the concept of the great artist so that it supports Chuck Berry as well as it does Marcel Proust, we might as well trash it altogether.

As with Charlie Chaplin or Walt Kelly or the Beatles, Chuck Berry's greatness doesn't depend entirely on the greatness or originality of his oeuvre. The body of his top-quality work isn't exactly vast, comprising three or perhaps four dozen songs that synthesize two related traditions: blues, and country and western. Although in some respects Berry's rock and roll is simpler and more vulgar than either of its musical sources, its simplicity and vulgarity are defensible in the snootiest high-art terms--how about "instinctive minimalism" or "demotic voice"? But his case doesn't rest on such defenses. It would be as perverse to argue that his songs are in themselves as rich as, say, Remembrance of Things Past. Their richness is rather a function of their active relationship with an audience--a complex relationship that shifts every time a song enters a new context, club or album or radio or mass singalong. Where Proust wrote about a dying subculture from a cork-lined room, Berry helped give life to a subculture, and both he and it change every time they confront each other. Even "My Ding-a-Ling," a fourth grade wee-wee joke that used to mortify true believers at college concerts, permitted a lot of 12-year-olds new insight into the moribund concept of "dirty" when it hit the airwaves; the song changed again when an oldies crowd became as children to shout along with Uncle Chuck the night he received his gold record at Madison Square Garden. And what happened to "Brown Eyed Handsome Man," never a hit among whites, when Berry sang it at interracial rock and roll concerts in Northern cities in the Fifties? How many black kids took "eyed" as code for "skinned"? How many whites?

How did that make them feel about each other, and about the song? And did any of that change the song itself?

Berry's own intentions, of course, remain a mystery. Typically, this public artist is an obsessively private person who has been known to drive reporters from his own amusement park, and the sketches of his life overlap and contradict each other. The way I tell it, Berry was born into a lower middle-class colored family in St. Louis in 1926. He was so quick and ambitious that he both served time in reform school on a robbery conviction and acquired a degree in hairdressing and cosmetology before taking a job on an auto assembly line to support a wife and kids. Yet his speed and ambition persisted. By 1953 he was working as a beautician and leading a three-piece blues group on a regular weekend gig. His gimmick was to cut the blues with country-influenced humorous narrative songs. These were rare in the black music of the time, although they had been common enough before phonograph records crystallized the blues form, and although Louis Jordan, a hero of Berry's, had been doing something vaguely similar in front of white audiences for years.

In 1955, Berry recorded two of his songs on a borrowed machine--"Wee Wee Hours," a blues that he and his pianist, Johnnie Johnson, hoped to sell, and an adapted country tune called "Ida Red." He traveled to Chicago and met Muddy Waters, the uncle of the blues, who sent him on to Leonard Chess of Chess Records. Chess liked "Wee Wee Hours" but flipped for "Ida Red," which was renamed "Maybellene," a hairdresser's dream, and forwarded to Allan Freed. Having mysteriously acquired one-third of the writer's credit with another DJ, Freed played "Maybellene" quite a lot, and it became one of the first nationwide rock 'n' roll hits.

At that time, any fair-minded person would have judged this process exploitative and pecuniary. A blues musician comes to a blues label to promote a blues song--"It was `Wee Wee Hours' we was proud of, that was our music," says Johnnie Johnson--but the owner of the label decides he wants to push a novelty: "The big beat, cars, and young love. It was a trend and we jumped on it," Chess has said. The owner then trades away a third of the blues singer's creative sweat to the symbol of payola, who hypes the novelty song into commercial success and leaves the artist in a quandry. Does he stick with his art, thus forgoing the first real recognition he's ever had, or does he pander to popular taste?

The question is loaded, of course. "Ida Red" was Chuck Berry's music as much as "Wee Wee Hours," which in retrospect seems rather uninspired. In fact, maybe the integrity problem went the other way. Maybe Johnson was afraid that the innovations of "Ida Red"--country guitar lines adapted to blues-style picking, with the ceaseless legato of his own piano adding rhythmic excitement to the steady backbeat--were too far out to sell. What happened instead was that Berry's limited but brilliant vocabulary of guitar riffs quickly came to epitomize rock 'n' roll. Ultimately, every great white guitar group of the early Sixties imitated Berry's style, and Johnson's piano technique was almost as influential. In other words, it turned out that Berry and Johnson weren't basically bluesmen at all. Through some magic combination of inspiration and cultural destiny, they had hit upon something more contemporary than blues, and a young audience, for whom the Depression was one more thing that bugged their parents, understood this better than the musicians themselves. Leonard Chess simply functioned as a music businessman should, though only rarely does one combine the courage and insight (and opportunity) to pull it off, even once. Chess became a surrogate audience, picking up on new music and making sure that it received enough exposure for everyone else to pick up on it, too.

Obviously, Chuck Berry wasn't racked with doubt about artistic compromise. A good blues single usually sold around 10,000 copies and a big rhythm and blues hit might go into the hundreds of thousands, but "Maybellene" probably moved a million, even if Chess never sponsored the audit to prove it. Berry had achieved a grip on the white audience and the solid future it could promise, and, remarkably, he had in no way diluted his genius to do it. On the contrary, that was his genius. He would never have fulfilled himself if he hadn't explored his relationship to the white world--a relationship which was much different for him, an urban black man who was used to machines and had never known brutal poverty, than it was for, say, Muddy.

Berry was the first blues-based performer to successfully reclaim guitar tricks that country and western innovators had appropriated from black people and adapted to their own uses 25 or 50 years before. By adding blues tone to some fast country runs and yoking them to a rhythm and blues beat and some unembarrassed electrification, he created an instrumental style with biracial appeal. Alternating guitar chords augmented the beat while Berry sang in an insouciant tenor that, while recognizably Afro-American in accent, stayed clear of the melisma and blurred overtones of blues singing, both of which enter only at carefully premeditated moments. His few detractors still complain about the repetitiveness of this style, but they miss the point. Repetition without tedium is the backbone of rock and roll, and the components of Berry's music proved so durable that they still provoke instant excitement at concerts two decades later. And in any case, the instrumental repetition was counterbalanced by unprecedented and virtually unduplicated verbal variety.

Chuck Berry is the greatest rock lyricist this side of Bob Dylan, and sometimes I prefer him to Dylan. Both communicate an abundance of the childlike delight in linguistic discovery that page poets are supposed to convey and too often don't, but Berry's most ambitious lyrics, unlike Dylan's, never seem pretentious or forced. True, his language is ersatz and barbaric, full of mispronounced foreignisms and advertising coinages, but then, so was Whitman's. Like Whitman, Berry is excessive because he is totally immersed in America--the America of Melville and the Edsel, burlesque and installment-plan funerals, pemmican, and pomade. Unlike Whitman, though, he doesn't quite permit you to take him seriously--he can't really think it's pronounced "a la carty," can he? He is a little surreal. How else can a black man as sensitive as Chuck Berry respond to the affluence of white America--an affluence suddenly his for the taking.

Chuck Berry is not only a little surreal but also a little schizy; even after he committed himself to rock 'n' roll story songs, relegating the bluesman in him to B sides and album fillers, he found his persona split in two. In three of the four singles that followed "Maybellene," he amplified the black half of his artistic personality, the brown-eyed handsome man who always came up short in his quest for the small-time hedonism American promises everyone. By implication, Brown Eyes' sharp sense of life's nettlesome and even oppressive details provided a kind of salvation by humor, especially in "Too Much Monkey Business," a catalog of hassles that included work, school, and the army. But the white teenagers who were the only audience with the cultural experience to respond to Berry's art weren't buying this kind of salvation, not en masse. They wanted something more optimistic and more specific to themselves; of the four singles that followed "Maybellene," only "Roll Over Beethoven," which introduced Berry's other half, the rock 'n' roller, achieved any real success. Chuck got the message. His next release, "School Day," was another complaint song, but this time the complaints were explicitly adolescent and were relieved by the direct action of the rock 'n' roller. In fact, the song has been construed as a prophecy of the Free Speech Movement: "Close your books, get out of your seat/Down the halls and into the street."

It has become a cliché to attribute the rise of rock and roll to a new parallelism between white teenagers and black Americans; a common "alienation" and even "suffering" are often cited. As with most clichés, this one has its basis in fact--teenagers in the Fifties certainly showed an unprecedented consciousness of themselves as a circumscribed group, though how much that had to do with marketing refinements and how much with the bomb remains unresolved. In any case, Chuck Berry's history points up the limits of this notion. For Berry was closer to white teenagers both economically (that reform school stint suggests a JD exploit, albeit combined with a racist judicial system) and in spirit (he shares his penchant for youthfulness with Satchel Paige but not Henry Aaron, with Leslie Fiedler but not Norman Podhoretz) than the average black man. And even at that, he had to make a conscious (not to say calculated) leap of the imagination to reach them, and sometimes fell short.

Although he scored lots of minor hits, Chuck Berry made only three additional Billboard Top Ten singles in the Fifties--"Rock and Roll Music," "Sweet Little Sixteen," and "Johnny B. Goode"--and every one of them ignored Brown Eyes for the assertive, optimistic, and somewhat simpleminded rock 'n' roller. In a pattern common among popular artists, his truest and most personal work didn't flop, but it wasn't overwhelmingly popular either. For such artists, the audience can be like a drug. A little of it is so good for them that they assume a lot of it would be even better, but instead the big dose saps their autonomy, often so subtly that they don't notice it. For Chuck Berry, the craving for overwhelming popularity proved slightly dangerous. At the same time that he was enlivening his best songs with faintly Latin rhythms, which he was convinced were the coming thing, he was also writing silly exercises with titles like "Hey Pedro." Nevertheless, his pursuit of the market also worked a communion with his audience, with whom he continued to have an instinctive rapport remarkable in a 30-year-old black man. For there is also a sense in which the popular artist is a drug for the audience, and a doctor, too--he has to know how much of his vital essence he can administer at one time, and in what compound.

The reason Berry's rock 'n' roller was capable of such insightful excursions into the teen psyche--"Sweet Little Sixteen," a celebration of everything lovely about manhood; or "Almost Grown," a basically unalienated first-person expression of teen rebellion that Sixties youth-cult pundits should have taken seriously--was that he shared a crucial American value with the humorous Brown Eyes. That value was fun. Even among rock critics, who ought to know better, fun doesn't have much of a rep, so that they commiserate with someone like LaVern Baker, a second-rate blues and gospel singer who felt she was selling her soul every time she launched into a first-rate whoop of nonsense like "Jim Dandy" or "Bumble Bee." But fun was what adolescent revolt had to be about--inebriated affluence versus the hangover of the work ethic. It was the only practicable value in the Peter Pan utopia of the American dream. Because black music had always thrived on exuberance--not just the otherworldly transport of gospel, but the candidly physical good times of great pop blues singers like Washboard Sam, who is most often dismissed as a lightweight by the heavy blues critics--it turned into the perfect vehicle for generational convulsion. Black musicians, however, had rarely achieved an optimism that was cultural as well as personal--those few who did, like Louis Armstrong, left themselves open to charges of Tomming. Chuck Berry never Tommed. The trouble he'd seen just made his sly, bad-boy voice and the splits and waddles of his stage show that much more credible.

Then, late in 1959, fun turned into trouble. Berry had imported a Spanish-speaking Apache prostitute he'd picked up in El Paso to check hats in his St. Louis nightclub, and then fired her. She went to the police, and Berry was indicted under the Mann Act. After two trials, the first so blatantly racist that it was disallowed, he went to prison for two years. When he got out, in 1964, he and his wife had separated, apparently a major tragedy for him. The Beatles and the Rolling Stones had paid him such explicit and appropriate tribute that his career was probably in better shape after his jail term than before, but he couldn't capitalize. He had a few hits--"Nadine" and "No Particular Place to Go" (John Lennon is one of the many who believe they were written before he went in) --but the well was dry. Between 1965 and 1970 he didn't release one-even passable new song, and he died as a recording artist.

In late 1966, Berry left Chess for a big advance from Mercury Records. The legends of his money woes at Chess are numerous, but apparently the Chess brothers knew how to record him--the stuff he produced himself for Mercury was terrible. Working alone with pickup bands, he still performed a great deal, mostly to make money for Berry Park, a recreation haven 30 miles from St. Louis. And as he toured, he found that something had happened to his old audience--it was getting older, with troubles of its own, and it dug blues. At auditoriums like the Fillmore, where he did a disappointing live LP with the Steve Miller Blues Band, Chuck was more than willing to stretch out on a blues. One of his favorites was from Elmore James: "When things go wrong, wrong with you, it hurts me too."

By 1970, he was back home at Chess, and suddenly his new audience called forth a miracle. Berry was a natural head--no drugs, no alcohol--and most of his attempts to cash in on hippie talk had been embarrassments. But "Tulane," one of his greatest story songs, was the perfect fantasy. It was about two dope dealers: "Tulane and Johnny opened a novelty shop/ Back under the counter was the cream of the crop." Johnny is nabbed by narcs, but Tulane, his girlfriend, escapes, and Johnny confidently predicts that she will buy off the judge. Apparently, she does, for there is a sequel, a blues. In "Have Mercy Judge," Johnny has been caught again, and this time he expects to be sent to "some stony mansion." Berry devotes the last stanza to Tulane, who is "too alive to live alone." The last line makes me wonder just how he felt about his own wife when he went to prison: "Just tell her to live, and I'll forgive her, and even love her more when I come back home."

Taken together, the two songs are Berry's peak, although Leonard Chess would no doubt have vetoed the vocal double-track on "Tulane" that blurs its impact a bit. Remarkably, "Have Mercy Judge" is the first important blues Berry ever wrote, and like all his best work it isn't quite traditional, utilizing an abc line structure instead of the usual aab. Where did it come from? Is it unreasonable to suspect that part of Berry really was a bluesman all along, and that this time, instead of him going to his audience, his audience came to him and provided the juice for one last masterpiece?

Berry's career would appear closed. He is a rock and roll monument at 50, a pleasing performer whose days of inspiration are over. Sometime in the next 30 years he will probably die, and while his songs have already stuck in the public memory a lot longer than Washboard Sam's, it's likely that most of them will fade away too. So, is he, was he, will he be a great artist? It won't be we judging, but perhaps we can think of it this way. Maybe the true measure of his greatness was not whether his songs "lasted"--a term which as of now means persisted through centuries instead of decades--but that he was one of the ones to make us understand that the greatest thing about art is the way it happens between people. I am grateful for aesthetic artifacts, and I suspect that a few of Berry's songs, a few of his recordings, will live on in that way. I only hope that they prove too alive to live alone. If they do, and if by some mishap Berry's name itself is forgotten, that will nevertheless be an entirely apposite kind of triumph for him.

https://www.robertchristgau.com/xg/music/berry-76.php

CHAPTER 22
CORETTA SCOTT KING (1927-2006)

Credit: Library of Congress

The widow of one of the most influential leaders in the world, Coretta Scott King provided Martin Luther King, Jr., with what he called the "love, sacrifices, and loyalty [without which] neither life nor work would bring fulfillment" (King, Stride, 11). An activist in her own right, Coretta King made numerous contributions to the struggle for social justice and human rights throughout her life.

Coretta Scott was born on 27 April 1927, near Marion, Alabama. Her parents, Obadiah "Obie" Scott and Bernice McMurray Scott were farm owners committed to ensuring that their children received the best education possible. Scott attended the private Lincoln High School in Marion, where she developed her interest in music. There she took formal vocal lessons, learned to read music, and played several instruments. By the age of 15, she had become the choir director and pianist of her church's junior choir.

After graduating from Lincoln, Scott won a partial scholarship to Antioch College, in Yellow Springs, Ohio, the same university her sister Edythe had attended as the first Black American student. While at Antioch, Scott studied voice and music education. She also became a member of the local chapter of the National Association for the Advancement of Colored People, as well as the Race Relations and Civil Liberties Committees. In an article, "Why I Came to College," published in Opportunity in 1948, Scott wrote that college graduates "had greater freedom of movement: they went on trips; they visited cities; they knew more about the world" (Scott, 42). She later credited Antioch with preparing her for her role in the civil rights movement, stating that "the college's emphasis on service to mankind reinforced the Christian spirit of giving and sharing" and provided "a new self-assurance that encouraged me in competition with all people" (Scott King, 43).

In 1951 Scott enrolled in Boston's New England Conservatory of Music with a grant from the Jessie Smith Noyes Foundation. In early 1952, her friend Mary Powell introduced her to King, then a doctoral candidate at Boston University's School of Theology. While initially wary of dating a Baptist minister, she was impressed by his sophistication and intellect and recalled King telling her: "You have everything I have ever wanted in a wife" (Scott King, 53). The two were married at the Scott family home near Marion on 18 June 1953. After the wedding, they returned to Boston to complete their degrees. Coretta Scott King earned her Bachelor of Music degree in June 1954.

Although Scott King was focused on raising the couple's four children: Yolanda Denise King (1955), Martin Luther King, III (1957), Dexter Scott King (1961), and Bernice Albertine King (1963), she continued to play a critical role in many of the civil rights campaigns of the 1950s and 1960s, performing in freedom concerts that included poetry recitation, singing, and lectures related to the history of the civil rights movement. The proceeds from these concerts were donated to the Southern Christian Leadership Conference.

Scott King also accompanied her husband around the world, traveling to Ghana in 1957 and India in 1959. She was particularly affected by the women she met in India. "As we traveled through the land, we were greatly impressed by the part women played in the political life of India, far more than in our own country" (Scott King, 162). In 1962, Coretta Scott King's interest in disarmament efforts took her to Geneva, Switzerland, where she served as a Women's Strike for Peace delegate to the 17-nation Disarmament Conference. Two years later, she accompanied her husband to Oslo for the awarding of the Nobel Peace Prize. She later recalled thinking: "What a blessing, to be a co-worker with a man whose life would have so profound an impact on the world" (Scott King, 12).

After King's assassination on 4 April 1968, Coretta Scott King devoted much of her life to spreading her husband's philosophy of nonviolence. Just days after his death, she led a march on behalf of sanitation workers in Memphis, Tennessee. Later that month, she stood in for her husband at an anti–Vietnam War rally in New York. In May 1968, she helped to launch the Poor People's Campaign, and thereafter participated in numerous anti-poverty efforts.

With a deep commitment to preserving King's legacy, almost immediately Coretta Scott King began mobilizing support for the Martin Luther King, Jr., Center for Nonviolent Social Change. As founding president of the King Center, she guided its construction next to Ebenezer Baptist Church, where King had served as co-pastor with his father, Martin Luther King, Sr.

Throughout the 1970s and 1980s, Scott King continued to speak publicly and write nationally syndicated columns and began efforts to establish a national holiday in honor of her husband. In 1983, she led an effort that brought more than a half-million demonstrators to Washington, D.C., to commemorate the 20th anniversary of the 1963 March on Washington for Jobs and Freedom, where King had delivered his famous "I Have a Dream" speech. As chairperson of the Martin Luther King, Jr., Federal Holiday Commission, she successfully formalized plans for the annual celebration of Martin Luther King, Jr., Day, which began in January 1986.

During the 1980s, Coretta Scott King reaffirmed her long-standing opposition to South African apartheid, participating in a series of sit-in protests in Washington that prompted nationwide demonstrations against South African racial policies. In 1986 she traveled to South Africa and met with Winnie Mandela. She also remained active in various women's organizations, including the National Organization for Women, the Women's International League for Peace and Freedom, and United Church Women.

Throughout her life, Coretta Scott King carried the message of nonviolence and social justice to almost every corner of the globe. On 30 January 2006, Coretta Scott King died in her sleep at a holistic health center in Rosarito Beach, Mexico. She was 78 years old.

https://kinginstitute.stanford.edu/encyclopedia/king-coretta-scott

CHAPTER 23
MAYA ANGELOU (1928-2014)

Credit: Maya Angelou, American poet and author. Image via Wikimedia Commons.

Poet, dancer, singer, activist, and scholar Maya Angelou was a world-famous author. She was best known for her unique and pioneering autobiographical writing style.

On April 4, 1928, Marguerite Ann Johnson, known to the world as Maya Angelou, was born in St. Louis, Missouri. Due to her parents' tumultuous marriage and subsequent divorce, Angelou went to live with her paternal grandmother in Stamps, Arkansas at an early age. Her older brother, Bailey, gave Angelou her nickname "Maya."

Returning to her mother's care briefly at the age of seven, Angelou was raped by her mother's boyfriend. He was later jailed and then killed when released from jail. Believing that her confession of the trauma had a hand in the man's death, Angelou became mute for six years. During her mutism and into her teens, she again lived with her grandmother in Arkansas.

Angelou's interest in the written word and the English language was evident from an early age. Throughout her childhood, she wrote essays, poetry, and kept a journal. When she returned to Arkansas, she took an interest in poetry and memorized works by Shakespeare and Poe.

Prior to the start of World War II, Angelou moved back in with her mother, who at this time was living in Oakland, California. She attended George Washington High School and took dance and drama courses at the California Labor School.

When war broke out, Angelou applied to join the Women's Army Corps. However, her application was rejected because of her involvement in the California Labor School, which was said to have Communist ties. Determined to gain employment, despite being only 15 years old, she decided to apply for the position of a streetcar conductor. Many men had left their jobs to join the services, enabling women to fill them. However, Angelou was barred from applying at first because of her race. But she was undeterred. Every day for three weeks, she requested a job application, but was denied. Finally, the company relented and handed her an application. Because she was under the legal working age, she wrote that she was 19. She was accepted for the position and became the first Black American woman to work as a streetcar conductor in San Francisco. Angelou was employed for a semester but then decided to return to school. She graduated from Mission High School in the summer of 1944 and soon after gave birth to her only child, Clyde Bailey (Guy) Johnson.

After graduation, Angelou undertook a series of odd jobs to support herself and her son. In 1949, she married Tosh Angelos, an electrician in the US Navy. She adopted a form of his surname and kept it throughout her life, though the marriage ended in divorce in 1952.

Angelou was also noted for her talents as a singer and dancer, particularly in the calypso and cabaret styles. In the 1950s, she performed professionally in the US, Europe, and northern Africa, and sold albums of her recordings.

In 1950, Black American writers in New York City formed the Harlem Writers Guild to nurture and support the publication of Black authors. Angelou joined the Guild in 1959. She also became active in the Civil Rights Movement and served as the northern coordinator of the Southern Christian Leadership Conference, a prominent Black American advocacy organization

In 1969, Angelou published I Know Why the Caged Bird Sings, an autobiography of her early life. Her tale of personal strength amid childhood trauma and racism resonated with readers and was nominated for the National Book Award. Many schools sought to ban the book for its frank depiction of sexual abuse, but it is credited with helping other abuse survivors tell their stories. I Know Why the Caged Bird Sings has been translated into numerous languages and has sold over a million copies worldwide. Angelou eventually published six more autobiographies, culminating in 2013's Mom & Me & Mom.

She wrote numerous poetry volumes, such as the Pulitzer Prize-nominated Just Give me a Drink of Water 'fore I Diiie (1971), as well as several essay collections. She also recorded spoken albums of her poetry, including "On the Pulse of the Morning," for which she won a Grammy for Best Spoken Word Album. The poem was originally written for and delivered at President Bill Clinton's inauguration in 1993. She also won a Grammy in 1995, and again in 2002, for her spoken albums of poetry.

Angelou carried out a wide variety of activities on stage and screen as a writer, actor, director, and producer. In 1972, she became the first Black American woman to have her screen play turned into a film with the production of Georgia, Georgia. Angelou earned a Tony nomination in 1973 for her supporting role in Jerome Kitty's play Look Away, and portrayed Kunta Kinte's grandmother in the television miniseries Roots in 1977.

She was recognized by many organizations both nationally and internationally for her contributions to literature. In 1981, Wake Forest University offered Angelou the Reynolds Professorship of American Studies. President Clinton awarded Angelou the National Medal of Arts in 2000. In

2012, she was a member of the inaugural class inducted into the Wake Forest University Writers Hall of Fame. The following year, she received the National Book Foundation's Literarian Award for outstanding service to the American literary community. Angelou also gave many commencement speeches and was awarded more than 30 honorary degrees in her lifetime.

Angelou died on May 28, 2014. Several memorials were held in her honor, including ones at Wake Forest University and Glide Memorial Church in San Francisco. To honor her legacy, the US Postal Service issued a stamp with her likeness on it in 2015. (The US Postal Service mistakenly included a quote on the stamp that has long been associated with Angelou but was actually first written by Joan Walsh Anglund.)

In 2011, President Barack Obama awarded Angelou the Presidential Medal of Freedom, the country's highest civilian honor. It was a fitting recognition for Angelou's remarkable and inspiring career in the arts.

https://www.womenshistory.org/education-resources/biographies/maya-angelou

CHAPTER 24
MARTIN LUTHER KING JR. (1929-1968)

Credit: Library of Congress

Martin Luther King, Jr., (January 15, 1929-April 4, 1968) was born Michael Luther King, Jr., but later had his name changed to Martin. His grandfather began the family's long tenure as pastors of the Ebenezer Baptist Church in Atlanta, serving from 1914 to 1931; his father has served from then until the present, and from 1960 until his death Martin Luther acted as co-pastor. Martin Luther attended segregated public schools in Georgia, graduating from high school at the age of fifteen; he received the B. A. degree in 1948 from Morehouse College, a distinguished Black institution of Atlanta from which both his father and grandfather had graduated. After three years of theological study at Crozer Theological Seminary in Pennsylvania where he was elected president of a predominantly white senior class, he was awarded the B.D. in 1951. With a fellowship won at Crozer, he enrolled in graduate studies at Boston University, completing his residence for the doctorate in 1953 and receiving the degree in 1955. In Boston he met and married Coretta Scott, a young woman of uncommon intellectual and artistic attainments. Two sons and two daughters were born into the family.

In 1954, Martin Luther King became pastor of the Dexter Avenue Baptist Church in Montgomery, Alabama. Always a strong worker for civil rights for members of his race, King was, by this time, a member of the executive committee of the National Association for the Advancement of Colored People, the leading organization of its kind in the nation. He was ready, then, early in December 1955, to accept the leadership of the first great Black nonviolent demonstration of contemporary times in the United States, the bus boycott described by Gunnar Jahn in his presentation speech in honor of the laureate. The boycott lasted 382 days. On December 21, 1956, after the Supreme Court of the United States had declared unconstitutional the laws requiring segregation on buses, Blacks and whites rode the buses as equals. During these days of boycott, King was arrested, his home was bombed, he was subjected to personal abuse, but at the same time he emerged as a Black leader of the first rank.

In 1957 he was elected president of the Southern Christian Leadership Conference, an organization formed to provide new leadership for the now burgeoning civil rights movement. The ideals for this organization he took from Christianity, its operational techniques from Gandhi. In the eleven-year period between 1957 and 1968, King traveled over six million miles and spoke over twenty-five hundred times, appearing wherever there was injustice, protest, and action; and meanwhile he wrote five books as well as numerous articles. In these years, he led a massive protest in Birmingham, Alabama, that caught the attention of the entire world, providing what he called a coalition of conscience. and inspiring his "Letter from a Birmingham Jail", a manifesto of the Black revolution; he planned the drives in Alabama for the registration of Blacks as voters; he directed the peaceful march on Washington, D.C., of 250,000 people to whom he delivered his address, "I Have a Dream", he conferred with President John F. Kennedy and campaigned for President Lyndon B. Johnson; he was arrested upwards of twenty times and assaulted at least four times; he was awarded five honorary degrees; was named Man of the Year by Time magazine in 1963; and became not only the symbolic leader of American blacks but also a world figure.

At the age of thirty-five, Martin Luther King, Jr., was the youngest man to have received the Nobel Peace Prize. When notified of his selection, he announced that he would turn over the prize money of $54,123 to the furtherance of the civil rights movement.

On the evening of April 4, 1968, while standing on the balcony of his motel room in Memphis, Tennessee, where he was to lead a protest march in sympathy with striking garbage workers of that city, he was assassinated.

https://www.nobelprize.org/prizes/peace/1964/king/lecture/

CHAPTER 25
RAY CHARLES (1930-2004)

Credit: Library of Congress

Ray Charles Robinson was born September 23, 1930, in Albany, Georgia, the first child of Aretha and Bailey Robinson. His father worked off and on for the railroads; his mother took in laundry. The family started out poor and stayed that way throughout the hard years of the Depression. "Even compared to other blacks," Charles recalled, "we were on the bottom of the ladder looking up at everyone else. Nothing below us except the ground"

Ray Charles was a poor, blind, newly orphaned teenager living in Tampa, Florida, in 1948 when he decided to move to Seattle, picking the city because it was as far away as he could get from where he was. He stayed only two years, but during that time he cut his first record and began to develop the genre-bending musical style that would make him an international star. Charles often spoke of Seattle as a pivotal point in his long and hugely successful career as a singer/songwriter. He met a lot of very good friends here, he told one interviewer. he liked the atmosphere. And the people were friendly and took to him right away. Seattle is the town where he made his first record. And if you ever wanted to say where he got his first start, he said you would have to say that.

The family moved across the border to Greenville, Florida, when Charles was a few months old. A second child soon followed; a son named George. Bailey Robinson became little more than an occasional visitor after that. "The old man wasn't part of my life," Charles wrote in his 1978 autobiography. "... to tell the truth, I wouldn't bet a lot of money he and my mother ever were married. He was a tall dude -- I remember that. But he was hardly ever around".

Despite the poverty, Charles recalled his early childhood as a happy time. He felt loved by two women: his mother, whom he called "Mama," and his father's first wife, a woman he called "Mother." He loved the singing he heard on Sundays at the Shiloh Baptist Church. Above all, he loved picking out boogie-woogie tunes on the upright piano owned by a neighbor named Wylie Pitman. "I was born with music inside me," he said. "And from the moment I learned there were piano keys to be mashed, I started mashing 'em, trying to make sounds out of feelings".

When he was about five, Charles witnessed the drowning death of his younger brother. The two boys had been in the backyard playing near a large metal tub their mother used for washing clothes when four-year-old George slipped over the edge and into the soapy water. Charles tried to pull him out, but his brother -- quickly weighted down by his wet clothing -- was too heavy. Charles ran indoors, screaming for his mother, but it was too late. It was the first major tragedy in a life that would have many other sorrows.

Not long after the drowning, Charles began to lose his vision, apparently as the result of untreated glaucoma. He was completely blind by the time he was seven. He credited his mother with preparing him to live without sight. She made him continue to draw water from the well, bring in the firewood, and do other chores, even though he often tripped and fell. You may be blind, she told him, but you're not stupid; you have to do things for yourself, no one else will do them for you. "She let me roam, let me make my own mistakes, let me discover the world for myself," he wrote. From this he developed a fierce independence and the ability to maneuver so adroitly that some people, later in his life, doubted that he was really blind.

His mother managed to get him accepted as a charity student at the Florida State School for the Deaf and the Blind (known at the time as the Institute for the Blind, Deaf and Dumb), in St. Augustine, about 130 miles southeast of Greenville. He stayed there for eight years, with time off for summers at home. He learned how to read Braille, to type, to weave baskets, and to repair radios and cars. He also studied music formally for the first time, mastering the piano and other instruments, including clarinet and saxophone. He learned to read and compose music in Braille. He played everything, from Chopin to jazz pianist Art Tatum. On the radio he listened to swing, country-western, and gospel.

Charles later summed up the effect of blindness on his career with three words -- "Nothing, nothing, nothing" -- and pointed out that he had begun playing music by the age of three, when he could still see, and he continued after age seven, when he lost his sight: "I was going to do what I was going to do anyway. So, blindness didn't have anything to do with it. It didn't give me anything. And it didn't take nothing".

Charles' mother died shortly before his 15th birthday. It was, he wrote later, the most devastating experience of his life. He felt like "truly a lost child." He left school and moved to nearby Jacksonville, where he stayed for a while with one of his mother's friends. He began trying to make a living as a musician, working as a sideman in small combos. "Work was very sparse," he wrote. "I might work a couple of nights and then no more for two weeks or three weeks -- whenever something came along. Hit and miss, really, that's what it was".

Eventually, he moved on to Tampa. But he found it difficult to survive as a musician in Florida. He also resented working for other people. He wanted to form his own group and make a fresh start in a new place. Too intimidated to try New York or Chicago, he asked a friend, a guitarist Garcia "Gosady"

McGee -- what city in the continental United States was farthest from Florida. McGee "took a map and went diagonal across it, and there was Seattle sittin' up in the Northwest, and I said let me go there and see what I can do".

R. C. Robinson arrived in Seattle in March 1948, after a five-day bus trip from Tampa. He found a town that was, as he put it "really open and smokin'." A vibrant jazz scene had sprung up in Pioneer Square and in the Central Area, nurtured by a wartime influx of Black Americans drawn by jobs in Puget Sound shipyards. There were more than 30 nightclubs in the area around Jackson Street, open all hours of the day and night. The competition for jobs in the clubs was fierce, Charles told jazz historian Paul de Barros. "Many cats had just left the armed-forces bands -- and don't think those outfits couldn't play," he said. "There were lots of musicians roaming the streets who'd blow your ass off the stand if you gave 'em half the chance" (de Barros, 151).

Despite his youth, Charles quickly established himself in the Seattle music community. Within days, he had earned a gig at the black Elks Club at 662 Jackson Street, playing piano and singing in a trio with his friend McGee, on guitar, and local bassist Milt Jarrett (sometimes spelled Garred). They called themselves the McSon Trio (after the "Mc" in McGee and the "son" in Robinson). The trio "was the first thing I had that I could honestly say was mine," Charles said later.

However, the McSon Trio belonged more to Nat "King" Cole than to Ray Charles. "When Ray came here, you could close your eyes and you'd swear Nat King Cole was singing," said jazz vocalist Ernestine Anderson, a teenager when she met Charles during his Seattle sojourn (Seattle Post-Intelligencer). Charles had yet to put his own stamp on his music. He deliberately mimicked Nat Cole, Charles Brown, and other popular artists. He later said the legacy of growing up poor made him hesitate to develop his own sound. "I could get a lot of work sounding like Nat Cole," he told interviewer Terry Gross. "I could work in night clubs. I could make a living with his sound".

Charles moved into a small apartment on 20th Avenue and equipped it with the essentials, including an electric piano and a combination radio/record player. He shopped on his own, cooked his own meals, did his own laundry. His independence greatly impressed the young Quincy Jones, another teenage musical prodigy, who showed up at the Elks Club one night to check out rumors he had heard about "a blind dude" who was "tearing the place up with his singing and playing." It was, Jones wrote in his autobiography, "love at first instinct for both of us" -- the beginning of a lifelong friendship and collaboration.

Jones, then 15, was amazed that the 17-year-old Charles had his own apartment, a well-stocked bar, three suits, and a bevy of girlfriends. He also marveled at the way Charles ignored his blindness. "I'd watch him cross the street without cane or dog, dodging traffic ... never missing a step," he wrote. "It was like somebody forgot to tell Ray he was blind. In fact, Ray never acted blind unless there was a pretty girl around, then he'd get all helpless and sightless, bumping into walls and doors" (Jones, 86). Jones went on to become one of the country's most successful composers and producers. His body of work includes collaborations with Charles on three important albums: The Genius (1959), Genius + Soul = Jazz (1961), and Back on the Block (1989).

In the racially divided Seattle of the 1940s, the McSon Trio played gigs for white audiences at such venues as the Seattle Tennis Club, University of Washington fraternities, and uptown ballrooms. They played for black audiences at after-hours clubs such as the Washington Social Club, the Black & Tan, the 908 Club, and the blues-oriented Rocking Chair, on 14th just off Yesler. Their popularity gained them a regular 15-minute spot on KRSC radio. Late in 1948, the group performed on KRSC-TV (predecessor to KING-TV), in one of the earliest live broadcasts in Seattle. At 18, Charles was getting his first taste of celebrity.

It was at the Rocking Chair that Charles met Jack Lauderdale, a record producer from Los Angeles. As Charles told the story, "Jack was there one night and heard us playing. He said, 'I'd like to sign you guys up to a contract. What would you think about that?' Oh, man, I was so excited! 'Wow! We're gonna get a record contract!' There was nothing about any advance or money up front. All the man said to me was he was gonna record me, and we'd have a hit".

The trio recorded "Confession Blues" (written by Charles) and "I Love You, I Love You" (written by his friend, Joe Lee Lawrence) in a small, primitive Seattle studio. It was released as a 78 in early 1949 -- credited to the Maxin Trio. It sold respectably enough that Lauderdale took the group to Los Angeles to make several other recordings for the Swingtime label, including "Rockin' Chair Blues," which pays tribute to Charles' Seattle days. "If you're feelin' low down, don't have a soul to care, just grab your hat and start for the Rockin' Chair," he sang. The record was a hit on "race records" (later called Rhythm and Blues) charts in late 1949.

Charles returned to Los Angeles in 1950 to record "Baby Let Me Hold

Your Hand," working with musicians who had played with Nat Cole. By this time, he was billed as "Ray Charles, the blind singing sensation." He had dropped his last name, partly in deference to the boxer, Sugar Ray Robinson, and partly in an effort to define himself as his own person -- not a Nat Cole clone. "I woke up one morning and started thinking: nobody knows my name," he said. "Everybody's calling me 'Hey kid -- you sound just like Nat Cole.' It was always 'Hey kid.' I started telling myself, 'Your mama always told you to be yourself and you got to be yourself if you want to make it in this business'".

One other legacy of Charles' Seattle years was an addiction to heroin. He discussed his addiction openly in his autobiography. It began, he said, with a desire to both emulate older musicians and prove his independence. Although he never served an extended jail sentence, he was arrested for possession of narcotics in 1955, 1961, and 1965. After his third arrest, he checked himself into a California sanatorium to kick his 17-year habit and stopped performing for a year, the only break during his long career.

Charles left Seattle in 1950 and began touring with blues guitarist Lowell Fulson. "We woke up one day and R.C. was here," said Ernestine Anderson, who occasionally sang with Charles in Seattle clubs. "We didn't know where he came from or how he got here. That's the way he left. We woke up one day and no Ray" (Seattle Post-Intelligencer).

He continued to refine his style during the next few years, melding blues and gospel, bebop and swing. He toured up and down the West Coast and throughout the South. His schedule kept him on the road for much of the year -- a regimen that he continued for more than half a century. He still managed to find studio time, although it was often in radio stations along the way.

After signing with Atlantic Records in 1952, he persuaded the label to let him record with his touring band. His first national hit, "I've Got a Woman," was recorded in 1954 in a radio station studio in Atlanta with his seven-piece band. It signaled the emergence of what became the classic Ray Charles – bluesy, tender, raw, intense, a mix of the secular (jazz) and the sacred (gospel). The record was followed by a string of other gospel-tinged hits, including "Drown in My Tears" and "Hallelujah I Love Her So."

In the mid-1950s, Charles expanded his band to include a group of female backup signers (the Raelettes), who provided gospel-like responses to his deep, raspy baritone. They became a permanent part of his music -- and they also hinted at his sometimes-volatile relationships with women.

On the road in the 1950s and 1960s, Charles often encountered the same kind of segregation that he had grown up with in the South. As a Black American, he stayed in rooming houses instead of the Hilton or the Sheraton; he had to make sure that the band stopped at a gas station that had rest rooms for "Colored;" at restaurants, he sometimes had to go around to the back door for a sandwich instead of a hot meal in the dining room. He would say years later that racism affected him just as it did any other black person at the time. "What I never understood to this day, to this very day, was how white people could have black people cook for them, make their meals, but wouldn't let them sit at the table with them," he said. "How can you dislike someone so much and have them cook for you? Shoot, if I don't like someone you ain't cooking nothing for me, ever".

Charles became a certified star with the 1959 release of "What'd I Say." The record broke the usual two and a half-minute mold for a radio song, with its extended "call and response" chorus and improvisational style. It was followed the next year by a version of Hoagy Carmichael's "Georgia on My Mind," a sweet ballad with strings and a vocal chorus. The song demonstrated Charles' versatility and his love for the South. In 1979, it became the official anthem of the state of Georgia.

He branched out into other musical genres in the 1960s and 1970s, including country-and-western ("Your Cheatin' Heart" and "I Can't Stop Loving You," both released in 1962); middle-of-the-road pop ("You Are My Sunshine," 1962); and British pop (releasing a version of the Beatles' "Eleanor Rigby" in 1968). At the same time, he continued to pay homage to his roots in jazz. He refused categorization. He confounded some of his fans by accepting an invitation to perform "America the Beautiful" for President Richard Nixon in 1972, but the song became one of his standards (he sang it again at the Republican National Convention in 1984). Drawing from jazz, gospel, blues, and country, he created a river that only he could navigate.

Music critic Patrick Macdonald credits Charles with first using the word "Soul" to describe his style of music. To Frank Sinatra, Charles was "The Genius." Quincy Jones put the two together and called Charles "The Genius of Soul."

He could be difficult. He was sometimes hard on his band members and background singers. His private life was, as The New York Times delicately put it, "complicated" (Pareles and Weinraub). He was divorced twice and fathered 12 children. Still, he remained a consummate performer almost to the very end of his life. He made more than 60 albums, won 12 Grammys (including one for "A Song for You" in 1993), and earned a string of honors, including induction into the Rock 'n' Roll Hall of Fame in 1986 and the Presidential Medal for the Arts in 1993. Along the way, he influenced generations of singers, from Sinatra to Elvis to Billy Joel.

Charles died at his home in Beverly Hills, California, on June 10, 2004, of liver disease. He was 73. He had recently recovered from hip replacement surgery and had planned to resume touring in June when he became ill. Earlier, he had completed work on his last album, a collection of duets with Norah Jones, B. B. King, Willie Nelson, Bonnie Raitt, James Taylor, and others. The album was released on August 31, 2004, under the title Genius Loves Company. It swept the Grammys in 2005, winning eight awards, including Album of the Year.

He saw his life primarily as an example of what anyone can accomplish. "I would like people to know that you can recover from a lot of adversity that you might have in your life if you keep pressing on," he told one interviewer. "In other words, you don't give up just because you get knocked down a few times".

His death unleashed a torrent of tributes, including this one from Ernestine Anderson: "The gods were smiling on us when he came to Seattle".

https://www.historylink.org/file/5707

CHAPTER 26
TONI MORRISON (1931-2019)

Credit: Deborah Feingold/Corbis/Getty Images

Toni Morrison is one of the most celebrated authors in the world. In addition to writing plays, and children's books, her novels have earned her countless prestigious awards including the Pulitzer Prize and the Presidential Medal of Freedom from President Barack Obama. As the first Black American woman to win the Nobel Prize in Literature, Morrison's work has inspired a generation of writers to follow in her footsteps.

Toni Morrison was born on February 18, 1931, in Lorain, Ohio. The second of four children, Morrison's birth name was Chloe Anthony Wofford. Although she grew up in a semi-integrated area, racial discrimination was a constant threat. When Morrison was two years old, the owner of her family's apartment building set their home on fire while they were inside because they were unable to afford the rent. Morrison turned her attention to her studies and became an avid reader. She was able to use her intellect on the debate team, her school's yearbook staff, and eventually as a secretary for the head librarian at the Lorain Public Library. When she was twelve years old, she converted to Catholicism and was baptized under the name Anthony after Saint Anthony of Padua. She later went by the nickname "Toni" after this saint.

In 1949, Morrison decided to attend a historically black institution for her college education. She moved to Washington, D.C. to attend Howard University. While in college, Morrison experienced racial segregation in a new way. She joined the university's theatrical group called the Howard University Players, and frequently toured the segregated south with the play. In addition, she witnessed how racial hierarchy divided people of color based on their skin tone. However, the community at Howard University also allowed her to make connections with other writers, artists, and activists that influenced her work. After graduating with a bachelor's degree in English, Morrison attended Cornell University to earn the Master of Arts in English. When she graduated in 1955, she began teaching English at Texas Southern University but returned to Howard University as a professor. While back at the university, Morrison taught the young civil rights activist Stokely Carmichael, and met her husband, Harold Morrison. The couple had two children, Harold, and Slade.

After teaching at Howard University for seven years, Morrison moved to Syracuse, New York to become an editor for the textbook division of Random House publishing. Within two years, she transferred to the New York City branch of the company and began to edit fiction and books by Black American authors. Although she worked for a publishing company, Morrison did not publish her first novel called The Bluest Eye until was she was 39 years old. Three years later, Morrison published her second novel called Sula, that was nominated for the National Book Award. By her third novel in 1977, Toni Morrison became a household name. Song of Solomon earned critical acclaim as well as the National Book Critics Circle Award. The success of her books encouraged Morrison to become a writer full time. She left publishing and continued to write novels, essays, and plays. In 1987, Morrison released her novel called Beloved, based on the true story of a Black American enslaved woman. This book was a Bestseller for 25 weeks and won countless awards including the Pulitzer Prize for Fiction. In 1993, Morrison became the first Black woman to win the Nobel Prize in Literature. Three years later, she was also chosen by the National Endowment for the Humanities to give the Jefferson Lecture and was honored with the National Book Foundation's Medal of Distinguished Contribution to American Letters.

Morrison's work continued to influence writers and artists through her focus on Black American life and her commentary on race relations. In 1998, Oprah Winfrey co-produced and starred in the film adaptation of Morrison's book, Beloved. The film also starred major Hollywood actors including Danny Glover, Thandie Newton, and Kimberly Elise. Following this, Morrison's books were featured four times as selections for Oprah's Book Club. While writing and producing, Morrison was also a professor in the Creative Writing Program at Princeton University. Her work earned her an honorary Doctorate degree from the University of Oxford, and the opportunity to be a guest curator at the Louvre Museum in Paris. In 2000, she was named a Living Legend by the Library of Congress. Morrison also wrote children's books with her son until his death at 45 years old. Two years later, Morrison published the last book they were working on together and received the Presidential Medal of Freedom in that same month. In June of 2019, director Timothy Greenfield-Sanders released a documentary of her life called Toni Morrison: The Pieces I Am. Morrison passed away two months later from complications of pneumonia.

https://www.womenshistory.org/education-resources/biographies/toni-morrison

CHAPTER 27
JAMES BROWN (1933-2006)

Credit: Library of Congress

James Brown, who grew up in Augusta, was one of the most influential musicians of the last half of the twentieth century. An original artist, fascinating showman, and tireless performer, Brown achieved legendary status, inspiring a generation of younger musicians. An inductee into both the Georgia Music Hall of Fame and the Rock and Roll Hall of Fame, he created a solid body of work that has withstood the passage of time and popular music trends.

Born in a one-room shack in the country outside Barnwell, South Carolina, on or around May 3, 1933 (although some sources give different dates), Brown grew up in severe poverty. His mother left the family when he was four, and when he was five his father and aunt moved with him to Augusta, Georgia. There, in a roadhouse on U.S. 1, Brown was brought up by two aunts while his father worked a series of odd jobs and appeared only sporadically. As a boy Brown also worked a variety of jobs and began to develop an interest in music, learning to play the drums, piano, and guitar. He won singing awards in several local talent shows.

When he was fifteen Brown was caught committing petty theft and was sentenced to eight to sixteen years in juvenile prison. While incarcerated, first in Rome and then in Toccoa, he formed a gospel group and earned the nickname "Music Box." He appealed to the parole board and was released shortly after his nineteenth birthday. He stayed in Toccoa, where he married and continued to make music, both gospel and rhythm and blues, with other local players. His band, the Flames, began to tour in the area. A Little Richard show in Toccoa convinced Brown and the Flames that they should move to Macon, Little Richard's home and a lively music center. A talent scout for King Records, based in Cincinnati, Ohio, heard a demo tape by Brown and the "Famous Flames." He sought them out, found them playing a show at a little club outside Milledgeville, and signed them to record for King.

Brown's first single, "Please Please Please," was released March 3, 1956. It was a major hit, going to number six on the rhythm and blues charts. Brown continued recording singles and scored a number one hit in 1958 with "Try Me." He and the Flames began a relentless touring schedule, earning Brown the epithet "the hardest-working man in show business." He developed a high-energy, dramatic stage show that thrilled audiences. The concert album Live at the Apollo, released in January 1963, captured the excitement of the shows, and became a best-seller.

Brown, along with Ray Charles and Sam Cooke, pioneered a distinct new form of wildly popular music known as "soul," a dynamic blend of gospel and rhythm and blues. Two singles in 1965, "Papa's Got a Brand-New Bag" and "I Got You (I Feel Good)," were milestones of soul. Both were number one on the rhythm and blues charts, and in the top ten on the pop charts. The pop ranking indicated that Brown was beginning to gain popularity with white listeners. For the next decade Brown was positioned at the top of the charts, releasing single after single and continuing the grueling touring schedule.

With "Say It Loud, I'm Black and I'm Proud," released in 1968 a few months after Martin Luther King Jr.'s assassination, Brown forcefully voiced the ideals of Black cultural nationalism. Yet Brown rejected violence and was criticized by some political militants for helping to calm angry crowds after King's assassination and for accepting U.S. president Lyndon Johnson's invitation to dine at the White House. But poet LeRoi Jones (later Amiri Baraka) called him "our number one Black poet," and in 1969 Look magazine's cover asked if he was the most important Black man in America.

That same year, Brown moved back to Augusta, where Black citizens held a James Brown Day in his honor and white citizens organized an unsuccessful campaign to prevent him from moving into an upper-class, all-white neighborhood. He traveled to Vietnam to perform for American troops and endorsed Richard Nixon for president in 1972. On songs from the late sixties and early seventies, like "Mother Popcorn," Brown continued to push musical barriers, and these new directions helped inspire the later sounds of funk, disco, and rap.

Brown's popularity declined in the late seventies, though he continued to perform and record. In 1988 his career came to a halt. A year of legal troubles—suspicions of drug abuse and convictions for assaulting his wife as well as resisting arrest—concluded with a police chase through the streets of Augusta. When the bullet-punctured tires of Brown's truck finally came to a stop, he was surrounded by fourteen police cars. These circumstances prompted Brown's lawyers to charge that the police had overreacted, but a jury found Brown guilty, and he was sentenced to six years in prison. He served part of the term and was granted early release in February 1991. He resumed touring and recording.

Retrospective CD compilations in the 1990s found new audiences for Brown's work among the young. In 2003 Brown was honored at the Kennedy Center in Washington, D.C., for his artistic achievements. In May 2005 the city of Augusta erected a statue of Brown in the downtown area where he grew up, and in May 2006 the city held its inaugural James Brown Soul of America Music Festival. The Augusta–Richmond County Coliseum was renamed the James Brown Arena in August 2006.

Though often outspoken about America's persistent racism, Brown espoused Black self-help and told audiences to make something of their lives by working hard, as did this man born in a one-room shack in the Jim Crow South. His frenetic stage shows established a much-imitated style, and his songs continue to find wide airplay and receptive listeners, both Black and white.

Brown continued to perform until the end of his life; he died of congestive heart failure in Atlanta on December 25, 2006. A procession and public viewing were held in his honor three days later at the historic Apollo Theater in New York City, and on December 30 a public memorial service and viewing was held at the James Brown Arena in Augusta. Paine College, a private, historically Black college in Augusta, presented an honorary degree to the singer at the end of the service.

https://www.georgiaencyclopedia.org/articles/arts-culture/james-brown-ca-1933-2006/

CHAPTER 28
QUINCY JONES (1933-PRESENT)

Credit: Library of Congress

An impresario in the broadest and most creative sense of the word, Quincy Jones' career has encompassed the roles of composer, record producer, artist, film producer, arranger, conductor, instrumentalist, television producer, record company executive, magazine founder and multimedia entrepreneur. As a master inventor of musical hybrids, he has shuffled pop, soul, hip-hop, jazz, classical, African, and Brazilian music into many dazzling fusions, traversing virtually every medium, including records, live performance, movies and television.

Quincy Jones was born on March 14, 1933, in Chicago, Illinois, and brought up in Seattle, Washington. While in junior high school, Jones began studying trumpet and sang in a Gospel quartet at age twelve. His musical studies continued at the prestigious Berklee College of Music in Boston, Massachusetts, where he remained until the opportunity arose to tour with Lionel Hampton's band as a trumpeter, arranger, and sometime-pianist. He moved on to New York and the musical "big leagues" in 1951, where his reputation as an arranger grew. By the mid-1950s, he was arranging and recording for such diverse artists as Sarah Vaughan, Ray Charles, Count Basie, Duke Ellington, and Dinah Washington.

In 1957, Jones decided to continue his musical education by studying with Nadia Boulanger, the legendary Parisian tutor to American expatriate composers such as Leonard Bernstein and Aaron Copeland. To subsidize his studies, he took a job with Barclay Disques, Mercury's French distributor. Among the artists he recorded in Europe were Charles Aznavour, Jacques Brel and Henri Salvador, as well as such visitors from America as Sarah Vaughan, Billy Eckstine and Andy Williams. Jones' love affair with European audiences continues through the present: in 1991, he began a continuing association with the Montreux Jazz and World Music Festival, which he serves as co-producer.

Jones won the first of his many Grammy Awards in 1963 for his Count Basie arrangement of "I Can't Stop Loving You." Jones' three-year musical association as conductor and arranger with Frank Sinatra in the mid-1960s also teamed him with Basie for the classic Sinatra At The Sands, containing the famous arrangement of "Fly Me To The Moon."

When he became vice-president at Mercury Records in 1961, Jones became the first high-level black executive of an established major record company. Toward the end of his association with the label, Jones turned his attention to another musical area that had been closed to blacks--the world of film scores. In 1963, he started work on the music for Sidney Lumet's The Pawnbroker, and it was the first of his thirty-three major motion picture

146

scores. In 1985, he co-produced Steven Spielberg's adaptation of Alice Walker's The Color Purple, which won eleven Oscar nominations, introduced Whoopi Goldberg and Oprah Winfrey to film audiences, and marked Jones' debut as a film producer.

In 1990, Jones formed Quincy Jones Entertainment (QJE), a co-venture with Time Warner, Inc. The new company, which Jones served as CEO and chairman, produced NBC Television's Fresh Prince Of Bel Air (now in syndication), and UPN's In The House and Fox Television's Mad TV. He is also the publisher of VIBE Magazine (as well as founder), SPIN and Blaze magazines. Also in 1990, his life and career were chronicled in the critically acclaimed Warner Bros. film, Listen Up: The Lives of Quincy Jones, produced by Courtney Sale Ross.

In 1994, Quincy Jones led a group of businessmen, including Hall of Fame football player Willie Davis, television producer Don Cornelius, television journalist Geraldo Rivera and businesswoman Sonia Gonsalves Salzman in the formation of Qwest Broadcasting, a minority-controlled broadcasting company which purchased television stations in Atlanta and New Orleans for approximately $167 million, establishing it as one of the largest minorities owned broadcasting companies in the United States. Quincy served as chairman and CEO of Qwest Broadcasting. In 1999, taking advantage of the rapid escalation of broadcast station values, Jones and his partners sold Qwest Broadcasting for a reported $270 million. In 1997, Quincy Jones formed the Quincy Jones Media Group.

The laurels, awards and accolades have been innumerable: Quincy has won an Emmy Award for his score of the of the opening episode of the landmark TV miniseries, Roots, seven Oscar nominations, the Academy of Motion Picture Arts and Sciences' Jean Hersholt Humanitarian Award, twenty-seven Grammy Awards, and N.A.R.A.S.' prestigious Trustees' Award and The Grammy Living Legend Award. He is the all-time most nominated Grammy artist with a total of seventy-nine Grammy nominations. In 1990, France recognized Jones with its most distinguished title, the Legion d' Honneur. He is also the recipient of the French Ministry of Culture's Distinguished Arts and Letters Award. Jones is the recipient of the Royal Swedish Academy of Music's coveted Polar Music Prize and the Republic of Italy's Rudolph Valentino Award. He is also the recipient of honorary doctorates from Howard University, the Berklee College of Music, Seattle University, Wesleyan University, Brandeis University, Loyola University (New Orleans), Clark Atlanta University, Claremont University's Graduate School, the University of Connecticut, Harvard University, Tuskegee University, New York University, University of Miami and The American

Film Institute. Jones was also named a 2001 Kennedy Center Honoree, for his contributions to the cultural fabric of the United States of America.

In 2001, Quincy Jones added the title "Best Selling Author" to his list of accomplishments when his autobiography Q: The Autobiography of Quincy Jones entered the New York Times, Los Angeles Times and Wall Street Journal Best-Sellers lists. Rhino Records released a four CD boxed set of Jones' music, spanning his more than five-decade career in the music business, entitled Q: The Musical Biography of Quincy Jones.

Celebrating more than fifty years performing and being involved in music, Jones' creative magic has spanned over six decades, beginning with the music of the post-swing era and continuing through today's high-technology, international multi-media hybrids. In the mid-1950s, he was the first popular conductor-arranger to record with a Fender bass. His theme from the hit TV series Ironside was the first synthesizer-based pop theme song. As the first black composer to be embraced by the Hollywood establishment in the 1960s, he helped refresh movie music with badly needed infusions of jazz and soul. His landmark 1989 album, Back On The Block--named "Album Of The Year" at the 1990 Grammy Awards-- brought such legends as Dizzy Gillespie, Ella Fitzgerald, Sarah Vaughan and Miles Davis together with Ice T, Big Daddy Kane and Melle Mel to create the first fusion of the be bop and hip hop musical traditions; while his 1993 recording of the critically acclaimed Miles and Quincy Live At Montreux, featured Jones conducting Miles Davis' live performance of the historic Gil Evans arrangements from the Miles Ahead, Porgy and Bess and Sketches of Spain sessions, garnered a Grammy Award for Best Large Jazz Ensemble Performance. As producer and conductor of the historic "We Are The World" recording (the best-selling single of all time) and Michael Jackson's multi-platinum solo albums, Off The Wall, Bad and Thriller (the bestselling album of all time, with over forty-six million copies sold), Jones stands as one of the most successful and admired creative artists/executives in the entertainment world.

https://www.thehistorymakers.org/biography/quincy-jones-41

CHAPTER 29
HANK AARON (1934-2021)

Credit: Baseball Hall of Fame

Born into humble circumstances in Mobile, Alabama, Hank Aaron ascended the ranks of the Negro Leagues to become a Major League Baseball icon. He spent most of his 23 seasons as an outfielder for the Milwaukee and Atlanta Braves, during which time he set many records, including a career total of 755 home runs. Aaron was elected to the Baseball Hall of Fame in 1982, and in 1999, MLB established the Hank Aaron Award to annually honor the top hitter in each league.

Born Henry Louis Aaron on February 5, 1934, in a poor Black section of Mobile, Alabama, called "Down the Bay," Hank Aaron was the third of eight children born to Estella and Herbert Aaron, who made a living as a tavern owner and a dry dock boilermaker's assistant.

Aaron and his family moved to the middle-class Toulminville neighborhood when he was 8 years old. Aaron developed a strong affinity for baseball and football at a young age and tended to focus more heavily on sports than his studies. During his freshman and sophomore years, he attended Central High School, a segregated high school in Mobile, where he excelled at both football and baseball. On the baseball diamond, he played shortstop and third base.

In his junior year, Aaron transferred to the Josephine Allen Institute, a neighboring private school that had an organized baseball program.

In late 1951, 18-year-old Aaron quit school to play for the Negro American League's Indianapolis Clowns. It wasn't a long stay, but the talented teenager left his mark by hitting .366 and leading his club to victory in the league's 1952 World Series. Additionally, he would become the last to play in both the Negro Leagues and the Major Leagues.

After signing with the Milwaukee Braves for $10,000, Aaron was assigned to one of the organization's farm clubs, the Class C Eau Claire Bears. He did not disappoint, earning Northern League Rookie of the Year honors in 1952. Promoted to the Class A Jacksonville Braves in 1953, Aaron continued to tear apart pitching with 208 hits, 22 homers and a .362 average.

Aaron made his Major League debut in 1954, at age 20, when a spring training injury to another Milwaukee Braves outfielder created a roster spot for him. Following a solid first year (he hit .280 with 13 home runs), Aaron charged through the 1955 season with a blend of power (27 home runs), run production (106 RBIs) and average (.328) that would come to define his long career.

After winning his first batting title in 1956, Aaron registered an outstanding 1957 season, taking home the National League MVP and nearly nabbing the Triple Crown by hitting 44 home runs, knocking in another 132 and batting .322.

That same year, Aaron demonstrated his ability to come up big when it counted most. His 11th inning home run in late September propelled the Braves to the World Series, where he led underdog Milwaukee to an upset win over the New York Yankees in seven games.

With the game still years away from the multimillion-dollar contracts handed to star players, Aaron's annual pay in 1959 was around $30,000. When he equaled that amount that same year in endorsements, Aaron realized there could be more in store for him if he continued to hit for power. "I noticed that they never had a show called 'Singles Derby,'" he once explained.

He was right, of course, and over the next decade and a half, the always-fit Aaron banged out 30 to 40 home runs on an annual basis. In 1973, at the age of 39, Aaron was still a force, clubbing 40 home runs to finish the year with a career total of 713, just one behind Babe Ruth. In 1974, after tying Ruth on Opening Day in Cincinnati, Ohio, Aaron came home with his team. On April 8, he banged out his record 715th home run off Al Downing of the Los Angeles Dodgers. It was a triumph and a relief, as more than 50,000 fans on hand cheered him on as he rounded the bases. There were fireworks and a band, and when he crossed home plate, Aaron's parents were there to greet him.

After finishing his record-breaking 1974 season with 20 home runs, Aaron joined the Brewers in his old big-league hometown of Milwaukee to take advantage of the new designated hitter rule that gave aging sluggers a chance to rest their legs. He played two more years, wrapping up his stellar career after the 1976 season.

As Aaron drew closer to home run No. 714, the chase to beat the Ruth's record revealed that world of baseball was far from being free of the racial tensions that prevailed around it. Letters poured into the Braves offices, as many as 3,000 a day for Aaron. Some wrote to congratulate him, but many others were appalled that a Black man should break baseball's most sacred record. Death threats were a part of the mix. Still, Aaron pushed forward. He didn't try to inflame the atmosphere, but he didn't keep his mouth shut, either, speaking out against the league's lack of ownership and management opportunities for minorities. "On the field, Blacks have been able to be super giants," he once stated. "But, once our playing days are over, this is the end of it and we go back to the back of the bus again."

Aaron, nicknamed "Hammerin' Hank," is widely regarded as one of the greatest players in the history of the sport. Over 21 years as an outfielder for the Milwaukee and Atlanta Braves and two final years as a DH for the Milwaukee Brewers, he compiled numerous records, including:

• Runs batted in (2,297)

• Extra-base hits (1,477)

• Total bases (6,856)

• All-star appearances (25)

• Years with 30 or more home runs (15 — since tied by Alex Rodriguez)

Aaron ranks second all-time in-home runs (755), third in hits (3,771), third in games played (3,298) and tied for fourth with Ruth in runs scored (2,174). Over the course of his career, he won two batting titles, led his league in homers and RBIs four times each, and won three Gold Gloves for fielding excellence.

In 1999, Major League Baseball introduced the Hank Aaron Award to honor the top hitter in each league. Initially determined by the compiling of points based on stats, it soon fell under the voting jurisdiction of broadcasters, with fans later joining the process.

The first two winners were Manny Ramirez of the Cleveland Indians and Sammy Sosa of the Chicago Cubs. Alex Rodriguez won the award a record four times during his years with the Texas Rangers and New York Yankees.

For more than three decades, Aaron held the Major League record with his 755 career home runs. Barry Bonds surpassed that mark on August 7, 2007, when he hit his 756th dinger at AT&T Park in San Francisco, California.

Aaron was not at the ballpark that night, prompting speculation that he would not acknowledge the accomplishments of Bonds, who had been accused of cheating through performance-enhancement drugs. However, the former home run king soon appeared on the scoreboard to extend his congratulations via a videotaped message.

"I move over now," said Aaron, "and offer my best wishes to Barry and his family on this historic achievement."

In April 1997, baseball returned to the city of Mobile, Alabama, when the minor league Mobile Baybears squared off against the Birmingham Barons at Hank Aaron Stadium. Known locally as "The Hank," the field honors its namesake, as well as other Mobile-born baseball players through its location at the corner of Satchel Paige Drive and Bolling Brothers Boulevard: Paige was the first Negro League player inducted into the Baseball Hall of Fame, while Milt and Frank Bolling also made it to the sport's top level.

After retiring as a player, Aaron moved into the Atlanta Braves front office as executive vice president, where he became a leading spokesman for minority hiring in baseball. He was elected to the Baseball Hall of Fame in 1982, and eight years later, he published his autobiography, I Had a Hammer. In 2002, he was honored with the Presidential Medal of Freedom. Slowed by hip replacement surgery in 2014, Aaron nevertheless made it to a ceremony in January 2016 in which he was awarded the Japanese Order of the Rising Sun, Gold Rays with Rosette. He was honored for his close relationship with Japanese home run king Sadaharu Oh, and for his efforts to promote the two countries' shared love of the game.

Aaron passed away on January 22, 2021.

https://www.biography.com/athlete/hank-aaron

CHAPTER 30
JIM BROWN (1936-PRESENT)

Credit: Library of Congress

Jim Brown was born on this date in 1936. He was a Black football player, actor and (current) civil rights advocate.

From Saint Simons, Ga. He was the son of Swinton and Theresa Brown. He came the New York to live with his mother, a domestic; first in Great Neck and then on Lee Avenue in Manhasset, Long Island. Brown attended Plandome Road Junior High, where his speed and strength through high school helped him dominate any sport. Many say his best game was lacrosse. By the time he was a senior, his athletic prowess was such that the Yankees offered him a minor-league contract. Brown switched from lacrosse to baseball in the spring to test himself in the sport.

After pitching and playing first base with some success, he decided his skills wouldn't get him to the major leagues, so he sent his regrets to Casey Stengel. Ken Molloy, a Manhasset attorney and later a State Supreme Court judge in Nassau County, steered Brown to his Alma Mater, Syracuse University. But the coaching staffs were against the idea of a Black athlete in the early 1950s and did not offer a scholarship. Molloy rounded up enough money and obtained a promise from the school that it would put Brown on scholarship if he were as good as advertised.

Brown emerged as the greatest athlete in Syracuse history. As a senior, Brown scored 43 points in a football game against Colgate, was a unanimous college All-American at running back, and was voted the MVP of the Cotton Bowl and an All-America choice in 1956. It has been said that Notre Dame's Paul Horning won that year's Heisman Trophy instead of Brown because he was white.

He was the Cleveland Browns' No. 1 draft pick in 1957 and the NFL's leading rusher in eight of his nine NFL seasons. He was named to the All-NFL team eight times, the league's Most Valuable Player in 1958 and '65, Rookie of the Year in 1957 and played in nine straight Pro Bowls. His 5.22 average per rushing attempt is an NFL record.

In 1966 Brown starred in the box office hit The Dirty Dozen. Shooting for The Dirty Dozen was repeatedly delayed, and ultimately conflicted with football training camp. It was then that Brown abruptly announced his retirement from football. He was 30 years old and at the height of his game. For some years after Brown retired from football, he continued to win major film roles in works such as Dark of the Sun, Ice Station Zebra, and 100 Rifles. Brown's movie career was only a memory by the early eighties, his ten-year publicity contract with Pepsi-Cola went un renewed and he found himself hustling Celebrity Bowling tournaments on TV for $20,000 paydays.

Brown admitted in People that his numerous relationships with women led him astray for a time. "I've done things I'm not particularly proud of," he said in Esquire, "but at least I'm honest enough to talk about them." He founded his own production company, Ocean Productions, to encourage minority participation in movie making. Also, Brown has been no stranger to the field of public service. As early as his playing days in Cleveland, he founded the Black Economic Union (BEU), which used professional athletes as facilitators in the establishment of Black-run enterprises, urban athletic clubs, and youth motivation programs. The BEU eventually folded, but Brown took his ideas to the Coors Golden Door program and Jobs Plus.

In 1986, he founded a new endeavor, Vital Issues, aimed at teaching life management skills and personal growth techniques to inner-city gang members and prison inmates. By 1989, Vital Issues had evolved into Amer-I-Can. Brown conducts sessions of from his home in the hills above Los Angeles. In 1992, Amer-I-Can won more than a million dollars in grant money to expand its programs into cities such as San Francisco and Cleveland. While he may not be the only athlete to reach out to others less fortunate than himself, Brown urges his peers to do more than "make gestures" when facing society's ills.

In due course, Brown does not want to be seen as yet another wealthy athlete who made his way in the world through his physical ability. "I was a highly paid, over-glamorized gladiator," he told the Washington Post. "The decision-makers are the men who own, not the ones who play. I was never under an illusion as to who was the boss." 2002 brought legal problems to Brown. He refused to take court-ordered counseling and community service for vandalizing his wife's car in 1999. The result is a 180-day misdemeanor jail term in Los Angeles.

https://aaregistry.org/story/jim-brown-athlete-actor-activist/

CHAPTER 31
MORGAN FREEMAN (1937-PRESENT)

Credit: James Patterson/Getty Images

Morgan Freeman, American actor whose emotional depth, subtle humor, and versatility made him one of the most-respected performers of his generation. Over a career that included numerous memorable performances on stage, screen, and television, Freeman was one of the few Black American actors who consistently received roles that were not specifically written for Black actors.

As a young man, Freeman had aspirations of being a fighter pilot; however, a stint in the air force (1955–59) proved disappointing, and he turned his attention to acting. He made his Broadway debut in an all-Black production of Hello Dolly! in 1967. In the 1970s he continued to work on the stage and also appeared on the educational children's television show The Electric Company as the character Easy Reader. Freeman's performance in the film Brubaker (1980) and on the soap opera Another World (1982–84), along with several enthusiastic reviews for his theatrical work in the early 1980s, led to more challenging film roles. His portrayal of a dangerous hustler in Street Smart (1987) earned Freeman his first Academy Award nomination, for best supporting actor. He was later nominated for a best-actor Oscar for his work in Driving Miss Daisy (1989), in which he re-created the role of Hoke after first performing it onstage. He evinced a disciplinarian principal in Lean on Me (1989), a hard-hearted Civil War soldier in Glory (1989), and an aging gunslinger in Unforgiven (1992). He made his directorial debut with the antiapartheid film Bopha! (1993). A third Oscar nomination came for his soulful turn as a convict in The Shawshank Redemption (1994)

Freeman later appeared in several crime dramas, including Se7en (1995), Kiss the Girls (1997), and Along Came a Spider (2001)—the latter two based on James Patterson novels—as well as The Sum of All Fears (2002). He won an Academy Award for best supporting actor for his performance as a former boxer in Clint Eastwood's Million Dollar Baby (2004) before appearing as Lucius Fox, a research and development guru, in Christopher Nolan's Batman Begins (2005). Freeman reprised the latter role in the sequels The Dark Knight (2008) and The Dark Knight Rises (2012). In Rob Reiner's The Bucket List (2007), he and Jack Nicholson played terminally ill cancer patients who make the most of their remaining time.

In 2008 Freeman returned to Broadway after nearly 20 years away from the stage, taking the role of Frank Elgin, a talented yet dispirited actor who has lost the will to perform, in The Country Girl. The following year he reteamed with Eastwood on Invictus, a drama in which he played Nelson Mandela, who sought to unite divided South Africa by supporting the national rugby team's quest to win the 1995 World Cup. Freeman later appeared as a former CIA agent in the action-comedy Red (2010); as a high-ranking U.S. politician in the thriller Olympus Has Fallen (2013) and its sequels, London Has Fallen (2016) and Angel Has Fallen (2019); and as a postapocalyptic survivalist in the science-fiction adventure Oblivion (2013). He also played a magician who exposes the tradecraft of his confreres in Now You See Me (2013) and its 2016 sequel. Freeman pursued less-suspenseful fare as well with roles in the sentimental dramas Dolphin Tale (2011) and its sequel, Dolphin Tale 2 (2014), and in The Magic of Belle Isle (2012).

Freeman went for laughs in the buddy comedy Last Vegas (2013), in which he starred opposite Robert De Niro, Michael Douglas, and Kevin Kline. He later voiced a wizard in The LEGO Movie (2014), a computer-animated adventure that featured renderings of LEGO toys as the characters and settings. His other roles in 2014 included an anti-artificial-intelligence activist in Transcendence and a psychology professor in Lucy. Freeman's later films included the comedies Ted 2 (2015); Going in Style (2017), a remake of the 1979 film about retirees who plan a bank heist; and Just Getting Started (2017), in which two rivals at a retirement community team up to save the woman of both their affections from her kidnappers.

Freeman later portrayed the toy maker Drosselmeyer in The Nutcracker and the Four Realms (2018), an adaptation of Pyotr Ilyich Tchaikovsky's 19th-century ballet. In The Comeback Trail (2020), Freeman starred with De Niro and Tommy Lee Jones and was cast as a mob boss. His credits from 2021 included the crime thriller Vanquish, the action comedy The Hitman's Wife's Bodyguard, and the sci-fi anthology TV series Solos.

https://www.britannica.com/biography/Morgan-Freeman

CHAPTER 32
BILL COSBY (1937-PRESENT)

Credit: Library of Congress

Bill Cosby, in full William Henry Cosby, Jr., American comedian, actor, and producer who played a major role in the development of a more-positive portrayal of Blacks on television but whose sterling reputation was tarnished by dozens of accusations of sexual assault over the course of many decades. In 2018 he was found guilty of drugging and sexually assaulting a woman, but his conviction was overturned three years later.

Cosby left high school without earning his diploma and joined the U.S. Navy in 1956. While enlisted he passed a high-school equivalency exam, and after his discharge he received an athletic scholarship to Temple University in Philadelphia in 1961. During his sophomore year he left Temple to entertain at the Gaslight Cafe in Greenwich Village, New York City, where he began to establish a trademark comedic style characterized by a friendly and accessible stage persona and a relaxed, carefully timed delivery. During the 1960s Cosby toured major U.S. and Canadian cities, commanding ever-higher performance fees. In 1965 he made his first appearance on The Tonight Show Starring Johnny Carson.

Cosby's first acting assignment, in the espionage series I Spy (1965–68), made him the first Black actor to perform in a starring dramatic role on network television. His portrayal of a Black secret agent won him three Emmy Awards and helped to advance the status of Black Americans on television. Cosby's subsequent projects for television included the series of Bill Cosby Specials (1968–71, 1975), the situation comedy The Bill Cosby Show (1969–71), the variety show The New Bill Cosby Show (1972–73), and the successful cartoon Fat Albert and the Cosby Kids (1972–84, 1989). He appeared in numerous commercials and on children's shows such as Sesame Street and Electric Company. He also made several feature films, which enjoyed limited success.

Cosby's most-successful work was The Cosby Show, which appeared on NBC from 1984 to 1992 and was one of the most-popular situation comedies in television history. The Cosby Show depicted a stable, prosperous Black family—Cosby's character was a doctor whose wife was a lawyer—and avoided racial stereotypes. The show had broad cross-cultural appeal and won several major awards. After the show ended, he starred in the series Cosby (1996–2000), in which his Cosby Show costar Phylicia Rashad again played his wife.

Cosby was awarded a doctorate in education from the University of Massachusetts in 1977 and was inducted into the Television Hall of Fame in 1984. His comedy records earned him eight Grammy Awards. In 1986 he wrote the best-selling book Fatherhood. In 1997 Cosby's son, Ennis, was shot and killed while changing a tire on a Los Angeles freeway; that same year he and his wife, Camille, founded the Hello Friend/Ennis William Cosby Foundation in their son's memory to fund teachers of students with learning disabilities. Cosby was outspoken about the need for Black Americans to pursue higher education and to support their families. In 2008 he released the hip-hop album Cosby Narratives Vol. 1: State of Emergency, which blended jazz, pop, and funk but shied away from the profanity he said was typical of most hip-hop music.

Allegations of past sexual assaults by Cosby gained increasing media coverage in the United States in the early 21st century. In 2005 he was accused of drugging and sexually assaulting Andrea Constand the previous year; at the time of the alleged incident, she was working at Temple University. Later in 2005 District Attorney Bruce L. Castor, Jr., announced that he would not charge Cosby, citing insufficient evidence. The comedian then gave a deposition in a civil suit brought by Constand, and in 2006 he settled out of court, paying her more than $3 million. That case spurred a number of other women to go public with their own stories of drug-induced sexual assault by Cosby, and in February 2014 a series of media interviews with some of his alleged victims made headlines. Those allegations and a much-viewed video of an October performance by comedian Hannibal Buress in which he called Cosby a rapist prompted even more women to accuse Cosby of past sexual misconduct. While he had not faced charges related to the new accusations, his reputation was so damaged by them that both NBC and Netflix pulled planned Cosby projects in November 2014.

In the following months the total number of women who accused Cosby of either attempting to drug them, drugging them, or drugging and raping them ballooned to more than 50. Cosby vehemently denied the accusations and publicly labeled some of his accusers as liars. He was subsequently sued by those women for defamation. In July 2015 court documents related to the 2005 civil suit against Cosby were unsealed, and it was revealed that he admitted at the time to having obtained prescription sedatives to give to women with whom he wanted to have sex.

In December 2015 a new district attorney in Montgomery County, Pennsylvania, charged Cosby with felony aggravated indecent assault for the 2004 incident involving Constand, just days before the statute of limitations was set to expire. In 2016 Cosby's legal team sought to have the case thrown out, alleging that Castor had actually declined to file charges as part of a deal in which Cosby agreed not to invoke his Fifth Amendment right against self-incrimination in the civil trial. Although Castor later supported the defense's claim, no written agreement existed, and Constand and her lawyers stated that they had no knowledge of such a deal. The criminal trial against Cosby was allowed to proceed, and it ultimately included his 2005 testimony. In 2017 the trial ended in a hung jury and a mistrial after six days of jury deliberation without a unanimous decision. A retrial began in April 2018, and that same month he was found guilty of drugging and sexually assaulting Constand. In September he received a sentence of 3 to 10 years in prison. Cosby appealed the verdict, and in June 2021 his conviction was overturned by the Supreme Court of Pennsylvania, which ruled that there was an enforceable agreement between Castor and Cosby. The court ordered the comedian's release and barred a retrial.

Cosby's legal issues continued, however. In 2014 Judy Huth had filed a civil suit against the comedian in California, alleging that he had sexually assaulted her in 1975, when she was 16 years old. (In that state the statute of limitations is extended for cases involving allegations of child molestation.) The trial began in 2022, and the jury ruled in Huth's favour. Cosby was ordered to pay $500,000 in compensatory damages.

Despite all of the bad he has done; he will always be remembered for being the black man who uplifted his entire black community.

https://www.britannica.com/biography/Bill-Cosby

CHAPTER 33
COLIN POWELL (1937- 2021)

Credit: GETTY IMAGES

Colin Luther Powell, the son of Jamaican immigrants, was born on 5 April 1937 in the Harlem section of New York City. He grew up in the South Bronx, where he graduated from Morris High School. At sixteen he entered the City College of New York. Attracted by the panache of the Pershing Rifles drill team, he joined the Army Reserve Officer Training Corps (ROTC). There he found a sense of direction. He became company commander of the Pershing Rifles, attained ROTC's highest rank of cadet colonel, and was named a "distinguished military graduate." When he graduated in 1958 with a Bachelor of Science in geology, Powell was commissioned a second lieutenant in the Regular Army.

During the next decade Powell mastered infantry tactics and unit leadership. After completing Infantry Officer Basic, Ranger, and Airborne schools, he joined the 3d Armored Division in West Germany as a platoon leader. He then transferred to Fort Devens, Massachusetts, to command a company of the 5th Infantry Division and in 1962 was promoted to captain.

From December 1962 to November 1963 Powell was assigned to Vietnam, where he served as an adviser to a South Vietnamese infantry battalion. Wounded during this tour, he received a Purple Heart. On his return, he completed the Infantry Officer Advanced Course at Fort Benning, Georgia; was promoted to major in 1966; and the following year became an instructor at the Infantry School. In 1968 he graduated from the Command and General Staff College, Fort Leavenworth, Kansas, second in a class of 1,244.

In June 1968 Major Powell returned to Vietnam, serving first as a battalion executive officer and then as Assistant Chief of Staff, Operations (G-3), and later deputy G-3, with the 23d Infantry Division (America). During this tour he received the Soldier's Medal for repeatedly returning to a burning helicopter to rescue others despite being injured himself.

Powell spent 1969 to 1973 in Washington, DC. Promoted to lieutenant colonel in 1970, he received a master's in business administration from George Washington University in 1971. In 1971 and 1972 he worked as an operations research analyst in the Planning, Programming and Analysis Directorate in the Office of the Assistant Vice Chief of Staff of the Army. Selected in 1972 as one of seventeen White House Fellows from among 1,500 applicants, he was assigned to the Office of Management and Budget (OMB) as Special Assistant to the Deputy Director.

Lieutenant Colonel Powell returned to a troop assignment in September 1973 as Commander of the 1st Battalion of the 32d Infantry, 2d Infantry

Division, guarding the Demilitarized Zone in the Republic of Korea. His next assignment, from 1974 to 1975, was as an operations research systems analyst in the Office of the Assistant Secretary of Defense for Manpower and Reserve Affairs. During 1975 and 1976 he was a student at the National War College, Fort Lesley J. McNair, Washington, DC. Promoted to colonel in 1976, Powell assumed command of the 2d Brigade, 101st Airborne Division (Air Assault), Fort Campbell, Kentucky, in April of that year.

Colonel Powell returned to the Office of the Secretary of Defense (OSD) in July 1977 as Executive to the Special Assistant to the Secretary and Deputy Secretary of Defense. After promotion to brigadier general in 1979 he continued in OSD as Senior Military Assistant to the Deputy Secretary until June 1981, when he became Assistant Division Commander for Operations of the 4th Infantry Division (Mechanized), Fort Carson, Colorado. In August 1982 General Powell became the Deputy Commanding General of the US Army Combined Arms Combat Development Activity, Fort Leavenworth, Kansas.

In July 1983 he returned to the Pentagon as Senior Military Assistant to Secretary of Defense Caspar Weinberger. Promoted to major general the following month, Powell continued as Weinberger's assistant until June 1986, when he assumed command of V Corps in Europe. He was promoted to lieutenant general in July.

Six months later, President Ronald Reagan summoned him to become the Deputy National Security Adviser under Frank Carlucci, for whom Powell had worked at OMB and in OSD. When Carlucci became Secretary of Defense, General Powell replaced him as National Security Adviser. He served in this position from December 1987 until the end of the Reagan presidency in January 1989. During this time, he organized and coordinated several summit meetings between President Reagan and other world leaders.

In April 1989 Powell received his fourth star and became Commander in Chief of Forces Command (CINCFOR), Fort McPherson, Georgia, responsible for the general reserve of US-based Army forces. Within months of his appointment as CINCFOR, President George H. W. Bush selected General Powell to be the twelfth Chairman of the Joint Chiefs of Staff. When Powell became Chairman on 1 October 1989, he was the first Black American, the first ROTC graduate, and, at fifty-two, the youngest officer to serve in the position.

General Powell's tenure as Chairman coincided with the end of the Cold War; his chairmanship saw more change in the world than that of any of his predecessors. Powell was the principal architect of the reorientation of US strategy and the reduction of the armed forces in response to the changed strategic environment. He directed the most significant change in national military strategy since the late 1940s, devising a strategy that focused on regional and humanitarian crises rather than on the Soviet Union. Powell's concept of a "base force" sufficient to maintain the United States' superpower status won Secretary of Defense Dick Cheney's and President Bush's support for a 25 percent reduction in the size of the armed forces.

The first Chairman to serve his whole tenure under the Goldwater-Nichols Department of Defense reforms, Powell devoted considerable energy to promoting joint culture in order to enhance the services' ability to fight together as a team. He guided the development of doctrine for joint warfare and was the driving force behind the expansion of the Atlantic Command's responsibilities, which transformed it from a principally naval headquarters into one with responsibility for ground and air forces based in the continental United States as well as East Coast naval forces. When the new US Atlantic Command (USACOM) came into existence on 1 October 1993, the day after Powell's retirement, it was a joint command designed to meet the military requirements of the post-Cold War world.

During Powell's chairmanship, the US Armed Forces made over two dozen operational deployments. An attempted coup against the Panamanian dictator Manuel Noriega on 3 October 1989 almost postponed Powell's welcoming ceremony at the Pentagon. Over the next two months, the Chairman worked with the Commander in Chief of US Southern Command to develop a contingency plan that would provide a large force should President Bush decide to intervene in Panama. After Panama declared a state of war with the United States and Panamanian soldiers killed an American officer and manhandled another officer and his wife, President Bush ordered the deployment of approximately 14,000 troops to Panama in late December. They joined almost 13,000 troops already there to execute Operation JUST CAUSE, which resulted in the defeat of the Panamanian forces and the downfall of Noriega.

General Powell played a central role in the preparation for and conduct of the Persian Gulf War. In response to Iraq's invasion of Kuwait in August 1990, President Bush ordered the deployment of some 250,000 US troops to Saudi Arabia in Operation DESERT SHIELD. Powell advised keeping all options open, exerting diplomatic and economic pressure while building up sufficient forces in the region to assure quick victory if the United States and its coalition partners concluded that military action was necessary. When Iraqi President Saddam Hussein did not withdraw his forces from Kuwait, Powell endorsed the President's decision to launch an offensive—Operation DESERT STORM—in January 1991. After it became clear in late February that the coalition forces had achieved an overwhelming victory, he supported the President's decision to suspend hostilities. The Persian Gulf victory boosted the military's standing with the American public, and General Powell became a well-known and popular figure. For his leadership during the war, he received a Congressional Gold Medal, struck in his honor, and the Presidential Medal of Freedom.

In addition to the combat operations in Panama and the Persian Gulf, US forces participated in a number of rescue and relief operations during Powell's chairmanship, including humanitarian relief operations to provide assistance to famine victims in Somalia and to victims of ethnic warfare in Bosnia in 1992 and 1993. While supporting limited use of US forces to contain the crisis in the Balkans and to assist the United Nations forces on the ground there, General Powell was reluctant to commit US forces to intervene directly in the war and thus become one of the belligerents. He forcefully argued against the commitment of US ground troops in either a peacemaking or combat role. In internal debates in the Bush and Clinton administrations and in published articles, he advocated the use of US forces in combat only when there were clear political objectives and the political willingness to commit sufficient resources to achieve these objectives. Although there was a perception of an uneasy relationship between the military and the new Clinton administration, especially over the issue of homosexuals in the military, General Powell enjoyed a close working relationship with President William J. Clinton.

When General Powell retired on 30 September 1993, the role of the Chairman of the Joint Chiefs of Staff had been substantially enhanced due to his aggressive exercise of the expanded powers granted the Chairman in the Goldwater-Nichols Act. His tenure as Chairman subsequently became the subject of debate among some scholars and commentators concerned with the role of the military in policy development.

At his retirement General Powell was awarded a second Presidential Medal of Freedom, this one with distinction. Later that year Queen Elizabeth II made him an honorary Knight Commander of the Bath. In retirement, Powell wrote a best-selling autobiography and became a frequent public speaker. As a member of the three-man delegation, headed by former President Jimmy Carter, that President Clinton sent to Haiti in September 1994, he played a key role in negotiating the peaceful transfer of power from the military dictatorship to the elected president. Powell cochaired the Presidents' Summit for America's Future in 1997 and subsequently launched and became chairman of America's Promise—The Alliance for Youth, a national organization to mobilize volunteer efforts to assist young people in developing the character and skills needed to become successful adults. A trustee of Howard University and a director of the United Negro College Fund, he also served on the board of governors of the Boys & Girls Clubs of America, on the advisory board of the Children's Health Fund, and on corporate boards. In 1998 he received the US Military Academy's Sylvanus Thayer Award for embodying the values expressed in the Academy's motto, "Duty, Honor, Country," and in 1999 the Air Force Academy awarded him the Thomas D. White Defense Award for his contributions to national defense. Powell was a member of the US delegation of observers for the 1999 presidential election in Nigeria, one of the steps in that nation's transition to democratic rule. He also served as the 65th United States Secretary of State, under President George W. Bush from 2001 to 2005.

https://www.jcs.mil/About/The-Joint-Staff/Chairman/General-Colin-Luther-Powell/

CHAPTER 34
JESSE JACKSON (1941-PRESENT)

Credit: AFGE - https://www.flickr.com/photos/afge/10196156245/

Civil rights leader and two-time Democratic presidential candidate Jesse Jackson born in 1941, became one of the most influential Black Americans of the late 20th century. He rose to prominence working within Martin Luther King Jr.'s Southern Christian Leadership Conference (SCLC) and was at the Memphis hotel with King when he was assassinated. Through PUSH, the organization he founded in 1971, Jackson pressed for broader employment opportunities for Black Americans. During the 1980s and 1990s he negotiated the release of dozens of international hostages and prisoners. In his 1984 and 1988 presidential campaigns, Jackson won 16 state contests and millions of votes, making him the first viable Black American candidate for president.

Jesse Louis Burns was born October 8, 1941, in Greensville, South Carolina. His mother, Helen Burns, was 16; his father, Noah Louis Robinson, was a former professional boxer and a married man. When Jesse was 2, Helen married Charles Jackson. Jesse lived with his grandmother Matilda until he was 13. Jesse then returned to Charles Jackson's house and in 1957 was adopted by his stepfather.

At Greenville's Sterling High School, Jesse Jackson graduated with offers for a minor league baseball contract and a Big Ten football scholarship. He spent a year at the University of Illinois at Urbana-Champaign before transferring to North Carolina Agricultural and Technical College in Greensboro, where he was quarterback and student body president. By the time Jackson graduated with a sociology degree in 1964, he had married Jacqueline Brown, a fellow student, and welcomed the first of their five children.

While in Greensboro Jackson had joined the Congress of Racial Equality and participated in marches and sit-ins. After graduation, he began divinity studies at the Chicago Theological Seminary and worked to organize student support for Martin Luther King Jr. In March of 1965 Jackson travelled to Alabama for the historic Selma to Montgomery march with King. A year later he left the seminary to work full-time for the SCLC.

Jackson was placed in charge of Operation Breadbasket, an SCLC initiative to monitor companies' treatment of Black Americans and to organize boycotts calling for fair hiring practices. By 1968 Jackson was part of King's inner circle and was with him when he was assassinated. Jackson claimed he had been the last person to speak with the dying leader, though others present challenged his account.

Ralph Abernathy was chosen to succeed King as the SCLC's leader; a position Jackson had wanted. Jackson returned to leading Operation Breadbasket but continued to chafe with Abernathy until 1971, when he resigned to start his own organization.

Jackson's new venture, People United to Save Humanity (PUSH), was similar to Operation Breadbasket, but its scope expanded with its leader's passions. In 1972 Jackson led a group to the Democratic National Convention that managed to oust Chicago Mayor Richard Daley's Illinois delegation.

In 1984 Jackson ran for the Democratic presidential nomination, winning five primaries and caucuses and more than 18 percent of votes cast. However, a comment he made to a reporter about Jews and his relationship with Nation of Islam leader Louis Farrakhan led to controversy during the campaign.

Jackson's multiracial National Rainbow Coalition grew out of his work in the 1984 campaign and merged with PUSH in 1996. Jackson ran for president again in 1988 and won 11 primaries and caucuses and nearly 20 percent of the vote.

Parallel to his domestic advocacy, in the 1980s and 1990s Jackson worked independently to secure the release of prisoners held by several anti-American regimes. He frustrated the Reagan administration by traveling to Syria in 1984 to win the release of a U.S. fighter pilot. Jackson also helped free 22 Americans held in Cuba on drug charges, as well as 27 Cuban political prisoners.

During the 1990s Jackson worked to free hostages from Iraq and Kuwait before the Persian Gulf War. He also secured the release of three U.S. soldiers captured during the Kosovo conflict.

In 2001 Jackson withdrew briefly from activism after admitting that he had a 2-year-old a daughter with a former member of his staff and had used Rainbow/PUSH funds to pay a portion of the expenses.

Jackson was an early supporter of Barak Obama's successful 2008 presidential campaign, though he later became a critic of certain Obama policies. On the night of Obama's election, Jackson was photographed on stage at the victory celebration, tears streaming down his face as he recalled Martin Luther King and others who had died in the struggle for civil rights.

https://www.britannica.com/biography/Jesse-Jackson

CHAPTER 35
HUEY PERCY NEWTON (1941- 1989)

Credit: ®AAREG 2022

Huey P. Newton was an Black American activist best known for founding the militant Black Panther Party with Bobby Seale in 1966.

In 1966, Huey P. Newton and Bobby Seale founded the left-wing Black Panther Party for Self Defense in Oakland, California. The organization was central to the Black Power movement, making headlines with its controversial rhetoric and militaristic style. Newton faced a number of criminal charges over the years and at one point fled to Cuba before returning to the U.S. and earning his doctorate. Struggling with drug and alcohol addiction in his later years, he was killed in 1989 in Oakland.

Huey Percy Newton was born on February 17, 1942, in Monroe, Louisiana. Newton helped establish the Black American political organization the Black Panther Party and became a leading figure in the Black Power movement of the 1960s. The youngest of seven siblings, he and his family moved to Oakland, California when Newton was a toddler. Though later stating he was close to his family, the youngster had a difficult time early in life, which was reflected in highly erratic behavior at school and on the streets.

Despite having multiple suspensions and run-ins with the law as a teen, Newton began to take his education seriously, finding inspiration when his older brother Melvin earned a Master's in social work. Although Newton graduated high school in 1959, he was considered barely literate. He nonetheless became his own teacher, learning to read by himself.

In the mid-1960s, Newton decided to pursue his education at Merritt College, during which time he received a months-long prison term for a knife assault, and later attended the University of San Francisco School of Law. It was at Merritt where he met Seale. The two were briefly involved with political groups at the school before they set out to create one of their own. Founded in 1966, they called their group the Black Panther Party for Self Defense. Unlike many of the other social and political organizers of the time, they took a more militant stance to the plight of Black communities in America. A famous photograph shows Newton (the group's minister of defense) holding a gun in one hand and a spear in the other.

The group set forth its political goals in a document entitled the Ten-Point Program, which called for better housing, jobs, and education for Black Americans. It also called for an end to economic exploitation of Black communities, along with military exemption. The organization itself was not afraid to punctuate its message with dramatic appearances. For example, to protest a gun bill in 1967, members of the Panthers entered the California Legislature armed. (Newton actually wasn't present at the demonstration.) The action was a shocking one that made news across the country, and

Newton emerged as a leading figure in the Black militant movement.

The Black Panthers wanted to improve life in Black communities and took a stance against police brutality in urban neighborhoods by mostly white cops. Members of the group would go to arrests in progress and watch for abuse. Panther members ultimately clashed with police several times. The party's treasurer, Bobby Hutton, was killed while still a teenager during one of these conflicts in 1968.

Newton himself was arrested the previous year for allegedly killing an Oakland police officer during a traffic stop. He was later convicted of voluntary manslaughter and sentenced to two to 15 years in prison. But public pressure "Free Huey" became a popular slogan of the day, helped Newton's cause. He was freed in 1970 after an appeals process deemed that incorrect deliberation procedures had been implemented during the trial.

In the 1970s, Newton aimed to take the Panthers in a new direction that emphasized democratic socialism, community interconnectedness and services for the poor, including items like free lunch programs and urban clinics. But the Panthers began to fall apart due to factionalism, with later allegations surfacing that the FBI, under J. Edgar Hoover, was clandestinely involved in the organization's unraveling. Key members left while Newton and Eldridge Cleaver, the party's minister of information, split ways.

By mid-decade, Newton faced more criminal charges when he was accused of murdering a 17-year-old sex worker and assaulting a tailor. To avoid prosecution, he fled to Cuba in 1974, but returned to the U.S. three years later. The murder case was eventually dismissed after two trials ended with deadlocked juries, while the tailor refused to testify in court in relation to assault charges.

Even with his legal troubles, Newton returned to school, earning a Ph.D. in social philosophy from the University of California, Santa Cruz, in 1980. In his final years, however, he suffered from major drug/alcohol problems and faced more prison time for weapons possession, financial misappropriations, and parole violations. The once popular revolutionary died on August 22, 1989, in Oakland, California, after being shot on the street.

Newton had published a memoir/manifesto Revolutionary Suicide in 1973, with Hugh Pearson later writing the 1994 biography The Shadow of the Panther: Huey Newton and the Price of Black Power in America. Newton's story was later depicted in the 1996 one-man play Huey P. Newton, starring Roger Guenveur Smith. A 2002 filmed presentation of the project was created by Spike Lee, and documentarian Stanley Nelson looked at the history of the Panthers in the 2015 film The Black Panthers: Vanguard of the Revolution.

https://www.biography.com/activist/huey-p-newton

CHAPTER 36
MUHAMMAD ALI (1942-2016)

Credit: Neil Leifer/Sports Illustrated/Getty Images

Muhammad Ali was a boxer, philanthropist and social activist who is universally regarded as one of the greatest athletes of the 20th century. Ali became an Olympic gold medalist in 1960 and the world heavyweight boxing champion in 1964.

Following his suspension for refusing military service, Ali reclaimed the heavyweight title two more times during the 1970s, winning famed bouts against Joe Frazier and George Foreman along the way. Diagnosed with Parkinson's disease in 1984, Ali devoted much of his time to philanthropy, earning the Presidential Medal of Freedom in 2005.

Ali was born on January 17, 1942, in Louisville, Kentucky. His birth name was Cassius Marcellus Clay Jr. At an early age, young Clay showed that he wasn't afraid of any bout — inside or outside of the ring. Growing up in the segregated South, he experienced racial prejudice and discrimination firsthand. At the age of 12, Clay discovered his talent for boxing through an odd twist of fate. After his bike was stolen, Clay told a police officer, Joe Martin, that he wanted to beat up the thief.

"Well, you better learn how to fight before you start challenging people," Martin reportedly told him at the time. In addition to being a police officer, Martin also trained young boxers at a local gym.

Clay started working with Martin to learn how to spar and soon began his boxing career. In his first amateur bout in 1954, he won the fight by split decision.

Clay went on to win the 1956 Golden Gloves tournament for novices in the light heavyweight class. Three years later, he won the National Golden Gloves Tournament of Champions, as well as the Amateur Athletic Union's national title for the light heavyweight division.

In 1960, Clay won a spot on the U.S. Olympic boxing team, and traveled to Rome, Italy, to compete. At six feet, three inches tall, Clay was an imposing figure in the ring, but he also became known for his lightning speed and fancy footwork. After winning his first three bouts, Clay defeated Zbigniew Pietrzkowski of Poland to win the light heavyweight Olympic gold medal.

After his Olympic victory, Clay was heralded as an American hero. He soon turned professional with the backing of the Louisville Sponsoring Group and continued overwhelming all opponents in the ring.

Clay joined the Black Muslim group Nation of Islam in 1964. At first, he called himself Cassius X before settling on the name Muhammad Ali. The boxer eventually converted to orthodox Islam during the 1970s.

Ali started a different kind of fight with his outspoken views against the Vietnam War. Drafted into the military in April 1967, he refused to serve on the grounds that he was a practicing Muslim minister with religious beliefs that prevented him from fighting. He was arrested for committing a felony and almost immediately stripped of his world title and boxing license. The U.S. Department of Justice pursued a legal case against Ali, denying his claim for conscientious objector status. He was found guilty of violating Selective Service laws and sentenced to five years in prison in June 1967 but remained free while appealing his conviction.

Unable to compete professionally in the meantime, Ali missed more than three prime years of his athletic career. Ali returned to the ring in 1970 with a win over Jerry Quarry, and the U.S. Supreme Court eventually overturned the conviction in June 1971. Ali had a career record of 56 wins, five losses and 37 knockouts before his retirement from boxing in 1981 at the age of 39.

Often referring to himself as "The Greatest," Ali was not afraid to sing his own praises. He was known for boasting about his skills before a fight and for his colorful descriptions and phrases.

In one of his more famously quoted descriptions, Ali told reporters that he could "float like a butterfly, sting like a bee" in the boxing ring. A few of his more well-known matches include the following:

Sonny Liston

After winning gold at the 1960 Olympics, Ali took out British heavyweight champion Henry Cooper in 1963. He then knocked out Sonny Liston in 1964 to become the heavyweight champion of the world.

Joe Frazier

In 1971, Ali took on Joe Frazier in what has been called the "Fight of the Century." Frazier and Ali went toe-to-toe for 14 rounds before Frazier dropped Ali with a vicious left hook in the 15th. Ali recovered quickly, but the judges awarded the decision to Frazier, handing Ali his first professional loss after 31 wins.

After suffering a loss to Ken Norton, Ali beat Frazier in a 1974 rematch.

In 1975, Ali and Frazier locked horns again for their grudge match in Quezon City, Philippines. Dubbed the "Thrilla in Manila," the bout nearly went the distance, with both men delivering and absorbing tremendous punishment. However, Frazier's trainer threw in the towel after the 14th round, giving the hard-fought victory to Ali.

George Foreman

Another legendary Ali fight took place in 1974 against undefeated heavyweight champion George Foreman. Billed as the "Rumble in the Jungle," the bout was organized by promoter Don King and held in Kinshasa, Zaire.

For once, Ali was seen as the underdog to the younger, massive Foreman, but he silenced his critics with a masterful performance. He baited Foreman into throwing wild punches with his "rope-a-dope" technique, before stunning his opponent with an eighth-round knockout to reclaim the heavyweight title.

Leon Spinks

After losing his title to Leon Spinks in February 1978, Ali defeated him in a September 1978 rematch, becoming the first boxer to win the heavyweight championship three times.

Larry Holmes

Following a brief retirement, Ali returned to the ring to face Larry Holmes in 1980 but was overmatched against the younger champion.

Following one final loss in 1981, to Trevor Berbick, the boxing great retired from the sport at age 39. Ali was married four times and had nine children, including two children he fathered outside of marriage. Ali married his first wife, Sonji Roi, in 1964; they divorced after one year when she refused to adopt the Nation of Islam dress and customs. Ali married his second wife, 17-year-old Belinda Boyd, in 1967. Boyd and Ali had four children together: Maryum, born in 1969; Jamillah and Liban, both born in 1970; and Muhammad Ali Jr.; born in 1972. Boyd and Ali divorced in 1976.

At the same time Ali was married to Boyd, he traveled openly with Veronica Porche, who became his third wife in 1977. The pair had two daughters together, including Laila Ali, who followed in Ali's footsteps by becoming a champion boxer. Porche and Ali divorced in 1986.

Ali married his fourth and final wife Yolanda ("Lonnie") in 1986. The pair had known each other since Lonnie was just six and Ali was 21; their mothers were best friends and raised their families on the same street. Ali and Lonnie couple remained married until his death and had one son together, Asaad.

In 1984, Ali announced that he had Parkinson's disease, a degenerative neurological condition.

Despite the progression of Parkinson's and the onset of spinal stenosis, he remained active in public life. Ali raised funds for the Muhammad Ali Parkinson Center in Phoenix, Arizona. And he was on hand to celebrate the inauguration of the first Black American president in January 2009, when Barack Obama was sworn into office.

A few years before his death, Ali underwent surgery for spinal stenosis, a condition causing the narrowing of the spine, which limited his mobility and ability to communicate.

In his retirement, Ali devoted much of his time to philanthropy. Over the years, Ali supported the Special Olympics and the Make-A-Wish Foundation, among other organizations. In 1996, he lit the Olympic cauldron at the Summer Olympic Games in Atlanta, an emotional moment in sports history.

Ali traveled to numerous countries, including Mexico and Morocco, to help out those in need. In 1998, he was chosen to be a United Nations Messenger of Peace because of his work in developing nations.

In 2005, Ali received the Presidential Medal of Freedom from President George W. Bush. Soon after Obama's 2009 inauguration, Ali received the President's Award from the NAACP for his public service efforts.

Ali opened the Muhammad Ali Center in his hometown of Louisville, Kentucky, in 2005.
"I am an ordinary man who worked hard to develop the talent I was given," he said. "Many fans wanted to build a museum to acknowledge my achievements. I wanted more than a building to house my memorabilia. I wanted a place that would inspire people to be the best that they could be at whatever they chose to do, and to encourage them to be respectful of one another."

Actor Will Smith played Ali in the biopic film Ali, released in 2001.

Ali died on June 3, 2016, in Phoenix, Arizona, after being hospitalized for what was reportedly a respiratory issue. He was 74 years old.

The boxing legend had been suffering from Parkinson's disease and spinal stenosis. In early 2015, the athlete battled pneumonia and was hospitalized for a severe urinary tract infection.

Years before his passing, Ali had planned his own memorial services, saying he wanted to be "inclusive of everyone, where we give as many people an opportunity that want to pay their respects to me," according to a family spokesman. The three-day event, which took place in Ali's hometown of Louisville, Kentucky, included an "I Am Ali" festival of public arts, entertainment and educational offerings sponsored by the city, an Islamic prayer program and a memorial service.

Prior to the memorial service, a funeral procession traveled 20 miles through Louisville, past Ali's childhood home, his high school, the first boxing gym where he trained and along Ali Boulevard as tens of thousands of fans tossed flowers on his hearse and cheered his name.

The champ's memorial service was held at the KFC Yum Center arena with close to 20,000 people in attendance. Speakers included religious leaders from various faiths, Attallah Shabazz, Malcolm X's eldest daughter, broadcaster Bryant Gumbel, former President Bill Clinton, comedian Billy Crystal, Ali's daughters Maryum and Rasheda and his widow Lonnie.

"Muhammad indicated that when the end came for him, he wanted us to use his life and his death as a teaching moment for young people, for his country and for the world," Lonnie said. "In effect, he wanted us to remind people who are suffering that he had seen the face of injustice. That he grew up during segregation, and that during his early life he was not free to be who he wanted to be. But he never became embittered enough to quit or to engage in violence."

Former President Clinton spoke about how Ali found self-empowerment: "I think he decided, before he could possibly have worked it all out, and before fate and time could work their will on him, he decided he would not ever be disempowered. He decided that not his race nor his place, the expectations of others, positive, negative or otherwise would strip from him the power to write his own story. "

Crystal, who was a struggling comedian when he became friends with Ali, said of the boxing legend: "Ultimately, he became a silent messenger for peace, who taught us that life is best when you build bridges between people, not walls."

"You have inspired us and the world to be the best version of ourselves,' Rasheda Ali spoke to her father. 'May you live in paradise free from suffering. You shook up the world in life now you're shaking up the world in death. Now you are free to be with your creator. We love you so much Daddy. Until we meet again, fly butterfly, fly."

Pallbearers included Will Smith and former heavyweight champions Mike Tyson and Lennox Lewis. Ali was buried at the Cave Hill National Cemetery in Louisville.

Ali's stature as a legend continues to grow even after his death. He is celebrated not only for his remarkable athletic skills but for his willingness to speak his mind and his courage to challenge the status quo.

https://www.biography.com/athlete/muhammad-ali

CHAPTER 37
JIMI HENDRIX (1942-1970)

Credit: @Bryce FlemmingAP Images/picture-alliance

Jimi Hendrix is the single most famous musician to ever emerge from the Pacific Northwest's music scene -- rose from extremely humble beginnings to establish himself as perhaps the most gifted and inventive guitarist of all time, one who would be globally recognized as a major force in twentieth-century music. Born and raised in Seattle, Hendrix absorbed the region's distinct rockin' R&B aesthetic of the "Louie Louie" era, learned to play guitar, and performed in a series of at least three teenaged dance combos between 1959 and 1961. After a couple minor brushes with the law, Hendrix joined the U.S. Army in 1961, and upon discharge in 1962 formed an R&B band in Nashville, and then toured the "chitlin' circuit" of Black American-oriented nightclubs. By 1964 Hendrix had made his way to New York where he was discovered by elite British rockers. Flown to London in September 1966, his new band, the Jimi Hendrix Experience, was a literal over-night sensation. In 1967 they slayed the Monterey Pop Festival's crowds, within months became a top concert draw, and their albums were instant psychedelic rock 'n' roll classics. In 1969 Hendrix headlined the legendary Woodstock festival. In 1970 the magnificent young musician died in his sleep.

The Hendrix family first arrived in the Pacific Northwest during the Alaska-Yukon-Pacific Exposition of 1909. Nora (nee Moore) Rose Hendrix (1883-1984) was a dancer with Lacy's Band and their traveling vaudeville troupe whose "The Great Dixieland Spectacle" show was featured at the expo's Dixieland pavilion. Her husband, Bertran Philander Ross Hendrix (1866-1934), was a stagehand/roadie for the organization. Family legend tells that after the exposition concluded in October 1909, the troupe was stranded without future bookings and disbanded.

By 1912 the couple had settled into Vancouver, B.C., and the following year brought them their first child, Leon Marshall Hendrix. Subsequent years brought additional offspring including James Allen Hendrix (1919-2002), who developed a love of competitive dancing by the 1930s. It was while attending a Fats Waller dance one night that Al, as he was called, met the pretty 16-year-old from the mining town of Roslyn, Washington -- Lucille Jeter (1925-1958) -- who would become his wife in 1942. Months later, on November 27, 1942, she bore their first child, Johnny Allen Hendrix, at Seattle's King County Hospital -- today's Harborview Medical Center.

By that time Al was stationed overseas with the U.S. Army, and he was not pleased with the name Lucille had bestowed upon their son. Young Lucille loved the nightlife and partying and in time Al would learn that she had not been entirely faithful to him -- with one probable partner in adultery being a fellow named Johnny Williams. Upon his return from service, Al legally renamed his son James Marshall Hendrix (in 1946).

By 1947 the Hendrix family was settled into a unit of Seattle's Rainier Vista Housing Projects, but their domestic home-life never really did settle down. Al and Lucille bickered and battled over her drinking and disappearing for days at a time as young Jimmy began attending kindergarten at Rainier Vista School. Meanwhile Al was totally surprised when Lucille gave birth to another boy, Leon Morris Hendrix, in January 1948. Other children -- who would be fostered out -- came along, including Joseph Hendrix (b. 1949), Cathy Ira Hendrix (b. 1950) and Pamela Marguerite Hendrix (b. 1951).

In December of that same year, the couple was finally divorced, and Al essentially took over raising Jimmy and Leon. While Jimmy began attending Horace Mann Elementary School, Al took on multiple menial jobs including janitor, gas station attendant, and finally gardener. During those days of struggle, Jimmy and Leon were both taken in at times by relatives, friends, neighbors, and perhaps a half-dozen foster homes.

But Al eventually stabilized his situation enough that Jimmy rejoined him (at the house he'd bought back in 1950 at 2603 S Washington Street) and Al did what he could to provide -- including bringing home an old used ukulele for his oldest son. By the mid-1950s Jimmy was enrolled at Leschi Elementary School where he played on their Fighting Irish football team. Jimmy and his boyhood pals -- like most all Seattle kids -- were huge fans of the Sea fair festival's hydroplane races on nearby Lake Washington, and he also loved listening to the radio and playing Al's small collection of jazz and blues records.

With the dawn of rock 'n' roll as a popular form of youth-oriented music in the 1950s, Jimmy and his pals became obsessed with the new sounds. Initially the only radio stations to feature big-beat music were tiny FM operations in Bremerton and Tacoma that aired specialty shows hosted by local pioneering Black American DJs like Bob Summerise (1925-2010) and Fitzgerald "Eager" Beaver (1922-1992). But by 1957 even pop/Top-40 stations had to play the early big hits by Elvis Presley -- and the subsequent legions of other Southern rockabillies and Hollywood-based wannabes that would emerge.

It was in September 1957 that Presley's band electrified Seattle with a concert at the Sicks' Stadium ballpark near the Hendrix's neighborhood -- but even though various publications have reported that the then-15-year-old Jimmy attended, no proof of that assertion exists, and his family's precarious financial state would seem to cast further doubt on it. What is certain is that a cartoon sketch of Presley and his guitar was drawn by young Jimmy and survives in his family's archives.

It was also in about 1957 that Al bought an old used acoustic guitar for $5 and gave it to Jimmy, who immediately began teaching himself to tune and play chords on it -- in particular, the foolproof-but-addictive three chords to the region's signature tune, "Louie Louie." Jimmy also began to jam to songs on the radio and to theme songs from various television shows. By 1958 Jimmy was studying at Meany Junior High School and making new friends. It was probably in 1959 that Al was able to afford a cheap Supro Ozark electric guitar from the Myers Music shop downtown.

Undoubtedly grateful, Jimmy must also have been a bit frustrated that his father was never able to spare the cash to match that guitar with an amplifier. For the next years would always be reliant on sharing or borrowing the amps of his friends. And it was with such neighborhood friends as Pernell Alexander, Butch Snipes, and Luther Rabb that he began jamming after school. Alexander and Rabb were among the members of the first band that Jimmy helped form: the Velvetones. Though the band-members were far too young to play nightclubs, they honed their skills playing teen-dances in venues including recreation halls at area housing projects including Yesler Terrace in Seattle's Central District. Before long Jimmy's left-handed guitar playing had advanced to the degree that his peers became admirers. The Velvetones even began to include his original tune, "Jimmy's Blues," in their dance sets.

Time passed and Jimmy was invited to join another band -- the Rocking Teens -- who soon changed monikers to the Rocking Kings. Meanwhile, Jimmy became enthralled with the sounds being created by various top-tier local bands -- especially Seattle's Dave Lewis Combo, the Playboys and Dynamics, and Tacoma's Wailers -- and he undoubtedly ached to belong to a group that had the potential to break out of the small-time scene of house party, community hall, and rec center gigs his bands had been trapped in.

That opportunity arose around 1960 when he was invited to join James Thomas and His Tomcats, a new combo assembled, managed, and fronted by an older guy who had a sense for business and successfully got his band booked at good gigs such as Sea fair picnics and military officers clubs ranging from the U.S. Naval facility to Everett's Paine Field to Fort Lewis to Moses Lake's Larson Air Force Base and back. By this time Jimmy had acquired a new Danelectro guitar to replace one stolen during a gig at the Birdland nightspot.

It was while attending Garfield High School that Jimmy first began to get himself in trouble. Years later he would claim that he was expelled for smart mouthing a teacher, but school records only show that he dropped out. Although he began to work alongside his father in the yard-care business, Jimmy had a greater taste for flashy clothes than he could afford, and he reportedly got involved in a few acts of burglary at retail shops. Even more seriously, in the spring of 1961 he was arrested twice in one week for the same crime of riding in a stolen car. Back in those days judges often allowed young defendants an optional out from being sentenced to jail: that of joining the military instead. By June Jimmy was sweating in basic training at Fort Ord, California, and soon after was stationed at Fort Campbell, Kentucky.

It was then that Jimmy mailed a letter to Al requesting that his Danelectro guitar be shipped down, and upon its arrival he would often practice playing it on base during his free hours. That was how he crossed paths with a bass-playing soldier named Billy Cox who heard this music from a distance and was immediately impressed by the unseen guitarist's profound technique and musical acumen, later reminiscing that it came from a creative musical space "somewhere between Beethoven and John Lee Hooker" (Shapiro and Glebbeek, pp. 60-61). The two troopers hit it off and soon formed a combo, the King Kasuals, to play gigs around the adjacent Clarksville, Tennessee area. Long-story-short: Jimmy had difficulty managing his personal finances and was always frustrating his bandmates by pawning his guitar to raise a few bucks. Worse yet, at one point he actually sold his guitar to another soldier. Upon being discharged from the 101st Airborne Division in 1962 he begged the fellow to loan it back so he could find work.

Interestingly, years later Hendrix would claim that he'd been cut loose by the army because he'd broken his ankle during a parachute-training jump. Yet in 2005 some of his military records were released under a Freedom of Information Act request (posted at TheSmokingGun.com), which reveal that the guitarist had been a rather problematic soldier -- one who, among other infractions, was "unable to conform to military rules and regulations," and was severely distracted "while performing duties" due to excessive "thinking about his guitar" -- which led to a recommendation that he be discharged under Army Regulation #635-208, the classification for "Undesirable" status.

In addition, Charles R. Cross's 2005 biography references other army medical documents that show that Jimmy actually declared himself to have homosexual tendencies (a surefire way to get mustered out early). Though Hendrix earned a bit of a reputation as a teller of tall tales, his service did finally end -- for whatever reason, or combinations thereof -- on July 2, 1962.

Upon Billy Cox's discharge around September, he and Jimmy scrambled around putting together a new lineup of the King Kasuals and aimed their sights on the black nightclub scene in Nashville. Scoring gigs at the Del Morocco and the Jolly Roger clubs the guys figured they were making inroads into the music biz, and they even reportedly hired on in support of a few soul stars including Carla Thomas, the Marvelettes, and Curtis Mayfield.

His father once recalled that at a couple points Jimmy became flush enough to afford train tickets back for visits to Seattle and it is also known that he visited his grandmother Nora in Vancouver during one Christmas season. That was where he sat in with, and briefly joined the town's top club act, Bobby Taylor, and the Vancouvers, who had an extended engagement at the Dante's Inferno venue.

Some sources have insisted that that was where the 1950s rock 'n' roll icon, Little Richard, first discovered Hendrix. What is certain is that in time the promising young guitarist would ultimately join the star's band, and tour and record ("I Don't Know What You've Got but It's Got Me") with them. Hendrix himself would later confuse the record by making some possibly fanciful claims in media interviews regarding which other stars he played with along the way -- singers like Sam Cooke and Jackie Wilson included -- but it is a fact that after winding up in New York City in early 1964 he did join the Isley Brothers band (even touring through Seattle once with them) and record a few songs including the minor radio hit, "Testify," which in hindsight contains a tantalizing little flash of his guitar-playing prowess.

Rejoining Little Richard, Jimmy ended up back on the West Coast and while in Los Angeles he played in a recording session for a girl singer, Rosa Lee Brooks, which produced another early disc with Hendrix's guitar-work, "My Diary." Then, settled back in New York City once again, Jimmy played with a few club bands including Curtis Knight and the Squires, and did recording sessions with Lonnie Youngblood -- and even one with the King Curtis Orchestra: Ray Sharpe's "Help Me," which was released by a major label, Atco Records.

In late 1965, he formed Jimmy James and the Blue Flames, and they played in various Greenwich Village coffee houses and nightclubs. Within months Jimmy's reputation as a phenomenal guitarist began to get traction. In 1966 he was spotted while performing by Linda Keith -- the British model and girlfriend to the Rolling Stone's guitarist Keith Richards.

She stepped up and invited Jimmy over to an after-gig party and discovered that the budding guitar god was actually a shy, polite, and perfectly charming young man who suffered from self-esteem issues, the lack of adequate income, and a lack of nutrition. Feeling the need to help him out, she returned to her upscale hotel room, grabbed one of Richard's Fender Stratocaster guitars and gave it to the grateful musician. In addition, Keith did everything she could to spread the word about Jimmy amongst all the British rock stars she knew.

Chas Chandler -- bassist with the Animals -- likewise agreed that Jimmy was a full-on rock star just waiting to be nurtured, packaged, and launched. He convinced Jimmy to fly with him back to London where he would quit the Animals and manage the guitarist's future career. Aboard that September 23rd flight Chandler informed his protégé that he was to be marketed with an intriguing new name: Jimi Hendrix.

Once in London, auditions were held and bass guitarist Noel Redding and drummer Mitch Mitchell were selected to form the Jimi Hendrix Experience, and gigs and tours commenced after minimal rehearsals. Rock 'n' roll was forever transformed by Hendrix's mind-blowing psychedelic guitar pyrotechnics and beautiful songwriting. The debut single, "Hey Joe," was an instant hit that was quickly followed by the ground-breaking masterpiece, "Purple Haze," and the Summer of Love classic album Are You Experienced.

Initial Brit media coverage was a mixed bag: Some critics were duly agog over the band's virtuosity, while others couldn't get over Hendrix's wild appearance and lobbed racial insults like "Mau Mau" towards the emerging star. As word began to leak back stateside, a few folks in Seattle began to puzzle as to whether this "Jimi" guitar hero was in fact, the town's own Jimmy Hendrix. That mystery was deepened when Chandler -- employing every possible opportunity to hype the musician as exotic and entirely different than any other rocker in England -- really began playing up the fact that Hendrix was an American.

In June 1967 the Jimi Hendrix Experience was booked to perform at the highly publicized Monterey International Pops Festival. It was there that their music and Jimi's stage show (famously featuring a guitar-smashing, flambe finale) catapulted them to the top of the pop charts. Within weeks the first advertisements for a Seattle concert date were published -- albeit with the majorly embarrassing typographical hometown error which announced that "Jimmy Hendricks" would soon appear at the Eagles Auditorium along with San Francisco's Moby Grape (Helix).

The year 1968 saw two additional album releases by the Jimi Hendrix Experience: Axis: Bold as Love and Electric Ladyland. Both proved to be critical and commercial successes. On February 12, 1968, Hendrix performed at the Seattle Center Arena, a venue not renowned for its acoustic qualities. Tom Robbins wrote in the Seattle countercultural newspaper Helix, "Listening to rock in the Arena is like making love in a file cabinet. It's a study in frustration." The next time the band returned to town they played on September 6, 1968, at the somewhat better Seattle Center Coliseum -- a venue they returned to on May 23, 1969.

But by June, the Experience had dissolved, and Jimi began playing with varying lineups of other musicians sometimes billed as the Gypsy Suns and Rainbows or as Sky Church (which included Billy Cox, Mitch Mitchell, and other players), which headlined the Woodstock rock festival in 1969. Jimi then formed a new trio, the Band of Gypsys, with Cox and ace drummer Buddy Miles (formerly with Akron, Ohio's soft soul hitmakers, Ruby and the Romantics).

Jimi also invested in his future by building a new facility, Electric Lady Studios, in New York City -- making him one of the very few young pop musicians to have his own recording studio. Then on July 26, 1970, he returned home to play one final gig here at Seattle's outdoor baseball park, Sicks' Stadium. Although there were reports that Hendrix held mixed feelings about his hometown, he always made a point of visiting local musician pals when visiting, and he even penned lyrics to an original song titled "West Coast Seattle Boy."

The brutal life as a rock star -- constant touring, endless hassles, over-indulging in food, drinks, and recreational drugs -- finally took its greatest toll on the man. On September 18, 1970, James "Jimi" Marshall Hendrix died at age 27 while asleep in London, not of an overdose as has been so often reported, but by choking on vomit while under the influence of barbiturates and red wine.

He was buried on October 1, 1970, at Greenwood Cemetery (today's Greenwood Memorial Park, 350 Monroe Avenue NE), in Renton, Washington. A memorial service was cancelled because of lack of time and because of official concerns about problems with crowds, but Seattle's music community came together on January 22, 1971, with a three-day tribute jam/concert with over 30 bands -- to benefit the hastily organized and scandal-plagued Jimi Hendrix Memorial Foundation -- at the Eagles Auditorium to honor a lost native son.

In retrospect Hendrix's contributions to music cannot be overstated. He was the magic missing link between existing traditional R&B forms and progressive interstellar acid rock of the Aquarian Age; the one guitarist who sent shivers of envious fear coursing through the veins of rock 'n' roll's leading guitar gods: Eric Clapton, Jeff Beck, and Pete Townshend; an undeniable instrumental genius who harnessed feedback, fuzztone, and wah-wah sounds to positive and influential effect. He was a major force in twentieth century music.

The high level of esteem his music is still held in by generations not yet born at the time of his death can be partially gauged by the estimated value of his estate -- which was reported as $40 million to $100 million back in 1995 when Al Hendrix succeeded in a legal brawl to regain control of it from various music biz entities. Since 1970 scores of books have been written about the man, movies have been screened, countless artists have covered his songs, and in June 2000 Seattle saw the Grand Opening of a $250-million music museum, the Experience Music Project, founded in honor of Jimi Hendrix.

https://www.historylink.org/file/2498

CHAPTER 38
ARETHA FRANKLIN (1942-2018)

Credit: © Colgate University

A gifted singer and pianist, Aretha Franklin toured with her father's traveling revival show and later visited New York, where she signed with Columbia Records. Franklin went on to release several popular singles, many of which are now considered classics. In 1987 she became the first female artist to be inducted into the Rock and Roll Hall of Fame, and in 2008 she won her 18th Grammy Award, making her one of the most honored artists in Grammy history.

The fourth of five children, Aretha Louise Franklin was born on March 25, 1942, in Memphis, Tennessee, to Baptist preacher Reverend Clarence La Vaughan "C. L." Franklin and Barbara Siggers Franklin, a gospel singer.

Franklin's parents separated by the time she was six, and four years later her mother succumbed to a heart attack. Guided by C. L.'s preaching assignments, the family relocated to Detroit, Michigan. C. L. eventually landed at New Bethel Baptist Church, where he gained national renown as a preacher.

Franklin's musical gifts became apparent at an early age. Largely self-taught, she was regarded as a child prodigy. A gifted pianist with a powerful voice, Franklin got her start singing in front of her father's congregation.

By the age of 14, she had recorded some of her earliest tracks at his church, which were released by a small label as the album Songs of Faith in 1956. She also performed with C. L.'s traveling revival show and, while on tour, befriended gospel greats such as Mahalia Jackson, Sam Cooke and Clara Ward.

At the age of 12, she became a mother for the first time with a son, Clarence. A second child, Edward, followed two years later — with both sons taking her family's name. Franklin would later have two more sons: Ted White, Jr. and Kecalf Cunningham.

After a brief hiatus, Franklin returned to performing and followed heroes such as Cooke and Dinah Washington into pop and blues territory. In 1960, with her father's blessing, Franklin traveled to New York, where after being courted by several labels, including Motown and RCA, she signed with Columbia Records, who released the album Aretha in 1961.

Though two tracks from Aretha would make the R&B Top 10, a bigger success came that same year with the single "Rock-a-bye Your Baby with a Dixie Melody," which crossed over to No. 37 on the pop charts.

But while Franklin enjoyed moderate results with her recordings over the next few years, they failed to fully showcase her immense talent. In 1966 she and her new husband and manager, Ted White, decided a move was in order, and Franklin signed to Atlantic. Producer Jerry Wexler immediately shuttled Franklin to the Florence Alabama Musical Emporium (FAME) recording studios.

"I Never Loved a Man (The Way, I Love You)"
Backed by the legendary Muscle Shoals Rhythm Section, Franklin recorded the single "I Never Loved a Man (The Way I Love You)." In the midst of the recording sessions, White had a fight with a member of the band, and White and Franklin left abruptly.

But as the single became a massive Top 10 hit, Franklin re-emerged in New York and was able to complete the partially recorded track, "Do Right Woman—Do Right Man."

Hitting her stride in 1967 and 1968, Franklin churned out a string of hit singles that would become enduring classics, showcasing Franklin's powerful voice and gospel roots in a pop framework.

In 1967, the album I Never Loved a Man (The Way I Love You) was released, and the first song on the album, "Respect" — an empowered cover of an Otis Redding track — reached No. 1 on both the R&B and pop charts and won Franklin her first two Grammy Awards.

She also had Top 10 hits with "Baby I Love You," "Think," "Chain of Fools," "I Say a Little Prayer," "(Sweet Sweet Baby) Since You've Been Gone" and "(You Make Me Feel Like) A Natural Woman."

Franklin's chart dominance soon earned her the title Queen of Soul, while at the same time she also became a symbol of Black empowerment during the civil rights movement.

In 1968 Franklin was enlisted to perform at the funeral of Dr. Martin Luther King Jr. during which she paid tribute to her father's fallen friend with a heartfelt rendition of "Precious Lord." Later that year, she was also selected to sing the national anthem to begin the Democratic National Convention in Chicago.

Amidst this newfound success, Franklin experienced upheaval in her personal life, and she and White divorced in 1969. But this did not slow Franklin's steady rise, and the new decade brought more hit singles, including

"Don't Play That Song," "Spanish Harlem" and her cover of Simon & Garfunkel's "Bridge Over Troubled Waters."

Spurred by Mahalia Jackson's passing and a subsequent resurgence of interest in gospel music, Franklin returned to her musical origins for the 1972 album Amazing Grace, which sold more than 2 million copies and went on to become the best-selling gospel album at the time.

Franklin's success continued throughout the 1970s, as she branched out to work with producers such as Curtis Mayfield and Quincy Jones and expanded her repertoire to include rock and pop covers. Along the way, she took home eight consecutive Grammy Awards for Best R&B Female Vocal Performance, the last coming for her 1974 single "Ain't Nothing Like the Real Thing."

But by 1975, Franklin's sound was fading into the background with the onset of the disco craze, and an emerging set of young Black singers, such as Chaka Khan and Donna Summer, began to eclipse Franklin's career.

She did, however, find a brief respite from slumping sales with the 1976 soundtrack to the Warner Brothers film Sparkle — which topped the R&B charts and made the Top 20 in pop — as well as an invitation to perform at the 1977 presidential inauguration of Jimmy Carter. In 1978 she also married actor Glynn Turman.

A string of chart failures ended Franklin's relationship with Atlantic in 1979. The same year, her father was hospitalized after a burglary attempt in his home left him in a coma. As her popularity waned and her father's health declined, Franklin was also saddled with a massive bill from the IRS.

However, a cameo in the 1980 film The Blues Brothers helped Franklin revive her flagging career. Performing "Think" alongside comedians John Belushi and Dan Aykroyd exposed her to a new generation of R&B lovers, and she soon signed to Arista Records.

Her new label released 1982's Jump To It, an album that enjoyed huge success on the R&B charts and earned Franklin a Grammy nomination. Two years later, she endured a divorce from Turman as well as the death of her father.

In 1985 Franklin returned to the top of the charts with a smash-hit album: the polished pop record Who's Zoomin' Who? Featuring the single "Freeway of Love," as well as a collaboration with the popular rock band The

Eurythmics, the record became Franklin's biggest-selling album yet.

Her follow-up, 1986's Aretha, also charted well and eventually went gold, and her duet with British singer George Michael, "I Knew You Were Waiting (For Me)," hit No. 1 on the pop charts.

In 1987 Franklin became the first female artist to be inducted into the Rock and Roll Hall of Fame and was also awarded an honorary doctorate from the University of Detroit. That same year, she released the album One Lord, One Faith, One Baptism, which won the Grammy for Best Soul Gospel Performance.

Following another relatively quiet period in her career, in 1993, Franklin was invited to sing at the inauguration of Bill Clinton, and the following year she received both a Grammy Lifetime Achievement Award and Kennedy Center Honors. She would also be the focus of multiple documentaries and tributes as the decade progressed.

Nearing its conclusion, Franklin reprised her former role in Blues Brothers 2000, released the gold-selling "A Rose Is Still a Rose" and stood in for Luciano Pavarotti, who was too ill to accept his Lifetime Achievement Award, with her rendition of "Nessun Dorma" commanding stellar reviews.

In 2003 Franklin released her final studio album on Arista, So Damn Happy, and left the label to found Aretha Records. Two years later, she was awarded the Presidential Medal of Freedom and became the second woman ever to be inducted into the UK Music Hall of Fame.

In 2008 she received her 18th Grammy Award for "Never Gonna Break My Faith" — a collaboration with Mary J. Blige — and was tapped to sing at the 2009 presidential inauguration of Barack Obama.

With 18 Grammys under her belt, Franklin is one of the most honored artists in Grammy history, ranked among the likes of Alison Krauss, Adele, and Beyoncé Knowles. In 2011 Franklin released her first album on her own label, A Woman Falling Out of Love.

To support the project, she performed several concerts, including a two-night stint at the famed Radio City Music Hall in New York. With fans and critics alike impressed with her performances, she successfully proved that the Queen of Soul still reigned supreme.

In 2014 Franklin underscored that point with Aretha Franklin Sings the

Great Diva Classics, which reached No. 13 on the pop charts and No. 3 R&B.

In February 2017, the 74-year-old Queen of Soul told Detroit radio station WDIV Local 4 that she was collaborating with Stevie Wonder to release a new album.

"I must tell you, I am retiring this year," she said in the interview, adding: "I feel very, very enriched and satisfied with respect to where my career came from and where it is now. I'll be pretty much satisfied, but I'm not going to go anywhere and just sit down and do nothing. That wouldn't be good either."

On August 12, 2018, it was reported that a "gravely ill" Franklin was bedridden in her Detroit home, surrounded by family and friends. As news of her condition spread, more luminaries paid a visit to express their well wishes, including Wonder and Jesse Jackson.

Four days later, on the morning of August 16, Franklin succumbed to her illness, which her family revealed to be pancreatic cancer.

A public viewing was held later that month at the Charles H. Wright Museum of African American History in Detroit, with fans camping out overnight for the chance to pay their respects to the iconic singer. Her televised funeral was set to be held at the city's Greater Grace Temple on August 31, with Wonder, Khan and Hudson among the scheduled performers, and Jackson, Clinton and Smokey Robinson highlighting the list of speakers.

In January 2018, it was announced that Franklin hand-picked singer and actress Jennifer Hudson to play her in an upcoming biopic. After being pushed back several times, Respect will be released on August 13, 2021.

https://www.biography.com/musician/aretha-franklin

CHAPTER 39
ARTHUR ASHE (1943-1993)

Credit: Nationaal Archief Fotocollectie Anefo Item number 927-7839

In 1968, the first-year amateurs and professionals could compete against each other in major events, the US Open was won by Arthur Ashe, a man who enjoyed a storied career between the lines and a dignified life as an ambassador of equality and goodwill; a life that tragically ended in 1993 after he contracted HIV from a blood transfusion following heart bypass surgery.

Younger generations of tennis fans may only recognize Ashe's name as the one that adorns the stadium at the Billie Jean King National Tennis Center at Flushing Meadows, NY, site of the US Open, or that starting in 1993 the USTA has kicked off the tournament with Arthur Ashe Kids' Day, a remembrance and celebration of the sport's most elegant and thoughtful ambassador. Ashe rose from segregation and racial roadblocks to become the first Black American male to win the US Open (1968), Australian Open (1970), and Wimbledon (1975). In 1963 he was the first Black American chosen to play Davis Cup for the United States, and in ten years representing his country, helped the US win five championships (1963, 1968, 1969, 1970, 1978).

Ashe was much more than a storied tennis player; he was an activist, author, educator, and a tireless campaigner for civil rights and racial equality, not only in the United States but worldwide, particularly against the apartheid systems of South Africa. "Arthur was a voice for all the minorities, and that goes for women, too," Pam Shriver told the New York Times in Ashe's obituary. "He brought a level of conscience to the game, whether he was speaking on South Africa or inner-city minorities or exclusionary policies anyplace. Arthur's influence on tennis didn't fade after he left the sport." Further evidence of Ashe's convictions came in 1972, when helped found the Association of Tennis Professionals (ATP), the organization that unionized the professional tour and protected the interests of its players.

On sunny August 29th in 1968, Ashe, then 25, became an unlikely US Open champion amongst a field that included four Australians who were all seeded ahead of him: Rod Laver, Tony Roche, Ken Rosewall, and John Newcombe. Having won the United States Amateur Championships over Bob Lutz at the Longwood Cricket Club in Boston earlier that summer earned Ashe the No. 5 seed. He was under no pressure to win the championship; that was reserved for the Aussies. At the time, he was in the midst of a three-year Army stint, and expectations were low. In the finals, Ashe defeated an unforeseen counterpart in Dutchman Tom Okker, seeded No. 8, who was also on a magical run. Ashe had won his previous three matches in straight sets and had secured a bit of luck when his quarterfinal opponent Cliff Drysdale upset Laver in the fourth round. The final played out in five-marathon sets – the first five-setter Ashe faced at the Open – 14-

12, 5-7, 6-3, 3-6, 6-3. The cornerstone of Ashe's game, serving and volleying, was magnificent that afternoon. He pounded 26 aces against Okker, and his whipping backhand was flawless – angled perfectly on crosscourt shots and crisply executed at the net.

"Arthur could beat any player on a given day or he could lose to a bad player if he was mishitting," recalled his Davis Cup captain Donald Dell. "All the elements fell in place. There were a lot of upsets, and he just took advantage of the opportunity."

Ashe had become the first American to win at Forest Hills since Tony Trabert in 1955, but the victory was somewhat bittersweet. At the time, Ashe was still an amateur and receiving a per diem as a member of the Davis Cup team, meaning he couldn't accept the $14,000 prize, which went to Okker. If there was any solace for Ashe after missing out on his first professional paycheck, on December 12, 1968, he became the No. 1 ranked U.S. player by the United States Lawn Tennis Association. He had a stellar 1968 season, helping to lead the U.S. Davis Cup team to the championship with a decisive 4-1 victory over Australia, which ended a five-year losing drought.

Born in Richmond, Virginia, Ashe began playing tennis at age 7 on courts at Brookfield Park, a segregated playground adjacent to his home. Seven years later he found a mentor in Hall of Famer Dr. Robert Johnson, who for two decades had assisted black tennis prodigies, including Althea Gibson. Even as a youth, Ashe was a cerebral player and Johnson's guidance was instrumental on how his pupil comported himself on the court. His on-court etiquette was among the finest in tennis history. His high school interscholastic career started at Maggie L. Walter High School, but was completed at Summer High School in St. Louis, where he could face stronger competition.

As the No. 5 ranked junior in the country, Ashe won the National Junior Indoor Championship in 1962 and was awarded a full scholarship to the University of California at Los Angeles. As a student at UCLA, Ashe attracted the attention of both Pancho Gonzales and Pancho Segura, who helped refine his game and encourage experimentation. He won both the NCAA Division I singles and doubles championships in 1965, defeating Mike Belkin of the University of Miami, 6-4, 6-1, 6-1 in singles and teaming with Ian Crookened to capture the doubles title. With Ashe in tow, the Bruins won the 1965 NCCA team championship.

Starting in 1959, when he made his major tournament debut at the U.S. Nationals, Ashe played twenty years, retiring in 1979. He was a fixture at the

U.S. Nationals/US Open, playing 18 times and earning a 53-17 record, the best of the four majors. He was a semifinalist in 1965 (losing to champion Manuel Santana 2-6, 6-4, 6-2, 6-4) and a finalist in 1972 (losing to Ilie Năstase in a sensational match that saw Năstase erase a 2-1 sets deficit, 3-6, 6-3, 6-7, 6-4, 6-3).

Ashe only competed at the Australian Nationals/Open six times, but became the first African-American to win the title in 1970, defeating five Aussies, including Dick Crealy in the final, 6-4, 9-7, 6-2. He earned his semifinal win when fellow American Dennis Ralston retired down 2-1 sets in the fourth. Ashe also was a finalist in 1966, 1967, and 1971, losing to Roy Emerson the first two years and Rosewall in 1971 as the defending champion. The red clay at Roland Garros was not especially suited for Ashe's game; he was a quarterfinalist twice (1970, 1971), but the fast grass at Wimbledon was a surface that appealed to his attacking, serve-and-volley style.

Ashe had been a semifinalist at Wimbledon in 1968 and 1969, and when he defeated No. 1 seed and heavy favorite Jimmy Connors in 1975, it was a throwback to his US Open championship run seven years earlier. The Wimbledon field was stacked with Connors, Rosewall, Björn Borg, Guillermo Vilas, and Năstase, all seeded higher. Ashe, nearing his 32nd birthday, had never defeated Connors in three previous meetings and was seeking his first Wimbledon title. His draw became more favorable as the fortnight progressed, Năstase out in the second round, Rosewall a fourth-round casualty, and Vilas ousted in the quarterfinals. He upset Borg in the quarterfinals and needed to prevail in five long sets against Roche in the semifinals. The final against Connors saw Ashe play perhaps his finest strategic and athletic match in a huge upset, 6-1, 6-1, 5-7, 6-4. His lateral movement on the baseline that afternoon was swift yet controlled; Connors had few openings to slip balls past his opponent. Ashe sliced his backhand low and deep, mixed up his pace, placed lobs effectively; instead of booming big first serves, he sliced his serve wide to both Connors's backhand and forehand and charged the net. His volleys were on point and the victory ranks as one of Wimbledon's biggest upsets. "I always thought I could win," Ashe said afterwards. "I was pretty confident. I had been playing well."

The years that Ashe won his upset-laden major singles titles were his finest. In 1968 he won 10 of 22 tournaments he entered and compiled a 72-10 match record. In 1975 he was even better – winning eight of 26 tournaments with a 97-18 record. Ashe defeated Borg at the Dallas WCT Finals, 3–6, 6–4, 6–4, 6–0.

He won a pair of major doubles titles, the first at the French in 1971 alongside Marty Riessen in a lengthy 6-8, 4-6, 6-3, 6-4, 11-9 victory over fellow Americans Tom Gorman and Stan Smith and a second in straight sets at the 1977 Australian with partner Tony Roche.

Ashe spent ten years ranked in the world's Top 10, rising to No. 2 in 1976.

In 1979, at age 36, Ashe suffered his first heart attack that required bypass surgery and led to his retirement. He suffered a second heart attack and subsequent bypass surgery in 1983, which he widely believed led to him contracting HIV in 1988. The prideful Ashe didn't disclose he had the disease until April 1992, wanting to make the announcement on his terms, but news leaks forced his announcement. At the end of 1992, Sports Illustrated named him its Sportsman of the Year, and a year later he created the Arthur Ashe Foundation for the Defeat of AIDS.

Ashe's health issues ended his storied tennis career, but jumpstarted his philanthropic, humanitarian, civic, and activist endeavors, which occupied his life for a decade. In 1988, he helped develop inner-city tennis programs and co-founded the National Junior Tennis League in New York City, Newark, Detroit, Atlanta, Kansas City, and Indianapolis. That same year he published his three-volume 1,600-page treatise A Hard Road to Glory: A history of the Black American athlete. He earned an Emmy for co-writing the television adaptation of the book.

The soft-spoken but highly principled Ashe has been showered with honors, tributes, and accolades in life and death. Among the most prominent came in 1993 when he was posthumously awarded the Presidential Medal of Freedom by President Bill Clinton. ESPN's ESPY Awards presents the Arthur Ashe Courage Award to a person in the sports world that exhibits courage in the face of adversity. His alma mater, UCLA opened The Arthur Ashe Student Health and Wellness Center in 1997. In 2007, USA Today listed Ashe as one of the Most Inspiring People of the Last 25 Years.

On his website, Ashe is quoted as saying, "Regardless of how you feel inside, always try to look like a winner. Even if you're behind, a sustained look of control and confidence can give you a mental edge that results in victory."

https://www.tennisfame.com/hall-of-famers/inductees/arthur-ashe

CHAPTER 40
DIANA ROSS (1944-PRESENT)

Credit: Courtesy Netherlands National Archives

Diana Ross began singing with friends as a teenager, and eventually formed the groundbreaking 1960s trio the Supremes, going on to have hits like "Come See About Me" and "You Can't Hurry Love." Ross left for a solo career in 1969, later reaching No. 1 with hits like "Ain't No Mountain High Enough" and "Love Hangover." She starred in the films Mahogany and Lady Sings the Blues as well, earning an Oscar nomination for the latter. Despite personal and professional ups and downs, Ross has withstood the test of time as a performer with a career that spans more than four decades.

Ross was born on March 26, 1944, in Detroit, Michigan. Developing a reputation as an accomplished performer, Ross began singing in the group the Primettes with friends Mary Wilson, Florence Ballard, and Barbara Martin as a teenager. Martin eventually dropped out, but the remaining members of the group went on to become the internationally successful 1960s R&B and pop trio the Supremes (later named Diana Ross and the Supremes).

Signed to Motown Records by famed producer and label founder Berry Gordy Jr., in 1961 the Supremes scored their first No. 1 hit with "Where Did Our Love Go?" (1964). The trio then broke music records by having a streak of four additional singles top the charts — "Baby Love" (1964), "Come See About Me" (1964) "Stop! In the Name of Love" (1965) and "Back in My Arms Again" (1965) — thus becoming the first U.S. group ever to have five songs in a row to reach No 1.

In all the group scored a monumental 12 No. 1 hits, including "I Hear a Symphony" (1965), "You Can't Hurry Love" (1966), "The Happening" (1967), "Love Child" (1968) and "Someday We'll Be Together" (1969). They thus established a phenomenal record, becoming the American vocal group with the most Billboard chart-toppers in history.

Ross left the Supremes for a solo career in 1969 and continued to be a musical mainstay the following year with the Top 20 "Reach Out and Touch Somebody's Hand" and the No. 1 "Ain't No Mountain High Enough."

Among an array of albums, other hit songs for Ross from the 1970s included "Touch Me in the Morning" (1973), "Theme From Mahogany (Do You Know Where You're Going To)" (1976) and sensual dance classic "Love Hangover" (1976), with all three tracks reaching No. 1 on the pop charts.

In 1972, she branched out into acting and starred in the Billie Holiday biopic Lady Sings the Blues. While the film received somewhat mixed reviews, Ross's performance garnered her an Academy Award nomination for Best Actress. The Blues soundtrack was a huge success and helped spurn new interest in Holiday as well. Ross went on to star in the films Mahogany (1975), co-starring Billy Dee Williams and Anthony Perkins, and The Wiz (1978).

The next decade started out on a strong note for Ross with the Nile Rodgers-produced, platinum-selling album Diana (1980), featuring the No. 1 hit "Upside Down" as well as the Top 5 track "I'm Coming Out." She had another Top 10 single with "It's My Turn" and then reached No. 1 again, this time with Lionel Richie on the 1981 duet "Endless Love," from the film of the same name.

On her new record label RCA, Ross released the albums Why Do Fools Fall in Love (1981), which offered two more Top 10 hits, and Silk Electric (1982), which had the Top 10 single "Muscles," written by Michael Jackson. Ross's sales gradually faltered, but she continued to record and perform. Returning to Motown Records near the end of the 1980s, she released the albums Workin' Overtime (1989) and The Force Behind the Power (1991), the latter having significant international success with its singles.

Albums put forth by Ross in the new millennium included Blue (2006), a jazz standard set taken from Motown's archives, and I Love You (2007), a collection of mostly pop covers.

In the 1990s, Ross made several appearances on the small screen. She starred in the 1994 television movie Out of Darkness, playing a woman with schizophrenia. Ross then took on lighter fare with Double Platinum (1999), starring as a famous singer who had abandoned her child to pursue her career. Well-known pop performer Brandy played her daughter. Some of the songs from the project were featured on Ross's 1999 album, Every Day Is a New Day.

Ross has also experienced personal difficulties. She got into a dispute with a security guard in 1999 at London's Heathrow Airport, and as a result was arrested and detained for four hours before being released. In late 2002, she was arrested for driving under the influence in Tucson, Arizona, for which she later was briefly sentenced to jail.

In 2000, Ross launched a Supremes tour, which was highly criticized for excluding original member Wilson and later addition Cindy Birdsong, with there being talks of financial disputes between Ross' and Wilson's camps. After experiencing low attendance, the tour was canceled following a short run.

In 2007, Ross suffered a great personal loss. Her father, Fred, died in November of that year. "He touched many lives, and he will be truly missed. I loved him very much," Diana Ross said in a statement. On tour at the time, she returned home to Detroit to be with her family.

Despite her personal and professional ups and downs, Ross has withstood the test of time as a performer with a career that spans more than four decades. She has won several major awards, including a Golden Globe, a Tony, and several American Music Awards. Ross was inducted into the Rock and Roll Hall of Fame in 1988 as part of the Supremes.

Ross was awarded for her hard work again in 2007 when she was presented with Black Entertainment Television's Lifetime Achievement Award. Also, that year, a few weeks after her father's death, Ross was honored by the Kennedy Center for her contributions to the arts. Vocalist Smokey Robinson and actor Terrence Howard were on hand to provide tributes to the superstar, and Ciara, Vanessa Williams and Jordin Sparks paid homage to Ross in song. In 2009, Ross jumped back into the limelight when it was revealed that pop icon Michael Jackson had requested the diva as an alternate guardian for his children.

In 2012 Ross received a Grammy Award for Lifetime Achievement; it would become her first Grammy ever, despite having been nominated twelve times. Four years later, Ross received the Presidential Medal of Freedom from Barack Obama, the nation's highest civilian honor. In 2017, she added to her collection with Lifetime Achievement honors at the American Music Awards.

Ross has been married twice: In 1971 she wed music business manager Robert Ellis Silberstein. After their divorce, she was married to Norwegian tycoon Arne Næss Jr. from 1986 to 1999. The legendary singer is the mother of five children: Rhonda (whom Ross had with Gordy Jr.), Tracee (of Girlfriends and Black-ish fame), Chudney, Ross, and Evan.

https://www.biography.com/musician/diana-ross

CHAPTER 41
ANGELA DAVIS (1944-PRESENT)

Credit: ARound Robin Production Company.

Educator, activist, and author Angela Davis became known for her involvement in a politically charged murder case in the early 1970s. Influenced by her segregated upbringing in Birmingham, Alabama, Davis joined the Black Panthers and an all-Black branch of the Communist Party as a young woman. She became a professor at UCLA but fell out of favor with the administration due to her ties. Davis was charged with aiding the botched escape attempt of imprisoned Black radical George Jackson and served roughly 18 months in jail before her acquittal in 1972. After spending time traveling and lecturing, Davis returned to the classroom as a professor and authored several books.

Angela Yvonne Davis is best known as a radical Black American educator and activist for civil rights and other social issues. She was born on January 26, 1944, in Birmingham, Alabama to Sallye and Frank Davis, an elementary school teacher and the owner of a service station, respectively. Davis knew about racial prejudice from a young age; her neighborhood in Birmingham was nicknamed "Dynamite Hill" for the number of homes targeted by the Ku Klux Klan. As a teenager, Davis organized interracial study groups, which were broken up by the police. She also knew several of the young Black girls killed in the Birmingham church bombing of 1963.

Angela Davis later moved north and went to Brandeis University in Massachusetts where she studied philosophy with Herbert Marcuse. As a graduate student at the University of California, San Diego, in the late 1960s, she joined several groups, including the Black Panthers. But she spent most of her time working with the Che-Lumumba Club, which was all-Black branch of the Communist Party.

Hired to teach at the University of California, Los Angeles, Angela Davis ran into trouble with the school's administration because of her association with communism. They fired her, but she fought them in court and got her job back. Davis still ended up leaving when her contract expired in 1970.

Outside of academia, Angela Davis had become a strong supporter of three prison inmates of Soledad Prison known as the Soledad brothers (they were not related). These three men—John W. Cluchette, Fleeta Drumgo, and George Lester Jackson—were accused of killing a prison guard after several Black inmates had been killed in a fight by another guard. Some thought these prisoners were being used as scapegoats because of the political work within the prison.

During Jackson's trial in August 1970, an escape attempt was made when Jackson's brother Jonathan entered the courtroom to claim hostages he could exchange for his brother. Jonathan Jackson, Superior Court Judge Harold Haley, and two inmates were killed in the ensuing shoot-out.

Angela Davis was brought up on several charges for her alleged part in the event, including murder. She went into hiding and was one of the FBI's "Most Wanted" before being caught two months later. There were two main pieces of evidence used at trial: the guns used were registered to her, and she was reportedly in love with Jackson. Her case drew the attention of the international press and after spending roughly 18 months in jail, Davis was acquitted in June 1972.

After spending time traveling and lecturing, Angela Davis returned to teaching. She served as a Distinguished Professor Emerita at the University of California, Santa Cruz, before retiring in 2008. Davis is the author of several books, including Women, Race, and Class (1980), Blues Legacies and Black Feminism: Gertrude Ma Rainey, Bessie Smith, and Billie Holiday (1999), Are Prisons Obsolete? (2003), Abolition Democracy: Beyond Empire, Prisons, and Torture (2005), The Meaning of Freedom: And Other Difficult Dialogues (2012) and Freedom Is a Constant Struggle: Ferguson, Palestine, and the Foundations of a Movement (2016).

https://www.history.com/topics/black-history/angela-davis

CHAPTER 42
ALICE WALKER (1944-PRESENT)

Born to sharecropper parents, Alice Walker grew up to become a highly acclaimed novelist, essayist, and poet. She is best known for her 1982 novel The Color Purple, which won the 1983 Pulitzer Prize for Fiction and soon was adapted for the big screen by Steven Spielberg. Walker is also known for her work as an activist.

Alice Malsenior Walker was born on February 9, 1944, in Eatonton, Georgia. The youngest daughter of sharecroppers, she grew up poor, with her mother working as a maid to help support the family's eight children.

At 8 years old, Walker was shot in the right eye with a BB pellet while playing with two of her brothers. Whitish scar tissue formed in her damaged eye, and she became self-conscious of this visible mark.

After the incident, Walker largely withdrew from the world around her. "For a long time, I thought I was very ugly and disfigured," she told John O'Brien in an interview that was published in Alice Walker: Critical Perspectives, Past and Present (1993). "This made me shy and timid, and I often reacted to insults and slights that were not intended." She found solace in reading and writing poetry.

Living in the racially divided South, Walker showcased a bright mind at her segregated schools, graduating from high school as class valedictorian.

With the help of a scholarship, Walker was able to attend Spelman College in Atlanta. She later switched to Sarah Lawrence College in New York. While at Sarah Lawrence, Walker visited Africa as part of a study-abroad program. She graduated in 1965—the same year that she published her first short story.

After college, Walker worked as a social worker, teacher, and lecturer. She became active in the civil rights movement, fighting for equality for all Black Americans.

Walker's experiences informed her first collection of poetry, Once, which was published in 1968. Better known now as a novelist, Walker showed her talents for storytelling in her debut work, Third Life of Grange Copeland (1970).

Walker continued to explore writing in all of its forms. In 1973, she published the poetry collection Revolutionary Petunias and the short story collection In Love and Trouble, which included the highly acclaimed "Everyday Use." The following year, she delivered her first children's book, Langston Hughes: American Poet. Walker also emerged as a prominent voice in the Black feminist movement.

Walker's career as a writer took flight with the publication of her third novel, The Color Purple, in 1982. Set in the early 1900s, the novel explores the Black American female experience through the life and struggles of its narrator, Celie. Celie suffers terrible abuse at the hands of her father, and later, from her husband. The compelling work won Walker both the Pulitzer Prize for Fiction and the National Book Award for Fiction in 1983.

In 1985, Walker's story made it to the big screen: Spielberg directed The Color Purple, which starred Whoopi Goldberg as Celie, as well as Oprah Winfrey and Danny Glover. Like the novel, the movie was a critical success, receiving 11 Academy Award nominations. Walker explored her own feelings about the film in her 1996 work, The Same River Twice: Honoring the Difficult. In 2005, The Color Purple became a Broadway musical.

Walker incorporated characters and their relations from The Color Purple into two of her other novels: The Temple of My Familiar (1989) and Possessing the Secret of Joy (1992), which earned great critical praise and caused some controversy for its exploration of the practice of female genital mutilation.

In 1998, Walker published her first novel in six years, By the Light of My Father's Smile. Next up was the short story collection The Way Forward Is with a Broken Heart (2000).

Proving time and time again to be a versatile writer, Walker followed with the novel Now Is the Time to Open Your Heart (2004), the essay collection We Are the Ones We Have Been Waiting For: Light in a Time of Darkness (2006) and the well-received picture book There Is a Flower at the Tip of My Nose Smelling Me (2006).

Walker also wrote about her experiences with the group Women for Women International in 2010's Overcoming Speechlessness: A Poet Encounters the Horror in Rwanda, Eastern Congo, and Palestine/Israel. She published another poetry collection, Hard Times Require Furious Dancing, that same year.

After more than four decades as a writer, Walker shows no signs of slowing down. In 2012, she released The Chicken Chronicles; in this latest memoir, she ruminates on caring for her flock of chickens. The following year, she published Cushion in the Road: Meditation and Wandering As the Whole World Awakens to Being in Harm's Way and the poetry collection

The World Will Follow Joy: Turning Madness into Flowers.

According to Walker's website, her books have been translated into more than two dozen languages and sold more than 15 million copies.

Through her involvement in civil rights activism, Walker met the New York City-born Jewish lawyer Melvyn Leventhal. Following their marriage in 1967, they became the first legally married interracial couple to live in Mississippi. The two had one daughter, Rebecca, before divorcing in 1976.

Walker later dated both men and women, including singer Tracy Chapman. She was also known for publicly feuding with her daughter, who described how she was neglected by her writer mom in her memoir Black, White, and Jewish: Autobiography of a Shifting Self (2000).

Along with her Pulitzer and National Book Award, Walker has been honored with the O. Henry Award and the Mahmoud Darwish Literary Prize for Fiction. Additionally, she was inducted into the California Hall of Fame in 2006 and received the LennonOno Peace Award in 2010.

In 2007, Walker's personal papers were made available to the public at Emory University in Georgia. In 2013, she was the subject of the acclaimed documentary Alice Walker: Beauty In Truth.

https://www.biography.com/writer/alice-walker

CHAPTER 43
CLARENCE THOMAS (1948-PRESENT)

Credit: The Oyez Project

Clarence Thomas is known for his quiet, stoic demeanor during oral arguments and his conservative viewpoint that challenges, if not surpasses, even Scalia's originalism. Thomas was born in a small town outside of Savannah, Georgia on June 23, 1948. His father left him, his older sister, and his mother two years later. His mother struggled to make ends meet as a single working mother, especially after giving birth to another son after Thomas' father left. After a fire left his family homeless, Thomas was sent to live with his maternal grandfather. Thomas' grandfather was his most influential role model. He ran several of his own businesses and instilled in Thomas a sense of discipline and strength. When Thomas was sixteen, he fought to earn admittance into a boarding school seminary to pursue his dream of becoming a Catholic priest. He was the first black student admitted to St. John Vianney and felt the pressure of being the sole representative of his race during his time there. Thomas had excellent grades but struggled with the racially charged bullying he endured. In 1967, Thomas entered Conception Seminary at the college level. At this stage in his education, Thomas struggled with the passive stance the Catholic Church had taken in addressing civil rights. He decided to abandon his dream of becoming a priest soon after Martin Luther King, Jr.'s assassination in 1968.

Thomas transferred to College of the Holy Cross and graduated in 1971 with a bachelor's degree in English Literature and a passion for civil rights that drove him to pursue a career in law. He attended Yale Law School as one of the first students to benefit from the open admissions program that offered positions to black students in all-white colleges. Years later, Thomas would grow to abhor affirmative action, as hiring partners and other white colleagues would credit his accomplishments not to hard work and dedication, but to the color of his skin and the measures schools took to recruit black students. Upon graduation, Thomas began working in the office of the Missouri Attorney General after being admitted to the Missouri bar in 1974. In 1977, he worked for Senator John C. Danforth as his legislative assistant. After four years working with Danforth, President Reagan appointed Thomas as the Assistant Secretary for Civil Rights in the U.S. Department of Education. A year later, Reagan propelled his career even further by appointing him Chairman of the U.S. Equal Employment Opportunity Commission. By this point in Thomas' life, he was still living with severe debt from student loans, an issue made worse by his addiction to alcohol. Once Thomas decided he could no longer afford to drink as he did, he quit drinking all together. Thomas served at the EEOC for eight years, and in 1990, President George H. W. Bush nominated Thomas to the U.S. Court of Appeals for the District of Columbia circuit.

As a 43-year-old with barely one year of experience on the judiciary under his belt, Clarence Thomas was quite young and inexperienced when George H. W. Bush nominated him to the Supreme Court in 1991. Thomas experienced a particularly rigorous and dramatic round of Senate hearings. A former employee at the EEOC, Anita Hill, accused him of sexual harassment. After the FBI investigated and returned with an inconclusive report, the Senate initially decided not to pursue the report and continued with the hearings. The accusation was leaked to the press, and women's rights groups across America demanded that the Senate further investigate the matter. Anita Hill was called to testify in front of the Senate. Thomas denied all the allegations and spoke out against the unprofessional nature of the proceedings. Eventually, the Senate confirmed Thomas in October 1991 by the narrowest margin in a century.

Clarence Thomas is the second black justice to serve on the Court. As a Supreme Court justice, Thomas is notorious for his lack of questions during oral arguments. While many justices use questions to show their opinion on an issue or communicate with the other justices as to their feelings on a case, Thomas remains silent – but that does not hinder the other justices from discerning his thoughts. His reputation of conservativism guides their predictions. He has shown his opinions to lean farther right than any other justice on the bench today. Though Thomas is known for his lack of engagement in the oral arguments, his intellect is indispensable to his conservative cohorts. He contributed heavily both to Scalia's opinion in District of Columbia v. Heller, a gun control case, and Kennedy's opinion in Citizens United v. Federal Election Commission, a major campaign finance law case. Thomas also penned the conservative majority decision in Good News Club v. Milford Central School, where he stated that the public school violated the First Amendment when it refused to allow a religious club from meeting there. He also wrote a dissent in Gonzales v. Raich that exhibited his relative ease at overturning decades of precedent. The Gonzales case focused on the Commerce Clause powers granted to Congress in the Constitution and whether they reach so far as to allow regulation of a woman growing medicinal marijuana for personal use as granted by her home state. Thomas argued that allowing the Commerce Clause and congressional regulation to reach into a situation where there was no direct connection to commerce was unconstitutional.

https://www.oyez.org/justices/clarence_thomas

CHAPTER 44
STEVIE WONDER (1950-PRESENT)

Credit:@discogs.com

Stevie Wonder made his recording debut at age 11, becoming a 1960s force to be reckoned with via chart hits like "Fingertips, Pt. 2," "I Was Made to Love Her" and "My Cherie Amour." Over the next decade, Wonder had an array of No. 1 songs on the pop and R&B charts, including "Superstition," "You Are the Sunshine of My Life" and "Higher Ground." He continued to churn out hits into the 1980s, including "I Just Called to Say I Love You" and "Part-Time Lover."

Wonder was born Stevland Hardaway Judkins on May 13, 1950, in Saginaw, Michigan. He was born six weeks early with retinopathy of prematurity, an eye disorder which was exacerbated when he received too much oxygen in an incubator, leading to blindness. Wonder showed an early gift for music, first with a church choir in Detroit, Michigan, where he and his family had moved to when he was four years old, and later with a range of instruments, including the harmonica, piano, and drums, all of which he taught himself before age 10. Wonder was just 11 years old when he was discovered by Ronnie White of the Motown band The Miracles. An audition followed with Motown founder Berry Gordy Jr., who didn't hesitate to sign the young musician to a record deal.

In 1962, the newly renamed Little Stevie Wonder, working with Motown songwriter Clarence Paul, among others, released his debut The Jazz Soul of Little Stevie Wonder, an instrumental album that showed off the youngster's remarkable musicianship. The same year he also released Tribute to Uncle Ray, where Wonder covered the songs of soul icon Ray Charles. Wonder then developed a major audience with Little Stevie Wonder the 12-Year-Old Genius, an album recorded live. The set's edited single "Fingertips, Pt. 2" became Wonder's first No. 1 song, reaching the top of both the R&B and pop charts.

Rather than rest on his laurels, the hard-working Wonder, who would go on to study classical piano, pushed to improve his musicianship and songwriting capabilities. After dropping "Little" from his stage name in the mid-1960s, he churned out the top 5 pop single "Uptight (Everything's Alright)," which reached No. 1 on the R&B charts. Wonder scored two more No. 1 R&B hits with a cover of Bob Dylan's "Blowin' in the Wind" and the jubilant "I Was Made to Love Her," with the latter reaching No. 2 on the pop charts. The 1968 album For Once in My Life offered even more successful singles with the title track, "Shoo-Be-Doo-Be-Doo-Da-Day" and "You Met Your Match," with Wonder serving as co-writer on all three songs. The following year saw the release of My Cherie Amour, with the romantic top 5 pop/R&B title ballad as well as the top 5 R&B "Yester-Me, Yester-You, Yesterday." Wonder would remain a consistent hitmaker over the next two decades, with the artist co-producing 1970's Signed, Sealed, Delivered; the album featured the No. 1 R&B title track and a top 5 R&B cover of the Beatles' "We Can Work It Out."

Due in part to innate talent, but also because of his deep commitment to his craft, Wonder faced the difficulty of staying relevant as a musician as he grew from boy to man, and his voice matured into a shining tenor. In 1971, Wonder negotiated a new contract with Motown that gave him almost total control over his records and greatly increased his royalty rate. It was an unprecedented concession by Gordy, but, artistically, just what Wonder needed. As the 1970s unfolded, the musician went through an unrivaled period of production. 1971's Where I'm Coming From, with its groovy top 10 single "If You Really Love Me," marked the first time Wonder had writing or co-writing credits for every song on an album.

1972's Music of My Mind offered the top 20 R&B/top 40 pop single "Superwoman (Where Were You When I Needed You)," an emotionally rich jazz-soul opus that highlighted Wonder's pioneering work in synthesized/electronic sounds. His 1972 album Talking Book offered two No. 1 hits, the jaunty funk jam "Superstition" and "You Are the Sunshine of My Life," a smile-inducing ode to love that exemplified Wonder's abilities as a romanticist. Next up was Innervisions, a meditative concept album that was simultaneously introspective, political, critical and full of wit. The record featured two socially conscious No. 1 R&B hits, "Higher Ground" and "Living for the City," as well as the humorous "Don't You Worry 'Bout a Thing," which reached No. 2 on the R&B chart. All three singles fared well on the pop charts as well.

Fulfillingness' First Finale, released after Wonder had survived a serious car accident that left him in a coma, displayed his trademark odes to romance and beauty while also looking squarely at spirituality and death. Wonder created a song that railed against President Richard Nixon—"You Haven't Done Nothin'," which reached No. 1 on both the pop and R&B charts and featured The Jackson 5. The sexy "Boogie on Reggae Woman" went to No. 1 on the pop chart as well, while the album tracks "Creepin'" and "They Won't Go When I Go" were eventually covered by Luther Vandross and George Michael, respectively.

Even with this array of accomplishments, it was the double album with EP set Songs in the Key of Life that many have hailed as Wonder's most legendary project and one of the greatest records of all time. Offering a rich span of songs with genre fusions aplenty, Songs covered everything from ethnic diversity in the U.S. and fantastic utopian communities to vengeful relationships and transcendent love. Songs had two pop/R&B No. 1 singles, both uptempo: the Duke Ellington tribute "Sir Duke" and the back-in-the-day paean "I Wish." Wonder had additional top 40 hits with "Another Star" and "As," while the harmonica laden "Isn't She Lovely," though not a charting single, nonetheless became a radio mainstay as it heralded the cherished birth of a daughter.

During this era, Wonder was working with other artists as well, including Minnie Riperton (the mother of Maya Rudolph) and the band Rufus, with Chaka Khan's vocals heard on the Wonder-penned top 5 track "Tell Me Something Good." Over the years, other artists struck gold with Wonder remakes, as seen with Aretha Franklin's No. 1 R&B cover of "Until You Come Back to Me (That's What I'm Gonna Do)." Among an array of honors, Wonder captured 15 Grammy Awards during the decade, with Innervisions, Fulfillingness' First Finale and Songs in the Key of Life each recognized as album of the year.

By those incredible lofty standards, the 1980s weren't nearly as successful for Wonder. Still, he continued to be a huge musical force. He ended the '70s with the double album Journey Through the Secret Life of Plants, an avant-garde set for an unreleased botanical documentary, featuring the top 5 pop/R&B ballad "Send One Your Love." 1980's Hotter Than July was a more succinct, commercial affair with the disco track "All I Do" as well as the No. 1 R&B hit "Master Blaster (Jammin')," a reggae-influenced tribute to Bob Marley, and the top 5 R&B, country-influenced number "I Ain't Gonna Stand for It." In 1982, Wonder teamed up with ex-Beatle Paul McCartney for the No. 1 U.S./U.K. single "Ebony and Ivory," a song promoting racial harmony that was featured on the McCartney album Tug of War. That same year, Wonder also released his greatest hits compilation Original Musiquarium I, which featured the No. 1 R&B/top 5 pop single "That Girl," as well as additional hits "Ribbon in the Sky" and "Do I Do," featuring Dizzy Gillespie.

In 1984, Wonder released the soundtrack for the Gene Wilder film The Woman in Red, which featured contributions from Dionne Warwick as well as the top 5 R&B hit "Love Light in Flight" and the massive No. 1 pop single "I Just Called to Say I Love You." Like so much of Wonder's work, the song appealed to a wide audience, paving the way for it to become Motown's biggest international hit of all time. The single also won Wonder an Academy Award for best original song. Wonder released his next album, Square Circle, in 1985, which featured the historic track "Part-Time Lover," the first song to ever reach No. 1 on the pop, R&B, adult contemporary and dance charts. The album Characters was released two years later, featuring two No. 1 R&B

hits—"Skeletons" and "You Will Know." In 1989, Wonder was inducted into the Rock and Roll Hall of Fame. Wonder continued his soundtrack contributions with his work for the 1991 Spike Lee film Jungle Fever, starring Wesley Snipes and Annabella Sciorra. For the Jungle Fever album, Wonder composed three more top 10 R&B singles: "Gotta Have You," "Fun Day" and "These Three Words." A few years later, Wonder released Conversation Peace; its first single, the easygoing "For Your Love," reached the top 20 R&B and earned two Grammys in 1996, the same year he received the Grammy Lifetime

In addition to his acclaimed artistry, Wonder has routinely tackled social issues through his music and appearances. He successfully spearheaded a movement to create a national holiday recognizing the birthday of Dr. Martin Luther King Jr., a celebration he sang about in the track "Happy Birthday" from Hotter Than July. ("Happy Birthday" became a major U.K. hit as well, reaching No. 2.) Wonder had dedicated his Oscar win to anti-apartheid activist/future president Nelson Mandela and had performed on the No. 1 charity singles "We Are the World," to raise money for famine relief in Africa, and "That's What Friends Are For," with Warwick, Elton John and Gladys Knight, benefiting the American Foundation for AIDS Research (amfAR).

Wonder has also been a longtime advocate for improving services for the blind and those with disabilities. In connection with the International Day of Persons With Disabilities, he was named a United Nations Messenger of Peace in 2009. In June 2013, Wonder continued his advocacy work when he announced he would make good on a promise to perform a concert in Marrakech for negotiators from the World Intellectual Property Organization when they agreed on an international treaty providing blind and visually impaired individuals around the world with more access to books. Following a 10-year hiatus, Wonder released the well-received A Time to Love in 2005, with guest appearances from India.Arie, Doug E. Fresh, McCartney, Bonnie Raitt and Prince, among others. Wonder also put out the concert DVD Live At Last: A Wonder's Summer Night in 2009. In 2014, Wonder received the Presidential Medal of Freedom from President Barack Obama. The following year, the singer/songwriter/musician was paid tribute by a pantheon of performers on the telecast Stevie Wonder: Songs in the Key of Life—An All-Star Grammy Salute, recognizing his classic 1976 album.

Wonder occasionally surfaced with new music as he progressed through his late 60s, recording the Golden Globe-nominated single "Faith" with Ariana Grande in 2016, as well as the song "Future Sunny Days," specifically written for the 2018 finale of the hit series Scandal.

Wonder married fellow Motown singer/songwriter Syreeta Wright in 1970, divorcing two years later. A skilled lyricist, she worked with Wonder on hits like "Signed, Sealed, Delivered I'm Yours" and "If You Really Love Me," while he worked with Wright on her albums Syreeta (1972) and Stevie Wonder Presents Syreeta (1974). Wright died of cancer in 2004. Wonder had his first child, Aisha, with Yolanda Simmons in 1975. His daughter was the inspiration for "Isn't She Lovely." The couple had a son, Keita, who was born in 1977. In 1983, he had a son, Mumtaz, with Melody McCulley. Wonder had a daughter, Sophia, and son, Kwame, with a woman whose name has not been publicized. Wonder married Karen Millard Morris in 2001. The couple had two sons, Kailand and Mandla, before their divorce was finalized in 2015. Meanwhile, Wonder began a relationship with Tomeeka Robyn Bracy; the couple had two children, before tying the knot in 2017.

https://www.biography.com/musician/stevie-wonder

CHAPTER 45
OPRAH WINFREY (1954-PRESENT)

Credit: @amacad.org/person/oprah-winfrey

Born to an unwed teenage mother, Oprah Winfrey spent her first years on her grandmother's farm in Kosciusko, Mississippi, while her mother looked for work in the North. Life on the farm was primitive, but her grandmother taught her to read very early, and at age three Oprah was reciting poems and Bible verses in local churches. Despite the hardships of her physical environment, she enjoyed the loving support of her grandmother and the church community, who cherished her as a gifted child.

Her world changed for the worse at age six, when she was sent to Milwaukee to live with her mother, who had found work as a housemaid. In the long days when her mother was absent from their inner-city apartment, young Oprah was repeatedly molested by male relatives and another visitor. The abuse, which lasted from the ages of nine to 13, was emotionally devastating. When she tried to run away, she was sent to a juvenile detention home, only to be denied admission because all the beds were filled. At 14, she was out of the house and on her own. By her own account, she was sexually promiscuous as a teenager. After giving birth to a baby boy who died in infancy, she went to Nashville, Tennessee to live with her father.

Vernon Winfrey was a strict disciplinarian, but he gave his daughter the secure home life she needed. He saw to it that she met a curfew, and he required her to read a book and write a book report each week. "As strict as he was," says Oprah, "he had some concerns about me making the best of my life and would not accept anything less than what he thought was my best." In this structured environment, Oprah flourished, and became an honor student, winning prizes for oratory and dramatic recitation.

At age 17, Oprah Winfrey won the Miss Black Tennessee beauty pageant and was offered an on-air job at WVOL, a radio station serving the Black American community in Nashville. She also won a full scholarship to Tennessee State University, where she majored in speech communications and performing arts. Oprah continued to work at WVOL in her first years of college, but her broadcasting career was already taking off. She left school and signed on with a local television station as a reporter and anchor.

In 1976, she moved to Baltimore to join WJZ-TV News as a co-anchor. There, she co-hosted her first talk show, People Are Talking, while continuing to serve as anchor and news reporter. She had found a niche that perfectly suited her outgoing, empathetic personality, and word soon spread to other cities. In January 1984, she was invited to Chicago to host a faltering half-hour morning program on WLS-TV. In less than a year, she turned AM Chicago into the hottest show in town. The format was soon expanded to an hour, and in September 1985 it was renamed The Oprah Winfrey Show.

A year later, The Oprah Winfrey Show was broadcast nationally, and quickly became the number one talk show in national syndication. In 1987, its first year of eligibility, the show received three Daytime Emmy Awards in the categories of Outstanding Host, Outstanding Talk/Service Program and Outstanding Direction. The following year, the show received its second consecutive Emmy as Outstanding Talk/Service Program, and Oprah herself received the International Radio and Television Society's "Broadcaster of the Year" Award. She was the youngest person ever to receive the honor.

By the time America fell in love with Oprah Winfrey the talk show host, she had already captured the nation's attention with her poignant portrayal of Sofia in Steven Spielberg's 1985 adaptation of Alice Walker's novel The Color Purple. Winfrey's performance earned her nominations for an Oscar and a Golden Globe Award as Best Supporting Actress. Critics again lauded her performance in Native Son, a movie adaptation of Richard Wright's classic 1940 novel.

Her love of acting and her desire to bring quality entertainment projects into production prompted her to form her own production company, Harpo Productions, Inc., in 1986. Today, Harpo is a formidable force in film and television production, as well as magazine publishing and the Internet. In 1988, Harpo Productions, Inc. acquired ownership and all production responsibilities for The Oprah Winfrey Show from Capital Cities/ABC, making Oprah Winfrey the first woman in history to own and produce her own talk show. The following year, Harpo produced its first television miniseries, The Women of Brewster Place, with Oprah Winfrey as star and executive producer. It was quickly followed by the TV movies There Are No Children Here (1993), and Before Women Had Wings (1997), which she both produced and appeared in.

Initially, The Oprah Winfrey Show followed a model established by other daytime talk shows, employing sensational stories and outrageous guests to attract viewers, but since the 1990s, Oprah began to emphasize spiritual values, healthy living and self-help, and her program became more popular than ever. Motivated in part by her own memories of childhood abuse, she initiated a campaign to establish a national database of convicted child abusers and testified before a U.S. Senate Judiciary Committee on behalf of a National Child Protection Act. President Clinton signed the "Oprah Bill" into law in 1993, establishing the national database she had sought, which is now available to law enforcement agencies and concerned parties across the country.

Oprah's show also continued to attract the top names in the entertainment industry; a 1993 interview with the reclusive entertainer Michael Jackson drew 100 million viewers, making it the most-watched interview in television history. Oprah Winfrey was named one of the "100 Most Influential People of the 20th Century" by Time magazine, and in 1998 received a Lifetime Achievement Award from the National Academy of Television Arts and Sciences.

Despite her complete dominance of the daytime talk show field, Oprah Winfrey had not given up her acting ambitions. In 1998, she produced and starred in the feature film Beloved, adapted from the book by the Nobel Prize-winning American author Toni Morrison. Winfrey has long used her television program to champion the works of authors she admires, including Morrison, and her longtime friend Maya Angelou. Her influence over the publishing industry exploded when she began her on-air book club in 1996. "Oprah Book Club" selections became instant bestsellers, and in 1999 Winfrey received the National Book Foundation's 50th-anniversary gold medal for her service to books and authors. She herself has authored five books. A book on weight loss, co-written with her personal trainer, received a publisher's advance fee reported to be the highest in history.

Oprah Winfrey's business interests have extended well beyond her own production company. She is one of the partners in Oxygen Media, Inc., a cable channel, and interactive network presenting programming designed primarily for women. With her success, she has also become one of the world's most generous philanthropists. In 2000, Oprah's Angel Network began presenting a $100,000 "Use Your Life Award" to people who are using their own lives to improve the lives of others. She now publishes two magazines: O, The Oprah Magazine, and O at Home. The launch of her first magazine was the most successful start-up in the history of the industry. When Forbes published its list of America's billionaires for the year 2003, it disclosed that Oprah Winfrey was the first Black American woman to become a billionaire.

The Oprah Winfrey Show remained as popular as ever, airing in 140 countries around the world. Many of her regular guests, including Dr. Phil McGraw and Dr. Mehmet Oz, have gone on to shows of their own, produced by Oprah's Harpo Productions. Over the years, she has also used her program to promote the many philanthropic ventures she supports. After filming a Christmas program in South Africa, she established the Oprah Winfrey Leadership Academy for Girls, near Johannesburg. Her legendary generosity has extended not only to her favorite charities, but to her loyal viewers. She celebrated the beginning of her 20th season on national television by giving every member of the studio audience a brand new Pontiac automobile.

Two decades after she first established herself as a national presence, Oprah Winfrey was still devoting much of her prodigious energy to film and television production. In 2005, she produced a film adaptation of Zora Neale Hurston's novel Their Eyes Were Watching God, with a screenplay by Suzan-Lori Parks. The same year, she produced a successful Broadway musical version of The Color Purple. As an actress, she has been heard in a number of successful animated films, including Charlotte's Web, Bee Movie and The Princess and the Frog.

In the 2008 presidential election, Winfrey publicly endorsed a political candidate for the first time, hosting a fundraiser for Senator Barack Obama and appearing with him at campaign events. It is widely believed that her support was crucial to his winning the Democratic nomination — and the presidency itself. In that election year, she also announced plans for a new broadcasting venture with the Discovery Health Channel, to be renamed Oprah Winfrey Network (OWN). In a 2010 interview on the Larry King program at the end of that year, she announced her decision to end her run on The Oprah Winfrey Show. The final broadcast took place on May 25, 2011, after 24 seasons and over 5,000 broadcasts. The end of the syndicated program was not the end of Oprah Winfrey's broadcasting career. She now hosts a nightly program, Oprah's Lifeclass, on the Oprah Winfrey Network.

Oprah Winfrey makes her principal home on a 42-acre ocean-view estate in Montecito, California, just south of Santa Barbara, but also owns homes in another six states and the island of Antigua. The business press measures her wealth in numerous superlatives: the highest-paid performer on television, the richest self-made woman in America, and the richest Black American of the 20th century. More difficult to calculate is her profound influence over the way people everywhere read, eat, exercise, feel and think about themselves and the world around them. She appears on every list of leading opinion-makers and has been rightly called "the most powerful woman in the world." Her wide-ranging philanthropic efforts were recognized by the Academy of Motion Picture Arts and Sciences in 2011 with a special Oscar statuette, the Jean Hersholt Humanitarian Award. In 2013, President Barack Obama awarded her the nation's highest civilian honor, the Presidential Medal of Freedom. Oprah Winfrey has also donated more than $20 million to the Smithsonian Institution's National Museum of African American History and Culture. On September 24, 2016, she participated in a dedication ceremony during the grand opening of the Washington, D.C. Museum, which includes the 350-seat Oprah Winfrey Theater, named in her honor.

https://achievement.org/achiever/oprah-winfrey/

CHAPTER 46
CONDOLEEZZA RICE (1954-PRESENT)

As a child Condoleezza Rice dreamed of becoming a concert pianist. Her love for international music translated into a successful career in international diplomacy. Throughout her career, Rice became the first Black American woman to hold several positions, including Secretary of State.

Condoleezza Rice was born on November 14, 1954, in Birmingham, Alabama. Her mother worked as a teacher and her father as a guidance counselor. At an early age, Rice was drawn to music. She learned how to play the piano and entered college as a music major. However, after taking a course in international politics, she changed her career aspirations. Rice earned a degree in political science from the University of Denver. In 1979, she studied Russian at Moscow State University. Rice graduated from University of Denver with a PhD in political science in 1981. One year later, she began her career as an assistant professor at Stanford University.

At Stanford, Rice enjoyed a successful teaching career. She was awarded several teaching awards and she quickly advanced. Rice was selected as the Provost of Stanford in 1993, making her the first woman and first Black American to hold this position. Under her leadership, Rice led the university out of a financial deficit. While at Stanford, she also co-founded the Center for a New Generation, an after-school program for underprivileged students.

Throughout her time teaching, Rice actively pursued a career in politics. In 1989, she advised President George H.W. Bush's administration on Soviet Union affairs. In 2000, she was appointed the National Security Advisor under President George W. Bush, becoming the first black woman to hold this position. In 2004, Rice was selected as the Secretary of State of the United States. She was the first Black American woman to hold this position. In her role, Rice worked to promote peace globally. She placed American diplomats throughout the Middle East, especially in areas of major turmoil. Rice also aided in peace talks with other countries. She called her style of diplomacy "transformational," a term that has since been used to describe other international policies.

Rice also works tirelessly to educate the public on international relations. In 2009, when her appointment as Secretary of State ended, Rice returned to teaching. She has published several books including her two autobiographies. Currently Rice works as the Denning Professor in Global Business and Economy at the Stanford Graduate School of Business. She also serves on the board of several companies including the Boys and Girls Club. Although she did not pursue a career as a musician, Rice continues to play the piano. She also supports the arts through several charities. While working in Washington DC, Rice took up golfing as a leisure activity. In 2012, her leisure activity gained her another first. She became one of the first female members admitted to Augusta National Golf Club, an organization that had excluded women for 80 years.

https://www.womenshistory.org/education-resources/biographies/condoleezza-rice

CHAPTER 47
RUBY BRIDGES (1954-PRESENT)

Credit: Photo: Getty Images

Ruby Bridges was born in Tylertown, Mississippi on September 8, 1954. At the age of two, she moved to New Orleans with her parents, Abon and Lucille Bridges, to seek better opportunities for their family.

When Ruby was in kindergarten, she was chosen to take a test to determine if she could attend an all-white school. This was due to the 1954 Supreme Court ruling of Brown vs. The Board of Education which ordered all schools to desegregate. Ruby was one of six students to pass the test and her parents decided to send her to an all-white elementary school to receive a better education.

On November 14, 1960, at the age of six, Ruby became the very first Black American child to attend the all-white public William Frantz Elementary School. Ruby and her Mother were escorted by federal marshals to the school. When they arrived, two marshals walked in front of Ruby, and two behind her. This image was captured by Norman Rockwell in his painting "The Problem We All Must Live With," which is now on display in the White House outside the Oval Office.

Ruby faced blatant racism every day while entering the school. Many parents kept their children at home. People outside the school threw objects, police set up barricades. She was threatened and even "greeted" by a woman displaying a black doll in a wooden coffin. Only one teacher, Barbara Henry, agreed to teach her. Ruby was the only student in Barbara Henry's class because all the other children had been pulled out by their parents. She was not allowed to go to the cafeteria or outside for recess with the other students. When she needed to use the restroom, she was escorted by a federal marshal. Ruby's family faced discrimination outside of the school as well. However, as the year went on, many families began to send their children back to school and the protests and civil disturbances stopped.

During Ruby's second year at William Frantz Elementary, she no longer needed to be escorted by federal marshals. She walked to school on her own & was in a classroom with other students. Ruby had paved the way for other Black American children!

https://www.hilbert.edu/social-justice-activists/ruby-bridges

CHAPTER 48
AL SHARPTON (1954-PRESENT)

Credit: © 1990-2022 by IMDb.com, Inc.

Born in Brooklyn, New York, on October 3, 1954, Reverend Alfred "Al" Sharpton has been preaching since age four. He was licensed and ordained at age nine. In 1971, he founded the National Youth Movement and for seventeen years he led the organization, registering young people to vote and giving them job opportunities. His direct-action and civil disobedience campaigns have brought attention to injustice in many areas.

Sharpton has pursued other interests while continuing to preach in his teens, he established a close bond with James Brown and developed a father-son relationship, eventually recording the record God Smiled on Me with him. In the 1970s and early 1980s, he worked as a youth organizer with boxing promoter Don King, while learning more about Black American politics and entertainment.

However, Sharpton never strayed far from activism. He formed the National Action Network in 1991 to fight for progressive, people-based social policies by providing extensive voter education and registration campaigns, economic support for small community businesses and by confronting corporate racism. That same year, Sharpton was stabbed in a Bensonhurst school yard. This represented a turning point for him. Eventually, he met and reconciled with his attacker.

Sharpton has never hesitated to act in support of Black Americans, from individuals seeking public offices to Abner Louima, a Haitian immigrant brutalized by Brooklyn police in 1997. Now he is also seeking to build a national multi-cultural, multi-racial movement addressing a range of issues. To that end, in 1999 Sharpton, former New York City Mayor Ed Koch and Harvard Law School professor Charles Ogletree formed "Second Chance", a program to serve non-violent felony offenders after their release from prison. Sharpton also orchestrated a massive protest when police shot unarmed Amadou Diallo 42 times in 1999. In 2001, Sharpton protested the U.S. Navy's bombing of the Puerto Rican Island of Vieques. Attempting to fight injustice wherever he finds it, Sharpton is following in the footsteps of Reverend Martin Luther King, Jr. and Reverend Jesse Jackson Sr.

https://www.thehistorymakers.org/biography/reverend-al-sharpton

CHAPTER 48
MICHAEL JACKSON (1958-2009)

Credit: © 2022 Apple Inc. and its affiliates

Michael Joseph Jackson was born on August 29, 1958, in Gary, Indiana, and entertained audiences nearly his entire life. His father, Joe Jackson (no relation to Joe Jackson, also a musician), had been a guitarist, but was forced to give up his musical ambitions following his marriage to Michael's mother Katherine Jackson (née Katherine Esther Scruse). Together, they prodded their growing family's musical interests at home. By the early 1960s, the older boys Jackie, Tito and Jermaine had begun performing around the city; by 1964, Michael and Marlon had joined in.

A musical prodigy, Michael's singing and dancing talents were amazingly mature, and he soon became the dominant voice and focus of the Jackson 5. An opening act for such soul groups as the O-Jays and James Brown, it was Gladys Knight (not Diana Ross) who officially brought the group to Berry Gordy's attention, and by 1969, the boys were producing back-to-back chart-busting hits as Motown artists ("I Want You Back," "ABC," "Never Can Say Goodbye," "Got to Be There," etc.). As a product of the 1970s, the boys emerged as one of the most accomplished black pop / soul vocal groups in music history, successfully evolving from a group like The Temptations to a disco phenomenon.

Solo success for Michael was inevitable, and by the 1980s, he had become infinitely more popular than his brotherly group. Record sales consistently orbited, culminating in the biggest-selling album of all time, "Thriller" in 1982. A TV natural, he ventured rather uneasily into films, such as playing the Scarecrow in The Wiz (1978) but had much better luck with elaborate music videos.

In the 1990s, the downside as a 1980s pop phenomenon began to rear itself. Michael grew terribly child-like and introverted by his peerless celebrity. A rather timorous, androgynous figure to begin with, his physical appearance began to change drastically, and his behavior grew alarmingly bizarre, making him a consistent target for scandal-making, despite his numerous charitable acts. Two brief marriages -- one to Elvis Presley's daughter Lisa Marie Presley -- were forged and two children produced by his second wife during that time, but the purposes behind them appeared image-oriented.

Michael Jackson died on June 25, 2009, in Los Angeles, California. His passion and artistry as a singer, dancer, writer, and businessman were unparalleled, and it is these prodigious talents that will ultimately prevail over the extremely negative aspects of his troubled adult life.

https://www.imdb.com/name/nm0001391/bio

CHAPTER 50
BARACK OBAMA (1961-PRESENT)

Credit: Official White House Photo by Pete Souza

Barack Obama served as the 44th President of the United States. His story is the American story — values from the heartland, a middle-class upbringing in a strong family, hard work and education as the means of getting ahead, and the conviction that a life so blessed should be lived in service to others.

When Barack Obama was elected president in 2008, he became the first Black American to hold the office. The framers of the Constitution always hoped that our leadership would not be limited to Americans of wealth or family connections. Subject to the prejudices of their time—many of them owned slaves—most would not have foreseen a Black American president. Obama's father, Barack Sr., a Kenyan economist, met his mother, Stanley Ann Dunham, when both were students in Hawaii, where Barack was born on August 4, 1961. They later divorced, and Barack's mother married a man from Indonesia, where he spent his early childhood. Before fifth grade, he returned to Honolulu to live with his maternal grandparents and attend Punahou School on scholarship.

In his memoir Dreams from My Father (1995), Obama describes the complexities of discovering his identity in adolescence. After two years at Occidental College in Los Angeles, he transferred to Columbia University, where he studied political science and international relations. Following graduation in 1983, Obama worked in New York City, then became a community organizer on the South Side of Chicago, coordinating with churches to improve housing conditions and set up job-training programs in a community hit hard by steel mill closures. In 1988, he went to Harvard Law School, where he attracted national attention as the first Black American president of the Harvard Law Review. Returning to Chicago, he joined a small law firm specializing in civil rights.

In 1992, Obama married Michelle Robinson, a lawyer who had also excelled at Harvard Law. Their daughters, Malia and Sasha, were born in 1998 and 2001, respectively. Obama was elected to the Illinois Senate in 1996, and then to the U.S. Senate in 2004. At the Democratic National Convention that summer, he delivered a much-acclaimed keynote address. Some pundits instantly pronounced him a future president, but most did not expect it to happen for some time. Nevertheless, in 2008 he was elected over Arizona Senator John McCain by 365 to 173 electoral votes.

As an incoming president, Obama faced many challenges—an economic collapse, wars in Iraq and Afghanistan, and the continuing menace of terrorism. Inaugurated before an estimated crowd of 1.8 million people, Obama proposed unprecedented federal spending to revive the economy and hoped to renew America's stature in the world. During his first term he signed three signature bills: an omnibus bill to stimulate the economy, legislation making health care more accessible and affordable, and legislation reforming the nation's financial institutions. Obama also pressed for a fair pay act for women, financial reform legislation, and efforts for consumer protection. In 2009, Obama became the fourth president to receive the Nobel Peace Prize.

In 2012, he was reelected over former Massachusetts Governor Mitt Romney by 332 to 206 electoral votes. The Middle East remained a key foreign policy challenge. Obama had overseen the killing of Osama bin Laden, but a new self-proclaimed Islamic State arose during a civil war in Syria and began inciting terrorist attacks. Obama sought to manage a hostile Iran with a treaty that hindered its development of nuclear weapons. The Obama administration also adopted a climate change agreement signed by 195 nations to reduce greenhouse gas emissions and slow global warming.

In the last year of his second term, Obama spoke at two events that clearly moved him—the 50th anniversary of the civil rights march from Selma to Montgomery, and the dedication of the National Museum of African American History and Culture. "Our union is not yet perfect, but we are getting closer," he said in Selma. "And that's why we celebrate," he told those attending the museum opening in Washington, "mindful that our work is not yet done."

https://www.whitehouse.gov/about-the-white-house/presidents/barack-obama/

CHAPTER 51
MICHAEL JORDAN (1963-PRESENT)

Credit: © Ralf-Finn Hestoft/CORBIS/Corbis via Getty Images

Basketball superstar Michael Jordan is one of the most successful, popular, and wealthy athletes in college, Olympic, and professional sports history.

Michael Jordan was born on February 17, 1963, in Brooklyn, New York, one of James and Deloris Jordan's five children. The family moved to Wilmington, North Carolina, when Michael was very young. His father worked as a General Electric plant supervisor, and his mother worked at a bank. His father taught him to work hard and not to be tempted by street life. His mother taught him to sew, clean, and do laundry. Jordan loved sports but failed to make his high school basketball team as a sophomore. He continued to practice and made the team the next year. After high school he accepted a basketball scholarship to the University of North Carolina, where he played under head coach Dean Smith.

In Jordan's first season at North Carolina, he was named Atlantic Coast Conference (ACC) Rookie of the Year for 1982. The team won the ACC championship, and Jordan made the clutch jump shot that beat Georgetown University for the championship of the National Collegiate Athletic Association (NCAA). Jordan led the ACC in scoring as a sophomore and as a junior. The Sporting News named him college player of the year for both years. He left North Carolina after his junior year and was selected by the Chicago Bulls of the National Basketball Association (NBA) as the third pick of the 1984 draft. Before joining the Bulls, Jordan was a member of the Summer 1984 United States Olympic basketball team that won the gold medal in Los Angeles, California.

When Jordan was drafted by the Chicago Bulls, they were a losing team, drawing only around six thousand fans to home games. Jordan quickly turned that around. His style of play and fierce spirit of competition reminded sportswriters and fans of Julius Erving (1950–), who had been a superstar player during the 1970s. Jordan's incredible leaping ability and hang time thrilled fans in arenas around the league. In his first season he was named to the All-Star team and was later honored as the league's Rookie of the Year.

A broken foot sidelined Jordan for 64 games during the 1985–86 season, but he returned to score 49 points against the Boston Celtics in the first game of the playoffs and 63 in the second game—an NBA playoff record. The 1986–87 season was again one of individual successes, and Jordan started in the All-Star game after receiving a record 1.5 million votes. He became the first player since Wilt Chamberlain (1936–1999) to score 3,000 points in a single season. Jordan enjoyed personal success, but Chicago did not advance beyond the first round of the playoffs until 1988. Jordan concentrated on improving his other basketball skills, and in 1988 he was named Defensive Player of the Year. He was also named the league's Most Valuable Player (MVP) and became the first player to lead the league in both scoring and steals. He was again named MVP in that year's All-Star game.

By adding such players as Scottie Pippen, Bill Cartwright, Horace Grant, and John Paxson around Jordan, the Bulls' management created a strong team that won the 1991 NBA title by defeating the Los Angeles Lakers. The next year, the Bulls repeated as NBA champions by beating the Portland Trail Blazers. In 1992 Jordan also played on the "Dream Team," which participated in the Summer Olympic Games in Barcelona, Spain. The Olympic Committee had voted to lift the ban on professional athletes participating in the games. The team easily won the gold medal, winning their eight games by an average margin of 43.7 points.

In 1993, after a tough playoff series with the New York Knicks, the Bulls met the Phoenix Suns for the NBA championship. When it was over, Jordan was again playoff MVP, and Chicago had won a third straight title. That summer Jordan's father, James, was murdered by two men during a robbery attempt. Jordan was grief stricken, and his father's death, combined with media reports about his gambling, led him to announce his retirement from professional basketball in October. Jordan had won three straight NBA titles, three regular season MVP awards, three playoff MVP titles, seven consecutive scoring titles, and he was a member of the All-Star team every year that he was in the league. In just nine seasons he had become the Bulls all-time leading scorer.

In 1994–95 Jordan played for the Birmingham Barons, a minor league baseball team in the Chicago White Sox system. Although the seventeen-month experiment showed that he was not a major league baseball player, the experience and time away from basketball provided a much-needed rest and opportunity to regain his love of basketball.

When Jordan returned to the Chicago Bulls during the 1994–95 regular season, people wondered, "Could he do it again?" He played well, but he was obviously rusty. The Bulls were defeated in the playoffs by the Orlando Magic. After a summer of playing basketball during breaks from filming the live-action cartoon movie Space Jam, Jordan returned with a fierce determination to prove that he had the ability to get back on top. The 1995–96 Bulls finished the regular season 72–10, an NBA record for most wins in a season, and Jordan, with his shooting rhythm back, earned his eighth scoring title. He also became the tenth NBA player to score 25,000 career points and second fastest after Chamberlain to reach that mark. The Bulls went on to win their fourth NBA championship, overpowering the Seattle

Supersonics in six games. Few who watched will ever forget how Jordan sank to his knees, head bent over the winning ball, in a moment of bittersweet victory and deep sadness. The game had been played on Father's Day, three years after his father's murder.

The defending champions had a tougher time during the 1996–97 season but entered the playoffs as expected. Sheer determination took the Bulls to their fifth NBA championship. Illness, injury, and at times a lack of concentration hurt the team. In the fifth game of the finals Jordan carried the team to victory despite suffering from a stomach virus. In the 1997–98 season the Bulls were again in the playoffs, and again they faced tough competition. As before, they were able to clinch the NBA championship, and Jordan claimed his sixth NBA finals MVP award.

Jordan's other professional life as a businessman was never off track. Profitable endorsements (ads in which he voiced his support for certain products) for companies such as Nike and Wheaties, as well as his own golf company and products such as Michael Jordan cologne (which reportedly sold 1.5 million bottles in its first two months), made Jordan a multimillionaire. In 1997 he was ranked the world's highest paid athlete, with a $30 million contract—the largest one-year salary in sports history—and approximately $40 million a year in endorsement fees.

Jordan retired for a second time in 1999, ending his career on a high note just after the official end of a labor dispute between NBA players and team owners. Many people saw him as the greatest basketball player ever, and his retirement was called the end of an era. In 2000 Jordan became part-owner and president of basketball operations of the Washington Wizards. This made him only the third Black American owner in the NBA. He also gained an ownership stake in the Washington Capitals hockey team. Also in 2000, Jordan celebrated the first year of his $1 million grant program to help teachers make a difference in their schools.

In September 2001, after months of rumors, Jordan announced that he was ending his three-year retirement to play for the Wizards at age thirty-eight. At a news conference to discuss his comeback, he said, "Physically, I know I'm not twenty-five years old, but I feel I can play the game of basketball on the highest level." The Wizards, who had won only nineteen games the season before, improved with the addition of Jordan. After being voted to play in his thirteenth All-Star game (during which he missed a slam dunk), Jordan had the Wizards in the race for the playoffs until suffering a knee injury and missing the last part of the season. He was also distracted in January 2002 when his wife Juanita, whom he married in 1989, filed for divorce. (They have three children.) The next month the divorce was called off. Jordan said he planned to play one more season for the Wizards.

https://www.notablebiographies.com/Jo-Ki/Jordan-Michael.html

CHAPTER 52
JAY-Z (1969-PRESENT)

Credit:Chrisplug.com

Born Shawn Corey Carter on December 4, 1969, Jay-Z grew up in Brooklyn's drug-infested Marcy Projects. He used rap as an escape and appeared on Yo! MTV Raps in 1989. After selling millions of records with his own Roc-A-Fella label, Jay-Z created his own clothing line. He wed popular singer and actress Beyoncé Knowles in 2008.

Rapper Jay-Z was born Shawn Corey Carter on December 4, 1969, in Brooklyn, New York. "He was the last of my four children," Jay-Z's mother later recalled, "the only one who didn't give me any pain when I gave birth to him, and that's how I knew he was a special child." Jay-Z's father, Adnes Reeves, left the family when Jay-Z was only 11 years old. The young rapper was raised by his mother, Gloria Carter, in Brooklyn's drug-infested Marcy Projects.

During a rough adolescence, detailed in many of his autobiographical songs, Shawn Carter dealt drugs and flirted with gun violence. He attended Eli Whitney High School in Brooklyn, where he was a classmate of the soon-to-be-martyred rap legend Notorious B.I.G. As Jay-Z later remembered his childhood in one of his songs ("December 4th"), "I went to school, got good grades, could behave when I wanted/ But I had demons deep inside that would raise when confronted."

Carter turned to rap at a very young age as an escape from the drugs, violence and poverty that surrounded him in the Marcy Projects. In 1989, he joined the rapper Jaz-O—an older performer who served as a kind of mentor—to record a song called "The Originators," which won the pair an appearance on an episode of Yo! MTV Raps. It was at this point that Shawn Carter embraced the nickname Jay-Z, which was simultaneously an homage to Jaz-O, a play on Carter's childhood nickname of "Jazzy," and a reference to the J/Z subway station near his Brooklyn home.

But even though he had a stage name, Jay-Z remained relatively anonymous until he and two friends, Damon Dash, and Kareem Burke, founded their own record label, Roc-A-Fella Records, in 1996. In June of that year, Jay-Z released his debut album, Reasonable Doubt. Although the record only reached No. 23 on the Billboard charts, it is now considered a classic hip-hop album, featuring songs such as "Can't Knock the Hustle," featuring Mary J. Blige, and "Brooklyn's Finest," a collaboration with Notorious B.I.G. Reasonable Doubt established Jay-Z as an emerging star in hip-hop.

Two years later, Jay-Z achieved even broader success with the 1998 album Vol. 2 ... Hard Knock Life. The title track, which famously sampled its chorus from the Broadway musical Annie, became Jay-Z's most popular single to date and won him his first Grammy nomination. "Hard Knock Life" marked the beginning of a fruitful period in which Jay-Z would become the biggest name in hip-hop.

In 2000, Jay-Z released The Dynasty: Roc La Familia, which was originally intended to become a compilation album for Roc-A-Fella artists, but Def Jam turned into a Jay-Z album. The album helped to introduce newcomer producers The Neptunes, Just Blaze, Kanye West, and Bink, which have all gone on to achieve notable success. This is also the first album where Jay-Z utilizes a more soulful sound than his previous albums. The Dynasty sold over two million units in the U.S. alone.

Over the span of those years, the rapper released a slew of No. 1 albums and hit singles. His most popular songs from this period include "Can I Get A ...", "Big Pimpin'", "I Just Wanna Love U", "Izzo (H.O.V.A.)" and "03 Bonnie & Clyde", a duet with future bride Beyoncé Knowles.

Jay-Z's most acclaimed album of this period was The Blueprint (2001), which would later land on many music critics' lists of the best albums of the decade. Its release was set a week earlier than initially planned in order to combat bootlegging. Recording sessions for the album took place during 2001 at Manhattan Center Studios and Baseline Studios in New York City. Contrasting the radio-friendly sound of Jay-Z's previous work, The Blueprint features soul-based sampling and production handled primarily by Kanye West, Just Blaze, and Bink, as well as Timbaland, Trackmasters, and Eminem, who also contributes the album's sole guest feature.

At the time of the album's recording, Jay-Z was awaiting two criminal trials, one for gun possession and another for assault, and had become one of hip hop's most dissed artists, receiving insults from rappers such as Nas, Prodigy, and Jadakiss. The album is also famous for both its producers Kanye West and Just Blaze's breakouts as major producers. West produced four of the thirteen tracks on the album, including the songs "Izzo (H.O.V.A.)" and the controversial "Takeover", which included diss lyrics aimed at rappers Nas and Prodigy, while Just Blaze produced three tracks, "Girls, Girls, Girls", "Song Cry", and "U Don't Know", also including the hidden bonus track "Breathe Easy (Lyrical Exercise)".

The Blueprint received universal acclaim from music critics, with praise being directed at Jay-Z's lyricism and the production. It is considered one of his best albums and has also been labeled as one of the greatest hip-hop albums of all time. Despite its release coinciding with the September 11 attacks, it sold over 427,000 copies in its opening week and debuted at number one in the US, holding the spot for three weeks. It was later certified 2x Multi-Platinum by the RIAA.

In 2019, the album was selected by the Library of Congress for preservation in the National Recording Registry for being "culturally, historically, or aesthetically significant"

In 2003, Jay-Z shocked the hip-hop world by releasing The Black Album and announcing that it would be his last solo record before retirement. Asked to explain his sudden exit from rap, Jay-Z said that he once derived inspiration from trying to outshine other great MCs, but had simply gotten bored due to a lack of competition. "The game ain't hot," he said. "I love when someone makes a hot album and then you've got to make a hot album. I love that. But it ain't hot."

During his hiatus from rapping, Jay-Z turned his attention to the business side of music, becoming president of Def Jam Recordings. As president of Def Jam, Jay-Z signed such popular acts as Rihanna, Ne-Yo and Young Jeezy and helped effect Kanye West's transition from producer to bestselling recording artist. But his reign at the venerable hip-hop label wasn't all smooth sailing; Jay-Z resigned as Def Jam's president in 2007, complaining about the company's resistance to change from ineffectual business models. "You have record executives who've been sitting in their office for 20 years because of one act," he lamented.

Jay-Z's other, ongoing business ventures include the popular urban clothing line Rocawear and Roc-A-Fella films. He also owns the 40/40 Club, an upscale sports bar with locations in New York and Atlantic City, and is a part owner of the New Jersey Nets basketball franchise. As Jay-Z once rapped about his business empire, "I'm not a businessman/ I'm a business, man."

In 2006, Jay-Z ended his retirement from making music, releasing the new album Kingdom Come. He soon released two more albums: American Gangster in 2007 and Blueprint 3 in 2010. This trio of later albums marked a significant departure from Jay-Z's earlier sound, incorporating stronger rock and soul influences in their production and offering lyrics tackling such mature subjects as the response to Hurricane Katrina; Barack Obama's 2008 election; and the perils of fame and fortune. Jay-Z says he's trying to adapt his music to befit his own middle age. "There's not a lot of people who have come of age in rap because it's only 30 years old," he says. "As more people come of age, hopefully the topics get broader and then the audience will stay around longer."

Jay-Z released his tenth album entitled American Gangster on November 6, 2007. After viewing the Ridley Scott film of the same name, Jay-Z was heavily inspired to create a new "concept" album that depicts his experiences as a street-hustler. The album is not the film's official soundtrack, although it was distributed by Def Jam. Jay-Z's American Gangster depicts his life in correlation to the movie American Gangster. At the start of the album's first single, "Blue Magic", Jay-Z offers a dealer's manifesto while making references to political figures of the late 1980s with the lyric: "Blame Reagan for making me to into a monster, blame Oliver North and Iran-Contra, I ran contraband that they sponsored, before this rhymin' stuff we was in concert."

In 2008, Jay-Z signed a $150 million contract with the concert promotion company Live Nation. This super deal created a joint venture called Roc Nation, an entertainment company that handles nearly all aspects of its artists' careers. In addition to Jay-Z himself, Roc Nation manages Willow Smith and J. Cole among others.

More recently, Jay-Z proved that he had both commercial and critical staying power. He teamed up with another famous member of rap royalty, Kanye West, for 2011's Watch the Throne. The album proved to be a triple hit, topping the rap, R&B and pop charts that August.

The song "Otis," which samples the late R&B singer Otis Redding, snagged several Grammy Award nominations and the recording was also nominated for Best Rap Album.

Two years after the release of a collaboration album with West, both rappers dropped solo albums within weeks of the other's release date. West's album, Yeezus (2013), was critically lauded for its innovation, while his mentor Jay-Z's album gained less than stellar reviews. The rappers 12th studio album, Magna Carta Holy Grail (2013), was seen as decent but failed to live up to the hip-hop stars larger-than-life reputation and his unhumbly titled album.

Very protective of his private life, Jay-Z did not publicly discuss his relationship with longtime girlfriend, popular singer, and actress Beyoncé Knowles, for years. The couple even managed to keep the press away from their small wedding, which was held on April 4, 2008, in New York City. Only about 40 people attended the celebration at Jay-Z's penthouse apartment, including actress Gwyneth Paltrow and former Destiny's Child members Kelly Rowland and Michelle Williams.

Since tying the knot, Jay-Z and Beyoncé became the subject of countless pregnancy rumors. They welcomed their first child, a daughter named Blue Ivy Carter, on January 7, 2012. Concerned about their privacy and safety, Jay-Z and Beyoncé rented part of New York's Lenox Hill Hospital and hired extra guards.

Shortly after the birth of his daughter, Jay-Z released a song in her honor on his website. On "Glory," he expressed his joy of becoming a father and revealed that Beyoncé had previously suffered a miscarriage. Jay-Z and Beyoncé also posted a message along with the song, saying "we are in heaven" and Blue's birth "was the best experience of both of our lives."

In 2016, he won a lawsuit for the song "Made in America" with Kanye West featuring Frank Ocean against Joel McDonald.

In early June 2017, posters were displayed in New York City and Los Angeles, as well as banner ads on the Internet promoting a Tidal-related project titled 4:44. A teaser ad was aired during the NBA Finals on June 7 featuring actors Mahershala Ali, Lupita Nyong'o and Danny Glover in a one-minute video, ending in "4:44 – 6.30.17, Exclusively on Tidal". On June 18, the project was confirmed to be a new Jay-Z album, and a clip featuring a song titled "Adnis" was posted on Sprint's YouTube page.

4:44 was released through Roc Nation and Universal Music Group, as an exclusive to Sprint and Tidal customers. The album is the first in a planned series of music exclusives from the Sprint–Tidal partnership. For a short time, on July 2, the album was made available for free digital download in Tidal's site. A physical edition was released on July 7, including three additional tracks. On the same day, the album was made available to other streaming platforms, such as Apple Music, Google Play Music and Amazon Music.

The album received widespread acclaim from critics, who praised its emotional and personal content. On July 5, the album was certified Platinum by the Recording Industry Association of America (RIAA), in recognition of one million copies purchased by Sprint and offered to consumers as free downloads. It debuted at number one on the U.S. Billboard 200, making it Jay-Z's 13th consecutive studio album to top the chart. The album spawned two singles, the title track "4:44" and "Bam", as well as several music videos, directed by a variety of high-profile collaborators. The album received a Grammy Award nomination for Album of the Year, while the title track was nominated for Song of the Year and "The Story of O.J." was nominated for

Record of the Year at the 60th Annual Grammy Awards.

On June 6, 2018, Jay-Z and Beyoncé kicked-off the On the Run II Tour in Cardiff, United Kingdom. Ten days later, at their final London performance, the pair unveiled Everything Is Love, their much-awaited joint studio album, credited under the name The Carters. The pair also released the video for the album's lead single, "Apeshit", on Beyoncé's official YouTube channel. The song won two awards from eight nominations at the 2018 MTV Video Music Awards.

He is a 2021 nominee for the 36th annual Rock & Roll Hall of Fame. He also appeared on the song "Jail" on Kanye West's 2021 album, Donda. And according to Forbes magazine he is hip-hop's first billionaire

https://www.hiphopscriptures.com/jay-z

CHAPTER 53
TIGER WOODS (1975-PRESENT)

Tiger Woods | *CREDIT: JAMIE SQUIRE/GETTY*

On April 13, 1997, Tiger Woods made golfing history when he won the prestigious Masters Tournament of golf. The win was a record breaker in many ways. Woods, at age twenty-one, was the youngest person ever to win the Masters Tournament. He beat the competition with a record-breaking score of 270 for seventy-two holes. He secured the win with a twelve-stroke lead, the largest victory margin in the history of the tournament. Woods, a man of ethnic complexity, further distinguished himself as the first non-white to win the Masters, and in doing so he helped to dissolve many stereotypical notions and attitudes regarding minorities in the sport of golf.

Tiger Woods was born Eldrick Woods on December 30, 1975, in Cypress, California. He was the only child of Earl and Kultida Woods. His parents identified their son's talent at an unusually early age. They said that he was playing with a putter before he could walk. The boy was gifted not only with exceptional playing abilities, but he also possessed a passion for the sport itself. Woods first came to notoriety on a syndicated talk show when he beat the famed comedian and avid golfer Bob Hope in a putting contest. The young boy was only three at the time, and he was quickly hailed as a prodigy. Not long after that, when he was five years old, Woods was featured on the popular television magazine That's Incredible!

Woods' father has never denied that he devoted his energies to developing his son's talent and to furthering the boy's career as a golfer. During practice sessions, Tiger learned to maintain his composure and to hold his concentration while his father persistently made extremely loud noises and created other distractions. "I was using golf to teach him about life…. About how to handle responsibility and pressure," his father explained to Alex Tresniowski of People.

All the while, Tiger's mother made sure that her son's rare talent and his budding golf career would not interfere with his childhood or his future happiness. His mother was a native of Thailand and very familiar with the mystical precepts of Buddhism, and she passed this philosophy on to her son.

As Woods' special talents became increasingly evident, his parents stressed personality, kindness, and self-esteem. They impressed upon their son that he was not to throw tantrums or be rude or think of himself as any better than the next person. John McCormick and Sharon Begley of Newsweek said of his parents, "[Tiger Woods is] best-known as perhaps the finest young golfer in history. But to his parents, it's more important that Tiger Woods is a fine young man. It took love, rules, respect, confidence and trust to get there."

In many ways Woods grew up as a typical middle-class American boy. He developed a taste for junk food and an affection for playing video games. He also spent a fair share of his time clowning around in front of his father's ever-present video camera. As for playing golf, there is no question that the sport was the focus of his childhood. He spent many hours practicing his swing and playing in youth tournaments. Woods was eight years old when he won his first formal competition. From that point he became virtually unstoppable, amassing trophies and breaking amateur records everywhere. Media accounts of the boy prodigy had reached nearly legendary proportions by 1994, when he entered Stanford University as a freshman on a full golfing scholarship.

During his first year of college, Woods won the U.S. Amateur title and qualified to play in the Masters tournament in Augusta, Georgia, in the spring of 1995. Although he played as an amateur-not for prize money-Woods' reputation preceded him. Biographer John Strege wrote about that first Masters tournament in Tiger: A Biography of Tiger Woods, "Golf great Nick Price was there. So were Nick Faldo, John Daly and Fuzzy Zoeller, all of them consigned to relative obscurity on this Monday of Masters week. All eyes were on Woods." By 1996, Woods had won three consecutive U.S. Amateur titles, an unprecedented accomplishment in itself. Woods was only twenty years old, yet there was not much else for him to accomplish as an amateur. He carefully weighed the advantages of finishing college against the prospect of leaving school and entering the sport of professional golf.

The temptation to turn professional was enhanced by lucrative offers of endorsement contracts. In August of 1996, Woods decided to quit college in order to play professional golf. Four months later in December, Woods celebrated his twenty-first birthday. He marked the occasion with a legal name change, from Eldrick to Tiger. Woods had been called Tiger by his father even as a youngster. The nickname stuck, and Woods had always been known to his friends, and to the press, as Tiger. It soon became evident that he was destined for success. Sports Illustrated named him 1996 "Sportsman of the Year," and by January of 1997, he had already won three professional tournaments. He was an early media sensation and remains so to this day.

In April of 1997, and only eight months into his professional career, Woods played in the prestigious Masters tournament held at Georgia's Augusta National Golf Club. The Masters title is perhaps the most coveted honor in the world of golf. In addition to a hefty prize purse, first-place winners are awarded a green blazer to symbolize their membership among the most elite golfers in the world. Contestants are typically well into their thirties or even their forties by the time they win the Masters Tournament.

That year Woods competed against golfing greats but managed to best the most seasoned competition.

When the tournament was over, Woods had made history as the youngest person ever to win the Masters title. His score was an unprecedented 270 strokes. His victory margin set another record-twelve strokes ahead of the runner-up. This feat was enhanced by the fact that Woods was the first man of color ever to win the title. He accepted all of these honors with grace and humility and gave tribute to the black golfers who came before him and helped pave the way. He also honored his mother (who is Asian) by reminding the world of his diverse ethnic background; he is Black American, Thai, Chinese, Native American, and Caucasian. He discouraged the press from labeling him exclusively as Black American, because it showed complete disregard for his mother's Asian heritage. During an interview for the Oprah Winfrey Show, he reiterated an innovative description that he had coined for himself as a child, "I'm a Cablinasian." He was quoted also by John Feinstein of Newsweek, concerning the issue of race, "I don't consider myself a Great Black Hope. I'm just a golfer who happens to be black and Asian."

Less than three months passed until July 6, 1997, when Woods won the Western Open. Critics attributed his astounding success to uncanny persistence and an extraordinary desire to win. "He thinks, therefore he wins," reported the Detroit News, on the day after the Western Open. Woods seemed unstoppable. Some of the greatest golfers in the world offered sportsmanly tribute to the young hero. His enormous popularity and unprecedented success prompted Frank Deford of Newsweek to write, "It's getting so that the only other famous person on the golf circuit is Tiger's caddie ... suddenly you understand there is no second-best golfer in the world.... It is just Tiger Woods." In less than one year as a professional golfer Woods' career winnings totaled over $1,000,000. In addition to prize money earned, he signed multi-million-dollar contracts to endorse a variety of products, from sports equipment to investment funds.

In 2004, Tiger Woods Married Elin Nordegren, a former model from Sweden. The couple had two children, a daughter (Sam Alexis Woods) and a son (Charlie Axel Woods). Sam was born in 2007 and Charlie in 2009. Towards the end of 2009, news related to Woods' marital infidelity with multiple women broke. The story was widely reported and dominated media headlines. Woods lost many endorsement deals in the wake of his infidelity scandal. Tiger and Elin divorced in 2010.

Woods dominated the sport for more than a decade without interruption, though he did take some time off in 2006 following the death of his father. He had two knee surgeries in 2008. He played and won the 2008 Masters after his first knee surgery but sat out the remainder of the season during a second knee surgery. He also took a brief hiatus following the infidelity scandal. Since that time, he has continued to play professional golf consistently — and a high level — but has been plagued by injury and multiple surgeries.

By early 2021, Woods had undergone a total of five back surgeries. In January of 2021, an announcement was made that Woods' plans for the 2021 season were on hold as he recovered from his most recent back surgery. On February 23, 2021, Woods was involved in a serious automobile accident leading to hospitalization and surgery for multiple open fractures to his right leg, along with other injuries

To many observers, Tiger Woods' rise to fame is tied to issues of race and ethnicity as well as to outstanding athletic performance on the golfing course. "Tiger threatened one of the last bastions of white supremacy," wrote Strege in his biography of Woods. Although accusations of racial discrimination had been leveled against the Professional Golf Association (PGA) for many years, little was done. According to Rick Reilly of Sports Illustrated, the Augusta National Tournament founder, Clifford Roberts, once remarked, "As long as I'm alive, golfers will be white, and caddies will be black." Policies were slowly changed to ensure that black golfers would be allowed to compete on a par with whites, but the Augusta National Golf Club didn't accept its first Black American member until 1990.

Woods, with his easy style, his unpretentious disposition, and his powerful 300-yard drives, successfully commanded the respect and attention of golf's predominantly white culture. "Golf has shied away from [racism] for too long," Woods commented to Time. "Some clubs have brought in tokens, but nothing really has changed. I hope what I'm doing can change that." Robert Beck of Sports Illustrated called the ethnically diverse golfer, "A one-man Rainbow Coalition." By all reports, he rises graciously to every occasion, handling the media as well as his peers, with tact and aplomb. Joe Stroud of the Detroit Free Press commented, "He is a photogenic young man…. He is about as remarkable a combination of power and finesse as I've ever seen."

Woods is credited too with popularizing the sport of golf, not only among blacks and other minorities, but among children of all backgrounds. Jennifer Mills of Cable-TV explained the depth of the Tiger Woods phenomenon, "He is bringing a whole new set of people to the golf course who have never been here before…. Kids of every race are dying to see him. They look up at what he's doing and for the first time feel, 'Hey, maybe I could do that.'" His personal sponsorship of programs for children has been reported for years, and at least one corporate sponsor found that in order to secure an endorsement from Tiger Woods the price would include the added cost of a generous donation to the Tiger Woods Foundation for inner-city children. A Time review of the twenty-five most influential people of 1997 reported, "Woods doesn't simply take his money and play. He conducts clinics for inner-city kids, and he … will create opportunities for youngsters who would otherwise never get a chance."

https://biography.yourdictionary.com/tiger-woods

CHAPTER 54
LEBRON RAYMONE JAMES (1984- PRESENT)

Credit: Image via Getty

LeBron James is an American basketball player with the Los Angeles Lakers. James first garnered national attention as the top high school basketball player in the country. With his unique combination of size, athleticism, and court vision, he became a four-time NBA MVP. After leading the Miami Heat to titles in 2012 and 2013, James returned to Cleveland and helped the franchise claim its first championship in 2016.

James was born on December 30, 1984, in Akron, Ohio. At an early age, James showed a natural talent for basketball. He was recruited by St. Vincent-St. Mary High School to join their basketball team in 1999. Overall, James scored 2,657 points, 892 rebounds and 523 assists during his four years there.

As a freshman, James averaged 18 points per game. He helped the team to a Division III state title by scoring 25 points in the championship game. Word of his advanced basketball skills spread, and James received several honors for his performance.

As a high school sophomore, James was chosen for the USA Today All-USA First Team. He was the first sophomore ever selected for this award. His team also won the Division III state title for the second year in a row.

The following school year, James was named PARADE magazine's High School Boys Basketball Player of the Year and Gatorade Player of the Year. Following the end of his junior year, James was such a strong player that he contemplated going pro.

Deciding to finish his education, James had a tremendous senior year on the court. He averaged 31.6 points per game, helping his team clinch their third state title. The St. Vincent-St. Mary High School team also earned the top national ranking that year. James would soon emerge as one of the National Basketball Association's leading players.

With his impressive record, it was no surprise that James was the first player picked in the 2003 NBA Draft straight out of high school. The Cleveland Cavaliers signed the powerful young forward, and he proved to be a valuable addition to the then-struggling franchise. The team had ended the previous season in eighth place in the Eastern Conference.

During the 2003-04 season, James made history when he became the first member of the Cavalier franchise to win the NBA Rookie of the Year Award. He also became the youngest player — at only 20 years old — to receive this honor.

Additionally, James, averaging 20 points per game at this time, became one of only three rookies to accomplish this feat, putting him in the same company as Michael Jordan and Oscar Robertson.

James continued to excel professionally in the NBA the following season, upping his average points per game to 27.2. He made NBA history again in 2005 when he became the youngest player to score more than 50 points in one game.

In 2006, James helped his team defeat the Washington Wizards in the first round of playoff action. From there, the Cavaliers took on the Detroit Pistons in the Eastern Conference semifinals. James scored an average of 26.6 per game in this postseason matchup, but it wasn't enough to secure victory for his team. While his team wasn't at the top of the rankings, James himself continued to receive special recognition for his abilities.

In 2006, James reached a new contract agreement with the Cavaliers. The team proved to be stronger competitors the following season, defeating Detroit to win the Eastern Conference. In the NBA Finals against the San Antonio Spurs, however, the Cavaliers lost their championship bid in four consecutive games.

During the 2007-08 season, James continued to help the Cavaliers improve their standing in the Eastern Conference. The team made it to the semifinals, where they were defeated by the Boston Celtics in seven games. In terms of individual performance, James had a stellar year, outperforming such rival players as Kobe Bryant and Allen Iverson by scoring an average of 30 points per game, the highest average in the NBA regular season.

Early in the 2008-09 season, sports journalists and fans began talking about James' future in the sport. He had the option to become a free agent in 2010, and there was much discussion as to where James would end up. Some journalists identified the New York Knicks as a potential suitor for the rising player.

James made several references to his impending free-agent status, but he was sure to downplay the matter. "I am focused on the team that I am on right now and winning a championship ... I don't think about making a change at this point," James told reporters.

Shortly after becoming a free agent, James announced that he would be joining the Miami Heat for the 2010-11 season. His fans in Cleveland were less than pleased, and many considered his departure a betrayal to his hometown.

Soon after James' announcement, Cleveland Cavaliers majority owner Dan Gilbert wrote an open letter declaring James' decision as "selfish," "heartless" and a "cowardly betrayal." Unfazed, James finished second in the league during his first season with the Heat, scoring 26.7 points per game.

The 2011-12 season saw major success for James and the Miami Heat. With his team's victory over the Oklahoma City Thunder in the NBA Finals, the superstar forward finally earned his first title. In the clinching Game 5, James scored 26 points, and had 11 rebounds and 13 assists. "I made a difficult decision to leave Cleveland, but I understood what my future was about," James told FOX Sports following the game. "I knew we had a bright future in Miami."

During the 2012-13 season, James made NBA history yet again: On January 16, 2013, at age 28, he became the youngest player to score 20,000 points, succeeding Bryant of the Lakers — who accomplished this feat when he was 29 — and becoming only the 38th player in NBA history to achieve this distinction. James made a jump shot the final seconds of the game, bringing his scoring total 20,001 and leading the Heat to a 92-75 victory over the Warriors.

Success followed the Heat to the end of the 2012-13 season: Following a hard-fought, six-game series against the Indiana Pacers to win the Eastern Conference, Miami outlasted the San Antonio Spurs in seven games to win its second consecutive NBA championship.

At the culmination of the 2013-14 season, Miami returned to the NBA Finals to face off against the Spurs again, this time losing to San Antonio after five games.

In July of 2014, after opting out of his contract with the Heat and considering other teams, James announced that he would be returning to the Cavaliers.

Hampered by back and knee problems, James missed 13 of 82 regular-season games in 2014-15. However, he was as dominant as ever when healthy, averaging 25.3 points and 7.4 assists per game. James led the Cavaliers to the NBA Finals, becoming the first player in nearly 50 years to reach the championship round in five consecutive seasons. However, injuries to star teammates Kevin Love and Kyrie Irving damaged his hopes of claiming a third title, and the Cavaliers lost to the Golden State Warriors in six games.

Over the course of 2015-16, the Cavs overcame the distraction of a mid-season coaching change and breezed through the playoffs to earn a rematch with the Warriors, marking the sixth straight NBA Finals appearance for "King James." In perhaps the crowning achievement of his career, he led his team back from a 3-1 deficit, scoring 41 points in both Games 5 and 6, before recording a triple-double in Game 7 to give the Cavs their first championship in franchise history.

Voted Finals MVP, James said, "I came back to bring a championship to our city. I knew what I was capable of doing. I knew what I learned in the last couple years that I was gone, and I knew if I had to — when I came back — I knew I had the right ingredients and the right blueprint to help this franchise get back to a place that we've never been. That's what it was all about."

The following year, James again paced himself and took charge when necessary, driving the Cavs through the Eastern Conference to make an incredible seventh consecutive appearance in the NBA Finals. This time, with former MVP Kevin Durant added to the mix, the Warriors proved too formidable for James and his teammates, claiming the championship in five games.

For all his accomplishments, James achieved another first early in the 2017-18 NBA season: After yelling at a referee during a late November win over the Heat, he was ejected for the first time in 1,082 career games.

The superstar likely felt like yelling often during the course of a frustrating campaign, as an offseason trade that sent Irving to Boston for Isaiah Thomas failed to bear fruit and forced the Cavs to make another major deal before the All-Star break.

After averaging a career-best 9.1 assists in the regular season, James had to dig deep just to get the team out of the first round of the playoffs, delivering a brilliant 45-point effort to sink the Pacers in Game 7. The Cavs were again pushed to the limit two rounds later by the scrappy Celtics, but James scored 81 points over the last two games to pull out the series win and make his eighth straight NBA Finals appearance.

Game 1 of the rematch against Golden State went down to the wire, thanks to James's 51-point outburst, but Cleveland guard J.R. Smith inexplicably dribbled out the clock with the game tied in regulation, before the Warriors pulled away for the win in overtime. That represented the Cavs' best chance to get a leg up on their opponents, as the Warriors won the next three games handily to claim their third title in four years.

Afterward, with questions swirling about his future with the team, James revealed that he had played out the series with a broken right hand after punching a whiteboard in the aftermath of the Game 1 loss.

On July 1, 2018, James announced that he was moving on to the next chapter of his career by signing a 4-year, $153.3 million contract with the Los Angeles Lakers, a storied franchise that counted Bryant, Kareem Abdul-Jabbar and Magic Johnson among its all-time greats.

The good vibes had worn off by midseason, as the Lakers sputtered through a 17-game stretch without their injured star.

With the team still struggling in late February 2019, James accused his teammates of losing focus over trade rumors, saying, "If you're still allowing distractions to affect the way you play, this is the wrong franchise to be a part of and you should just come in and be like, 'Listen, I can't do this.'"

When the Lakers were officially eliminated from playoff contention in March 2019, it snapped James' personal marks of 13 consecutive postseasons and eight straight NBA Finals appearances. Capping a difficult first season in Los Angeles, the Lakers announced that their star would miss the final six games because of his lingering groin injury.

Things got off to a much better start the following season, thanks in large part to the addition of athletic big man Anthony Davis to the roster. Spearheading the Lakers' rise to the top of the standings was James, who became the first player to record a triple-double against all 30 NBA teams in November 2019.

The following month, James added another accolade to his ever-growing list by earning AP Male Athlete of the Decade honors.

James participated in eight straight NBA championships from the 2010-11 season to the 2018-19 season. During that time, he captured three championship rings: twice with the Heat (2011-12 and 2012-13) and once with the Cavaliers (2015-16).

James was selected for the NBA All-Star Game for the first time in 2005 and would go on to earn a spot in the annual showcase in each of the next 15 seasons.

In January 2018, the NBA announced that James and Golden State Warriors guard Stephen Curry had topped the ballots and would serve as captains for that year's All-Star Game.

In 2006, James was named the Most Valuable Player in the NBA All-Star Game, a feat he would repeat in 2008 and 2018. James has also been named NBA MVP four times, in seasons 2008-09, 2009-10, 2011-12 and 2012-13.

In January 2018, at age 33, James surpassed Bryant as the youngest player to accumulate 30,000 career points and became the seventh player in NBA history to achieve that milestone. The feat put him just more than 8,000 points shy of Abdul-Jabbar's all-time record of 38,387 points.

In 2019, James surpassed Jordan's career tally of 32,292 points to move into fourth place on the all-time list. In January 2020, he eclipsed Bryant's total of 33,643 points to slide into third place, one night before his predecessor's shocking death in a helicopter accident.

After 16 NBA seasons, James' stats included regular season per-game averages of:
- 27.2 points
- 38.6 minutes
- 0.736 free-throw percentage
- 0.343 3-point field-goal percentage
- 0.504 field-goal percentage
- 1.2 offensive rebounds
- 6.2 defensive rebounds
- 7.2 assists
- 0.8 blocks
- 1.6 steals
- 3.5 turnovers

James competed on the U.S. Olympic basketball team during three Summer Olympic Games, in 2004, 2008 and 2012. James made his Olympic debut at the 2004 Summer Games in Athens, Greece. He and his teammates won bronze medals after defeating Lithuania. Argentina took home the gold after beating Italy in the finals.

In the summer of 2008, James traveled to Beijing, China, to play with the likes of Bryant, Jason Kidd and Dwyane Wade on the U.S. Olympic basketball team. This time around the U.S. team brought home the gold after defeating Spain in the final round.

James competed at his third Olympic Games in 2012, at the Summer Olympics in London, along with Durant, Bryant, Carmelo Anthony and several other top players. The U.S. basketball team took the gold medal — James' second consecutive Olympic gold.

In 2003, James signed several endorsement deals, including a deal with Nike for $90 million that could net him over $1 billion over his lifetime.

Other endorsements include Intel, Verizon, Coca-Cola, Beats by Dre and Kia Motors.

In the 2016-17 season, James collected a $31 million salary, making him the third player to earn that much after Jordan and Bryant. The NBA superstar went on to sign a four-year, $153.3 million contract with the Lakers in July 2018. He's also a co-owner of the production company SpringHill Entertainment and has invested in Blaze Pizza.

In February 2019, Forbes magazine's estimated James' yearly earnings at $88.7 million, making him the NBA's highest-earning player for the fifth year in a row.

On January 1, 2012, James proposed to his high school sweetheart, Savannah Brinson. The couple married in a private ceremony with about 200 guests in San Diego on September 14, 2013.

James and Brinson have two sons and one daughter together. In October 2004, James welcomed his first son LeBron Jr. On June 14, 2007, Brinson gave birth to their second son, Bryce Maximus James. Their third child, daughter Zhuri James, was born on October 22, 2014.

Outside of the NBA, James has worked to help others. He established the LeBron James Family Foundation in 2004, along his mother Gloria, to help out children and single-parent families in need.

Among its many programs, the organization builds playgrounds in economically disadvantaged areas and hosts an annual bike-a-thon.

One of the world's most recognizable athletes, James hasn't been shy about expressing his views on social media. Among other issues, he displayed his support for Trayvon Martin after the teen's death in 2012, and he has clashed with U.S. President Donald Trump.

James waded into delicate territory in October 2019, after Houston

Rockets GM Daryl Morey posted a tweet in support of Hong Kong's pro-democracy protesters that ignited a Chinese media boycott of NBA preseason games in the country. James said he believed Morey was "misinformed" about the situation, although he later tweeted that he mainly took issue with the executive posting comments that could have exposed traveling players to danger.

The basketball superstar has also shown a playful side on social media, such as when he posted a picture of cartoon character Arthur clenching his first during the Cavaliers' slow start to the 2017-18 season.

James starred in Space Jam 2, the 2021 sequel to the 1996 hit starring Jordan. "The Space Jam collaboration is so much more than just me and the Looney Tunes getting together and doing this movie," James told The Hollywood Reporter.

"It's so much bigger. I'd just love for kids to understand how empowered they can feel and how empowered they can be if they don't just give up on their dreams."

https://www.biography.com/athlete/lebron-james

ABOUT THE AUTHOR
MAHAM THE MENTOR

Credit: @ MahamtheMentor.com

Maham the Mentor also known as Phillip (Kevin) DuBriel was born April 29, 1977, with his twin in Los Angeles. His biological father (Black Male) was murdered on New Year's Eve of 1977, almost five months before he was born. His biological mother (White Female) was found dead from a drug overdose October 9th, 1977, just four months after he was born. Leaving behind his sister, brothers, and himself. His parents' personal lifestyle led them to their deaths, and they were all put up for adoption.

Maham the Mentor and his twin were separated from the rest of his siblings in hopes that they would be adopted faster. They were moved through seven different foster homes before they were adopted by the DuBriel family consisting of Marsha Metoyer (Creole/ Black) and John DuBriel (Creole/ Black), Maham the Mentor was one year old. At the time of his adoption, the DuBriels lived in Long Beach, but moved to Albuquerque, New Mexico while he was still a baby. The DuBriels were good parents; they taught him right from wrong and the importance of family values. There was a lot of family there and there was a lot of love. Moving was normal for the DuBriel family. At five he moved to Colorado Springs, Colorado. Where he lived was nice, great people, real cold, snowed a lot, but no family. His parents got a divorce when he was seven; he was still living in Colorado Springs at the time. With only his mother and twin they moved to Arlington, Texas. Life in Texas was not as good as other places he had lived. The environment in Arlington was oozing with racism. Most people did not even know they were being racist, it was just normal for them. He did not live in Texas long, at nine, he moved to Fresno. Back in California again. He had plenty of family there, but none in Fresno. Maham the Mentor's first job was delivering the Fresno Bee (newspaper). He only stayed there for a couple of years, too. At about 10, he moved to Marksville, Louisiana. Talking about a culture shock, He was a city boy and Marksville was extremely country. He learned to appreciate the openness. It was nice and he seemed to be related to everybody in that part of Louisiana. Louisiana did not last, either. At 11 he moved to Dallas, by this time, he was just starting the sixth grade. His mom now had a live-in boyfriend name Michael (Black Male).

Maham the Mentor, as a child, could be a good kid but he stayed into trouble, moving so much. He learned how to make friends easily, being tough. He was always well liked and had plenty of friends. He was also a great athlete. In school he was always behind because he moved so much. he was a poor student except math and P.E. In Jr. High he failed most of everything. he started passing classes in high school, because his stepmother told him, he wasn't smart enough to pass anything and that he should drop-out and get a job. Passing allowed him to play sports, he was good in everything. The last grade he completed was the eleventh; he was sent to prison while he was still in the twelfth grade, and he just was 18.

Maham the Mentor started getting into trouble when he moved to Dallas. His mom's new boyfriend, Michael was the worst thing that could have happened to him. He hated everything about him, and he hated him back. They fought all the time, and he was only 12. He hated being home, so he stayed in the streets as much as possible. His neighborhood at that time was full of gangs. Gangbanging was a normal way of life in this time and era, especially in that part of the city, and he, at that time, was no different than anybody else.

Maham the Mentor joined a little gang call BGP at 12 and did all the gangbanging stuff. Life as a gangster, did not last too long. In his apartment complex, he was shot in a gang shoot-out by another gang member and then pistol-whipped by a couple of Dallas Police officers, all in the same night. He was only 13. They moved to a different neighborhood in Dallas. His new neighborhood was not gang infested like the last one, but what it lacked in gang activity, it made up in drug activity. It was never his intentions to get involved in anything drug related, but it was not long before selling drugs seemed extremely attractive to him. Selling drugs was something he became good at, and he made plenty of money doing it. Gangbanging and selling drugs had pretty much ruined his consciousness. He only cared about his family, his so-called friends, and his neighborhood. He was a nightmare to anyone who crossed him. Breaking the law was normal for him; he sold drugs daily, robbed and shot at people occasionally. He was known in the neighborhood for being a good friend or your worst enemy.

Maham the Mentor did not drink alcohol or use any drugs. He hated cigarettes, but he started smoking weed when he was around 18. While still in high school, he caught an Aggravated Robbery with a deadly weapon and an Attempt Murder case and was sentenced to 15 years in prison. He went in and came out in one piece. He ended up doing 10 years and nine months on that 15. Once out, he was getting his life back on track, but the world as he knew it would change again. Fresh out of prison, he was doing great, then BAM! His dad died from a massive heart attack while trying to come see him. Words cannot fully explain the pain he felt when his dad died. He had been working hard so his dad could be proud of him and now his dad was gone. His dad was one of his biggest supporters. His lost caused him to lose focus of his priorities, He soon found himself back in prison, with two drug related cases and a gun charge.

Maham the Mentor true transformation came on his second trip to prison. His criminal history, along with his new charges, made him look like he deserved a Life sentence. He had now hit the lowest point in his life, and he finally felt it was necessary to ask God for help. He did not wish to be free, but he asked God to give him something he could do, something reasonable. He promised God, if he blessed him with the opportunity to walk as a free man again, he would be a testament to His power. He ended up getting three eight-year sentences, all running concurrently. God did His part and now he wanted to his part. He noticed when he was free, all employers wanted people with computer skills. So, once in prison, He signed up for computer classes to improve self, educationally. When he was finally called to the Education Dept. to talk to the school counselor about taking Business Computer Information System (BCIS) classes, he found out that he could go to college under a grant but couldn't go to college without taking the THEA test. But his Educational Average (EA) score was 9.9 (too low), and it had to be at least an 11.0. He started BCIS, studied, and retook the EA test and made a 12.1. He then took and passed the THEA test and began college. He went to college while taking six hours (six months courses) BCIS and Computer Information Technology (C.I.T.). He maintained a 4.0 GPA in both trade courses earning 24 college credits for C.I.T. September 2012; he became the first person in his immediate family to graduate from college. He graduated from Trinity Valley Community College (TVCC) with honors in Applied Science for CIT and Horticulture; He maintained an "overall" 3.72 GPA with 92 credited hours. The first trip to prison He stayed in trouble (G4), now, His second trip, he was an outside trustee (G1) for over three years.

Maham the Mentor life has been extremely unique so far. He has had a lot of good times and a lot of bad times, but he has never given up on himself. His experiences have turned him into a very serious person, with a very positive attitude about his future. He knows, that if he puts his mind to it, nothing is impossible. Before becoming aware that he wanted to be a mentor. He was already studying to be an entrepreneur and learning about business and accounting.

Maham the Mentor was paroled out of prison in 2014. He immediately helped his twin brother with starting his own company called Superior Wash, a Truck washing service business in Memphis, TN. It took a couple of years, but the business has been successful and steady growing. Maham the Mentor was fully discharged from ALL Criminal Cases in 2016. He lives a free life as a Mentor, Servant-Leader, Entrepreneur, truck driver and brother. He lives in Castle Hills in Carrollton, Tx. He is the Founder and CEO of Maham the Mentor Books LLC. He is the Founder and Executive Director of the Society of Is-Real. A Youth Development Organization.

And he's also a volunteer for numerous non-profit organizations like the MOF (Miles of Freedom) organization, who helps Ex-offenders getting out of prison. And the PEP (Prison Entrepreneurship Program) which he won #1 Entrepreneur in his class, helps ex-offenders transform back into to society from prison and starting businesses. And OGU (Original Gangster University), which is all about stopping the violence in the Dallas and other cities around the Nation.

Maham the Mentor Books, LLC

Mahamthementor.com
PO Box 117032
Carrollton, Tx 75011-7032